Professor Oliner has given us a lucid and comprehensive account of the literature, including international movements on forgiveness and reconciliation. The stories are moving and they provide something badly needed in today's violent world—hope for the future.

—Nel Noddings, Ph.D., Jacks Professor Emeriti of Child Education at Stanford University. Author of *Caring: A Feminine Approach to Ethics and Moral Education, Women and Evil, Educating Moral People*, and *Happiness and Education.*

Samuel P. Oliner's book, *Altruism, Intergroup Apology, Forgiveness, and Reconciliation* (With assistance from Piotr Olaf Zylicz), is the culmination of Oliner's many years of research on altruism. It weaves together multiple threads of his studies into a golden-tinged, tapestry showing the power and pervasiveness of altruism and love. This tour de force should be read by individuals, government officials, peace workers, and anyone dealing in international relations and intergroup dialogues. Heeding its lessons could change the world.

—Everett Worthington, Ph.D., Professor and Chair of the Department of Psychology at Virginia Commonwealth University. Published 17 books and many articles and scholarly chapters, mostly on forgiveness including his recent book, *Five Steps to Forgiveness: The Art and Science of Forgiving.*

Samuel P. Oliner has dedicated his research career to deepening our understanding of altruistic behavior. Now he has taken a lifetime of study, insight, and practice to the level of altruism between groups especially in the form of intergroup forgiveness. With the assistance of Piotr Olaf Zylicz, Oliner has produced the finest book on this topic I have ever read! In a world of intergroup conflict and hatred, this may well be the most urgent book of the decade. It is also a fitting tribute to Sam Oliner's remarkable life.

—Stephen G. Post, Ph.D., Professor, Department of Bioethics, Case School of Medicine and President of the Institute for Research on Unlimited Love. Author of several books including *Why Good Things Happen to Good People* (with Jill Neimark) and editor of *Altruism and Health.*

Highly respected for his research on altruism, particularly on rescuer behavior in genocidal situations, Samuel Oliner expands his insightful attention to consider apology, forgiveness, and reconciliation, which are each as controversial as they are important. Interdisciplinary and comprehensive, this thoughtful book is timely and much needed.

—John Roth, Ph.D., Edward J. Sexton Professor of Philosophy and Director of the Center for the Study of the Holocaust, Genocide, and Human Rights; and Chair, Department of Philosophy and Religious Studies at Claremont McKenna College. Author or editor of a number of books, including *Approaches to Auschwitz: The Holocaust and Its Legacy* (with Richard L. Rubenstein) and *Different Voices: Women and the Holocaust* (with Carol Rittner).

Altruism, Intergroup Apology, Forgiveness, and Reconciliation is an intellectually stimulating and morally significant work exploring one of the most important issues of our time.

—Michael Berenbaum, Ph.D., was Ida E. King Distinguished Professor of Holocaust Studies at Richard Stockton College and the Director of the United States Holocaust Research Institute at the U.S. Holocaust Memorial Museum. Author of numerous books, including *Anatomy of the Auschwitz Death Camp* and *After Tragedy and Triumph.*

Samuel Oliner's book is a well done, well written and thorough presentation of the science of positive human behavior intermingled with an extended contemplation of human goodness in its myriad of forms.

—Fred Luskin, Ph.D., Co-Director of the Stanford-Northern Ireland HOPE Project; served as the Director of the Stanford Forgiveness Project. Currently a Senior Fellow at the Stanford Center on Conflict and Negotiation. Author of *Forgive for Good.*

In reading this book, I was captivated not only by the thoughtfulness of Sam Oliner's reasoning but also by the realization that it was written by one who personally suffered the ravages of the Holocaust. Orphaned, hunted, and terrorized for three years as a Jewish adolescent in Poland, Oliner demonstrates the remarkable ability to emerge from the darkness to shed light on the world of healing and to strive to improve the human condition for all.

—Robert Krell, M.D., Emeritus Professor of Psychiatry at the University of British Columbia and Survivor of the Holocaust. He co-authored an updated, translated edition of Judith Hemmendinger Feist's book, *The Children of Buchenwald: Child Survivors and Their Post-War Lives.*

Altruism, Intergroup Apology, Forgiveness, and Reconciliation

Altruism, Intergroup Apology, Forgiveness, and Reconciliation

SAMUEL P. OLINER, Ph.D.
Emeritus Professor of Sociology
Humboldt State University
Arcata, California

assisted by

PIOTR OLAF ZYLICZ, Ph.D.
Warsaw School of Social Psychology
Warsaw, Poland

PARAGON HOUSE
ST. PAUL, MN

We owe a special debt of gratitude to scholars who read and evaluated the manuscript.

First Edition 2008

Published in the United States by
Paragon House
1925 Oakcrest Avenue Ste 7
St. Paul, MN 55113-2619

The paper used in this publication meets the minimum requirements of American
National Standard for Information—Permanence of Paper for Printed Library Materials,
ANSIZ39.48-1984.

Manufactured in the United States of America

10 9 8 7 6 5 4 3 2 1

For current information about all releases from Paragon House,
visit the Web site at http://www.paragonhouse.com

Contents

You Can Give Without Love,
But You Can't Love Without Giving.

—E.L. McKenzie

It is time to pull down the walls, it is time to capture the
dogmas, and bury them in the wilderness. It is time to
live in the accidents of the everyday.

—Iain Crichton Smyth

Acknowledgments . . . . *xiii*
Preface . . . . *xv*

1
Introduction 1

2
Altruism 7
The Nature of Altruism *8*
Overview of an Altruistic Inclination *8*
Altruism and Health *27*

3
Manifestations of Altruism in Different Religious Traditions 35
Judaism *37*
Christianity *41*
Islam *44*

Buddhism *46*
Hinduism *50*
Taoism *52*
Confucianism *54*
Native American Traditions *56*
Commonality among World Religions *59*

4
Apology 63

Interpersonal Apology *64*
Effective and Ineffective Apologies *70*
Intergroup Apology *72*
Case Studies of Group Apology *79*
Summary *117*

5
Forgiveness 121

Religion and Forgiveness *132*
Love, Empathy, and Forgiveness *142*
Biology and Forgiveness *148*
Interpersonal and Intergroup Forgiveness *150*
Summary *166*

6
Reconciliation and Restorative Justice 169

Interpersonal Reconciliation *172*
Intergroup Reconciliation *176*
Factors in Reconciliation *177*
Religion and Reconciliation *179*
Restorative Justice and Reconciliation *186*
Commissions and Tribunals *190*
Three African Approaches to Reconciliation after Human Rights Abuses . . *191*
Summary *197*

7

Collective Guilt, Apology, and Reconciliation: The Polish Case 199

Do Collective Guilt or Responsibility Exist?. *200*

In Search of Contemporary Examples of Group-Based Guilt *202*

Toward the Admission of Collective Guilt and its Consequences *203*

Research on Collective Guilt or Responsibility *205*

Types of Arguments Provided against Collective Guilt/Responsibility . . . *208*

Types of Arguments Favoring Collective Guilt/Responsibility *208*

Interviews with Dr. Marek Edelman and

    Former President Aleksander Kwaśniewski *211*

Some Conclusions of the Jedwabne Debate *218*

8

Conclusion 229

Appendix A. *237*
    Methodology

Appendix B. *245*
    List of Intergroup Apologies (Not Exhaustive)

Appendix C. *251*
    Surveys and Scales

Endnotes. *263*

References *271*

Index *303*

ACKNOWLEDGMENTS

This book would not be possible without the help of many people including faculty and students. I am grateful to all these individuals and foundations that have supplied us with valuable advice and financial support. The Templeton Foundation and The Institute for Research on Unlimited Love have enabled us to complete this book. There are a number of individuals whom I would like to acknowledge for their participation. Janet Zich and Michele Francesconi revised and improved the manuscript. Jeffrey Gunn and Jack Shaffer originally reviewed the manuscript. Mark Bauermeister, Jason Whitley, and Matthew Jelen, graduate students at Humboldt State University, helped with editing. I especially acknowledge Rosemary Yokoi, editor at Paragon House, who guided me with valuable advice through the publication process. There are, of course, others inadvertently left out to whom I express my appreciation as well.

PREFACE

Humans have proven their capacity to be monstrous. We think of Jeffrey Dahmer, who lured 17 men and boys into his apartment and murdered them; Timothy McVeigh, who murdered some 160 people in the Oklahoma City bombing; and Pol Pot, whose Khmer Rouge slaughtered 1.7 million people in Kampuchea. It has been said that man is an enemy-making animal.

There are a number of ideas about how and why atrocities happens (Oliner and Gunn 2006). One explanation is that something in human society—something structural but almost approaching the level of instinct—induces violence, hatred, and megalomania in humans, especially at the behest of political ideologues like Stalin, Mao, and Hitler.

Over time, many people have been abused or unjustly treated in some serious way. In fact, in our research sample, 92.8 percent of respondents reported that they had been hurt emotionally, psychologically, or physically by family, friends, or strangers. Whether the source of their pain is historical or contemporary, it frequently results in the desire for revenge on the real or perceived victimizers. But revenge does not have to be the solution.

This book wrestles with the question of how individuals, groups, and governments can collectively bring about a more humane and peaceful world. Its primary focus is to suggest four central antidotes to the violence, polarization, and alienation that pervade our society. The first three are altruism, genuine apology, and forgiveness, which under the right conditions can lead to the fourth, reconciliation.

The work has already begun. Currently there are more than 20 truth and reconciliation commissions around the world, some of which have facilitated positive outcomes. There are nearly 100 nations, groups, and religious, political, and business leaders that have apologized to others for harm done (French 1991; see list in Appendix B). Among these is Germany, which apologized to Israel for the Holocaust, and Poland and Ukraine, which recently undertook a mutual apology for the 1943 Volyn Massacres perpetrated on each other's people. It is encouraging to see that apology and forgiveness is an idea whose time has come.

The data gathered for this book (elaborated upon in Appendix A) consists of two sources: 1) the published literature on the topic of reconciliation and the role of apology in the healing of past group transgressions,[1] and 2) the information gathered from a nonrandom sample of 435 respondents in the United States and 84 in Poland. Dr. Zylicz collected data from one hundred respondents; however we used only 84 in our analysis.

The part of our research that comes from intellectual work done by others focuses on several groups that have apologized for massacres, slavery, and genocide. We discuss the apologies offered recently by Pope John Paul II and the nations of Germany, the United States, Poland, Ukraine, Rwanda, Guatemala, South Africa, Australia, Canada, Ireland, and Japan. Our own research includes a nonrandom sample of 519 respondents, consisting of college students from Humboldt State University and the College of the Redwoods, *moral exemplars*,[2] clergy, and a sample of what we call "general population," who are neither students nor clergy members. The study also includes a nonrandom sample of 84 respondents from Poland in order to compare responses from two different cultures. In the Polish sample, we are particularly interested in the respondents' attitudes toward *collective* and *individual guilt*. [3]

We administered several scales for these samples, which include measures of altruism, empathy, forgiveness, social responsibility, daily spiritual experience, and reconciliation. We interviewed the samples in depth and tape-recorded and transcribed the interviews. From these data, we were able to make some generalizations about correlations among religiosity, altruistic inclination, apology, forgiveness, and reconciliation.

This research tied up themes that have driven my work for the past quarter century. In previous projects I have grappled with the factors influencing the human capacity for altruism. I have examined the courage of everyday people as they performed heroic acts (*Do Unto Others* 2003) and asked why some European Gentiles risked their lives to rescue Jews in Nazi-occupied Europe (*The Altruistic Personality*, 1988 co-authored with Pearl Oliner; *Toward a More Caring Society* co-authored with Pearl Oliner, 1995; *Who Shall Live: The Wilhelm Bachner Story* co-authored with Kathleen Lee, 1996; *Altruism, Forgiveness, Empathy, and Intergroup Apology*,

2005; Manifestations of Radical Evil: Structure and Social Psychology, 2006).
Dr. Pearl Oliner and I, along with other editors, have taken a wider view
of the philosophical, psychological, and historical perspectives on altruism
(*Embracing the Other* 1992). This book focuses on reconciliation based on
an empathic involvement in apology and forgiveness processes. A concern
for how to improve our world underlies all my work.

1

INTRODUCTION

For several years I have been thinking about the state of the world and its suffering, and I have asked myself how extensive is the role of apology and forgiveness in helping to heal these hurts. One reason for my interest is that I have personally experienced apology and answered with forgiveness, and the experience left a deep impression on me.

In 1945, I came out of hiding in Poland, where I had lived under Nazi occupation. It was perhaps one of the most joyous experiences of my life, because suddenly the Soviet armies had liberated me and I was free, no longer afraid of being turned over to the Nazis who had killed my family. My joy increased as I learned of other Jewish survivors released from the camps, or those who had come out of hiding and ended up with me in Gorlice, in southern Poland. I was particularly thrilled to realize that Oskar Oliner, my father's cousin, and his wife, Hena, had survived; and they were happy that I had, too. They shared their home and their affection with me for several months, until they decided to leave for the American-occupied zone in Germany. I was greatly disappointed that they did not take me, a boy of 15, with them. I felt alone and hurt, but I understood that they must have had a good reason for leaving me behind. Later, I too left Poland. In August 1945, I arrived in Germany and soon found myself in a displaced persons' camp near Munich. In late 1945, the British government, in conjunction with the British Jewish refugee community, took 2,000 orphans to Britain. I was one of those orphans, and I stayed in England for five years. Leaving England at 20 years of age, I arrived in the United States and found that Oskar and Hena Oliner were residents of Brooklyn. They warmly embraced me and invited me to stay with them in their apartment. I was not sure that I quite forgave them for leaving me in Poland when they left for the West, but one day as we were having a meal in their house, Oskar and Hena apologized to me with teary eyes for having left me behind while they emigrated first to Germany and then to the United States. It was a moving experience for me as I realized the regret they felt. Their apology certainly reversed the resentment I had harbored toward them, and I forgave them.

In the mid 1980s, my wife, Dr. Pearl Oliner, and I attended a conference in Germany. We met some German scholars, some of whom later became associated with our research on the rescuers of Jews in Nazi-occupied Europe. One professor, a political scientist, invited us to his apartment in Berlin. He was a gracious host and knew of my background. After a few drinks, he grew a little sentimental and said, "If we Germans live a thousand years, we will never be able to wipe out the horror that we have perpetrated against the Jewish people." At that moment I was moved to tears, and I started explaining that it wasn't he who had perpetrated these murders, it was a cancer in German history at the time. As Pearl and I left, I hugged him and said to him, privately, "It's not your fault. Don't think that way. The world is going to be a brighter place."

More recently, in the mid 1990s, I went back to southern Poland to my native village of Zyndranowa, located close to the Slovak border, where my grandfather and other relatives had lived. When the Nazis murdered my relatives—along with 700 other victims—in the nearby Blonda Forest, their neighbors obtained their homes and lands. When I arrived there, the woman who now owns my grandfather's land said that she was very sorry about what had happened to my family, and she felt very badly that she now owned the land. She had purchased the land from the communists, who had it when the Polish Communist government took over Poland after the Nazis were driven out. I felt better and assured her that I did not come to claim the land or my grandfather's house.

These events have given me insight into the positive and healing process of apology. Therapists, marriage counselors, and other healers have written about the interpersonal process of apology and forgiveness and reported the role of these processes in healing interpersonal pain and repairing relationships. The scholarly literature of the last three decades indicates that more research is focusing on the topic. One prominent psychologist, Everett Worthington, detailed a tragic event in his life in which his mother was murdered by two intruders; he was consumed by pain, anger, and a strong desire for revenge. He concluded that his burden of rage was self-defeating and realized it would be better for his psychological health to forgive the murderers. Many people have asked me over the years whether I hate Germans because they exterminated my family in August 1942 and buried them in two mass graves. Initially, right after the war in 1945, I was very angry and thought I would hurt any German person I came across. Subsequently, as I matured and understood the kind of processes in human behavior that lead some people to harm or murder others, I felt more empathic toward the harm-doers.

The underlying goal of most of the research I have conducted over the past 25 years has been to try to account for altruistic behavior and to figure out how to encourage and sustain it. In studying a variety of helping, caring, and risking behaviors in several settings—rescuers in Nazi-occupied Europe, military heroes, Carnegie Heroes (Carnegie Heroes are those individuals who risked their lives to save total strangers from certain death), 9/11 heroes, hospice volunteers, L'Arche volunteers, philanthropists, and other altruistic actors—my colleagues and I have sought to pinpoint motivating factors for altruistic behavior. We have asked: Is there a single motivating explanation for sustained moral activity on behalf of others? What traits can we see among those individuals who are engaged in helping those in need on a sustained basis? We found that there seems to be a linear relationship between empathy, altruistic behavior, love, apology, and forgiveness that frequently leads to reconciliation and a restoration of harmonious relationships. Empathy seems to be a crucial ingredient: no real apology or forgiveness, or indeed reconciliation, is possible if it is based solely on self-interest. Taking the place of the other is what allows people to take the risks necessary for repairing human relations, on both interpersonal and intergroup levels.

We begin our book, in Chapter 2, with a discussion of altruism, its attributes, and motivating factors. We note what appears to be a positive relationship among altruism, apology, and forgiveness. We discuss the variables that help explain altruistic behavior. The chapter includes a brief discussion of moral exemplars and how they exhibit caring behavior, and it examines manifestations of altruism in different cultures and religious traditions.

Chapter 3 includes a brief examination of eight specific religious traditions—namely Judaism, Christianity, Islam, Buddhism, Hinduism, Taoism, Confucianism, and Native American religions—to trace similarities and differences in the attributes of altruism, how it is exhibited in those cultures, and to discern positive outcomes for the welfare of society.

Chapter 4 addresses the topic of apology. While there is substantial literature on interpersonal apology, we focus on intergroup apology by 11 groups that have made public apologies for harm done to others. These apologies were made on behalf of groups in Ireland, Poland, Ukraine, the United States, Australia, Canada, Rwanda, Japan, Germany, Guatemala, and South Africa. Here, too, we look at similarities and differences in motivations for apology, as well as the outcomes.

Chapter 5 examines research on interpersonal and intergroup forgiveness, as well as focusing on its various settings. Important motivators for forgiving include spirituality, altruism, love, empathy, the need to re-humanize the enemy, and the desire for reconciliation (Galambush 2007). This chapter also examines forgiveness and social justice.

Chapter 6 addresses complex questions raised by the relationships among apology, forgiveness, and reconciliation. Does apology always lead to reconciliation? How do these concepts fit together into restorative justice?

Chapter 7 is called Collective Guilt, Apology, and Reconciliation: The Polish Case. The concept of collective guilt is hotly debated among scholars. It lies at the root of the relationship between intergroup apology and forgiveness and their efficacy in bringing about meaningful reconciliation between groups. We use the massacre at Jedwabne as an example.

In Chapter 8 we conclude that there are actions that can create a more just and caring world. In concert with the current revival of some of the practical spirit of those pioneers in American sociology, who felt that studying a problem was the prelude to solving it, we feel that social theory and research can and should be applied directly to the problems of our world. This idea of "public sociology" (Burawoy 2004) is particularly appropriate, considering that the problems we face are complex, and the consequences of not solving them are severe. Sociology has a history of studying societal ills and applying this knowledge toward solutions. According to public sociologist Michael Burawoy:

> Thus, Karl Marx recovered socialism from alienation; Emile Durkheim redeemed organic solidarity from anomie and egoism. Max Weber, despite premonitions of "a polar night of icy darkness," could discover freedom in rationalization and extract meaning from disenchantment. On this side of the Atlantic, W. E. B. Du Bois pioneered pan-Africanism in reaction to racism and imperialism, while Jane Addams tried to snatch peace and internationalism from

the jaws of war (Burawoy 2004: 5).

We feel it is possible to materially improve the world by inculcating and disseminating the practice of true apology and forgiveness and by building processes that allow for reconciliation and restorative justice. We will show there is evidence that healing of past hurts is possible. The key to this healing lies in the human capacity for empathy, or taking the place of the other. Altruism, remediation, and apology can form the basis for forgiveness. Apology and forgiveness have frequently proven to be the basis for interpersonal reconciliation. Now, when most serious problems are the product of troubled group relations, we find that many of these same processes apply to intergroup reconciliation as well. The ability to act altruistically is within us all, and most importantly, we have the ability as a society to enhance our altruistic tendencies.

2

Altruism

My family had a small farm and a grocery store business, kind of a supermarket, and on the farm my mother raised chickens every year, so she raised hundreds and hundreds of chickens and turkeys, and she sold them for a few cents each in order to supplement our income. She also gave a lot away to people that needed them. She did fund-raising dinners for every organization that you could imagine, from the elementary school PTA to the local churches. She was a Red Cross volunteer. She did all those kinds of things. She had two of us and when my cousins' parents divorced, then they moved in with us, so she raised two other children who were not hers. She adopted them as her own and actually paid for both of them to go through college and graduate school.

—*A teacher and social worker, Humboldt County, California*

What prompts such selfless kindness? Altruistic behavior is the product of many influences and motivations. This chapter will directly address the nature of altruism and its correlates, including empathy, reciprocity, personal morality and moral goals, learned caring norms, courage, self-esteem, and religious faith and spirituality.

THE NATURE OF ALTRUISM

By altruism, we mean helping another person or group of people who are in need of help and welcome it, where help is voluntary and the helper expects no external reward. Altruism is associated with both apology and forgiveness—they are really two sides of the same coin. There are numerous examples of both conventional, or "ordinary," altruism and heroic altruism, which we shall discuss below.

For some time now theologians, philosophers, anthropologists, sociologists, and other social scientists have asked the question, how do societies survive? Some maintain that altruism is part of the answer and that its importance is reflected in the fact that it is partially a product of evolutionary processes. These thinkers view altruism as the glue that holds groups of people together, helping them function, cooperate, and simply exist. Conversely, some question the very existence of altruism, maintaining instead that giving help to others and cooperating within groups are really selfish acts that benefit the helper in some way. These benefits may be tangible, in the form of a tax benefit for the philanthropist, for example; or they may be intangible, earning the giver prestige or self-satisfaction. Philosopher Sir Thomas Browne tells us that by being compassionate we make others' misery our own and so, by relieving them, relieve ourselves also. In a recent book edited by Stephen Post (2007), 39 researchers noted a strong positive correlation between altruistic behavior and both physical and mental health. This behavior—found in most cultures, belief systems, and societies—works to create a more just, friendly, and caring worldand contributes to social solidarity.

Although it is clear that not all acts portrayed as altruistic are truly without intended benefit to the giver, the positive outcome that benefits the other is what matters.

OVERVIEW OF AN ALTRUISTIC INCLINATION

Social scientists and other scholars have had a long and ongoing argument about the nature of human behavior. They ask: Do human beings internalize a tradition and ethic of caring for others, or are they naturally brutish and inhumane toward each other? Are they selfish and unforgiving, or selfless and forgiving? Are they both good and evil? What makes such moral exemplars—such as Mahatma Gandhi, who passively resisted injustice by conducting hunger strikes for India's freedom, and Elie Wiesel, who fights for humanity, truth, and justice in a post-Holocaust world—act for what they believe in, rather than simply ponder the issues and do nothing? What made Pope John Paul II ask for forgiveness for 2,000 years of persecution of the Jews and other groups?

The tragedy that occurred on September 11, 2001 inspired many Americans to get involved with their fellows. We saw this on both a local and a global basis in the reaction to natural disasters, such as Hurricane Katrina in the United States and the devastating tsunami in Asia. These daily acts of ordinary goodness, and the selfless heroism of people who care for others, need to be recognized and celebrated. Media coverage of compassionate, altruistic acts could inspire caring even in the most apathetic and create in them the desire to do acts of goodness.

Nobel Peace Prize winner Elie Wiesel, said this to the American Congress in 1999:

> I think the greatest source of infinite danger in this world is indifference. I have always believed that the opposite of love is not hate, but indifference. The opposite of life is not death, but indifference. The opposite of peace is not war, but indifference to peace and indifference to war. The opposite of culture, the opposite of beauty, and the opposite of generosity is indifference. Indifference is the enemy, and the context is memory. As long as we remember, there is a chance; if we forget that, all that really matters is forgotten (Wiesel 1999).

Wiesel's message is that no matter where injustice takes place in the world, that place then becomes the center of the universe, and all thought must be focused there to alleviate suffering and restore justice. As a philosopher, historian, playwright, and novelist, he raises his voice against injustice everywhere.

The Oliners have found that most personality (Oliner and Oliner 1988) consists of a relatively enduring, internally determined predisposition that underlies behavior. Personality, as distinct from attitudes and values, reflects cognitive representation of appropriate behavior—a standard regarding what one should do. The Oliners emphasize the affective components of personality manifested in emotions and behavior. In a recent study of motivations for helping behavior (Oliner 2003), I have found a variety of self-reported explanations for helping. Among them is personal efficacy, a desire to contribute, an increased sense of self-esteem, standing up for beliefs, love of people, resourcefulness, an ability to face challenges, spirituality/religiosity, and self-confidence in the moral rightness of their actions.

In a social-psychological context, motivation for altruism can be found within the general mindset of the individual. The eight stages of psychological awareness of others that are relevant to our study have been well defined by Dennis Krebs and Frank Van Hesteren (1992). We include a brief description of these stages, because they show us convincingly how and at what point an individual develops into a caring and altruistically inclined person.

The first stage of prosocial behavior of children encompasses such things as *smiling and cooing* in response to stimulation. This stage is followed by *egocentric accommodation*, which are behaviors oriented to fulfilling their own needs. Next is the *cooperative stage*, which is doing one's share in concrete exchanges with others. Then comes *mutual altruism*, that is, being sensitive to the audience of the generalized other, to other people. This stage is aimed at fulfilling shared roles of obligation and avoiding social disapproval and even sustaining a good reputation and upholding friendship—that is, securing a place in the community. *Conscientious altruism* is oriented toward fulfilling an internalized obligation to assist in maintaining the institutions of the society and not violate the expectations of one's group. *Autonomous altruism*, the next stage of altruistic development, is based on more internalized, higher order principles. This stage is guided by internally held values such as upholding human dignity and the human rights of liberty and justice for all. *Integrated altruism* transcends self and integrates the individual with humanity in general. Finally, there is *universal love*, also known as *agape*. This stage is the most mature and most inclusive. It is an ethical, responsible, universal love, encompassing service and sacrifice for humanity and upholding the dignity of the recipient of such help (Krebs and Van Hesteren 1992).[4]

Stephen Post (2003) sees a correlation between love and altruism. His definition of unlimited love is perhaps the most concise. He says, "In essence, unlimited love is an abiding other-regarding perspective and emotional attunement that affirms and serves all of humanity unselfishly and unconditionally, without any exception whatsoever." Similarly, John Templeton (1999) suggests that unlimited love is a form of love that rises above every conceivable limit to embrace all of humanity in joy, creativity, compassion, care, and generativeness; it lies at the heart of all valid and worthwhile spiritual, religious, and derivative philosophical traditions. Unlimited love is often associated with a divine presence that underlies the cosmos and makes life a meaningful gift. Indeed, the life of unlimited love probably begins with the sense that every life is a gift.

The uncertainties of contemporary society is a hot topic for both lay and scholarly writers, and some argue that our society has lost its moral moorings. This is an inequitable, violent, and oppressive world. Its variety of ills and injustices often cause anger, alienation, and even willingness to die. There are groups of people all over the world who carry a grievance—real or imagined, current or from the distant past—and they look for someone to blame. They feel powerless. They compare themselves to the powerful and wonder how their plight can be ignored, how their suffering can be disregarded. The suicide bombers we see in the Middle East are one example of this. The terrorists of 9/11 saw the Western world as highly unjust and felt that their action was a direct attack on those responsible. This human ability to simplistically carve out groups of individuals into friends and enemies, and to arbitrarily distinguish between "Good" and "Evil", righteous and infidel, the deserving and the undeserving, and so on, may be at the root of the horrible massacres and genocides of the past century (Oliner and Gunn 2006).

When people take such an either-or view, all complexities are lost. Psychiatrist John E. Mack (2003) maintains that people see separation and difference more easily than unity and connection. In order to offer a solution, Mack maintains that we must find the connection among all human beings. Unless nation states and other institutions address this seriously, we will forever be suffering from the problems of "us" and "them," of friend and enemy. Both Vaclav Havel and Albert Einstein also have maintained the need to rid ourselves of these destructive and straight-jacketed views of the world. Without a global revolution in the sphere of human consciousness, which includes all of humanity, nothing will change for the better in the sphere of our being. We must use our root intuitive powers to transform the bases of our relationships to those of love and understanding.

Altruism and Its Correlates

Altruism is putting the needs of others first. An altruistic act is one that helps those in need when the actor is not seeking any gain. It is possible to distinguish two types of altruism: *heroic* altruism, which is voluntary and involves high risk to the helper; and *conventional* altruism, which also is voluntary and is largely associated with women but does not involve high risk to the helper. Heroic altruism risks the helper's life or well-being by performing the act. Those who fall into this category include rescuers of Jews in Nazi-occupied Europe, the Carnegie Heroes, holders of the Victoria Cross, and Congressional Medal of Honor winners. Conventional altruism involves little or no risk to one's life. Examples of conventional altruists include hospice volunteers and millions of others who give their time without compensation.

Throughout the last few decades correlations have been explored among personality traits and background experiences and altruistic behavior. The National Opinion Research Center and the University of Chicago (Smith 2003) measure the extent of behaviors and values in society at large. Tom W. Smith, director of the General Social Survey, used a national, full-probability sample of adult Americans and found several statistically significant relationships. Americans who attend church regularly, or who pray regularly, are more likely to engage in acts of kindness than those who do not pray or attend church. The study found that those with group memberships were more likely to engage in those behaviors than those who were less involved with groups. What the study did not find may be just as significant: There appears to be no correlation between size of community with acts of kindness.

Our previous research, looking at altruistic behavior in various settings (Oliner 2003, 2004), found a number of common motivating factors. Learned beliefs and values passed on by parents and the community are by far the most significant factors that motivated helping behavior. More than three out of four (78 percent) of the Carnegie Heroes we interviewed discussed the importance of parental guidance and internalization of their parents' norms and values. Many reported that they were taught at some point in their lives that people are supposed to care for one another, and they clearly felt that being a helper was intimately connected with their own sense of self. This includes learned values of caring and social responsibility acquired from the moral community in which they lived and from their parents.

Mike W. Martin, in his book *Love's Virtues* (1996), enumerates some positive social processes, which he calls virtues. Among those he discusses in some detail are morality, caring, faithfulness, respect for the other, fairness, courage, wisdom, and gratitude. He calls these "moral" virtues, because they involve affirming the moral works of a person. Caring, he maintains, is love's central virtue. This, of course, dovetails with the idea that love is not truly "love" unless one cares for another unselfishly.

In our several publications on rescuers of Jews in Nazi-occupied Europe during World War II (Oliner 1993, 2000, 2003; Oliner and Oliner 1988), we divided the population of 300 million European people who lived under Nazi occupation into four groups. These groups consisted of perpetrators (killers and collaborators), victims (Jews, gypsies, gays, priests, ministers, and others), rescuers (heroes, helpers), and bystanders (by far the largest group). It is an unfortunate characteristic of modern society that the largest number of people were bystanders, individuals who could have been involved with saving lives in Nazi-occupied Europe but did nothing. Although the "good Germans" who did not directly participate in the killings were originally considered to be non-guilty bystanders, it is only through the complicity of bystanders—who were guilty of unquestioning obedience to evil leaders—that the Holocaust was possible (Barnett 1999).

A dramatic example of bystanders involves a recent group of mountaineers who ignored British climber David Sharp's need for assistance as they continued past him to the summit of Mt. Everest; climbing enthusiasts are eager to reach the summit of Everest to snap a picture of their grand feat. But at what expense? "How glorious is a summit if you have to step over, and ignore, a dying fellow human being in order to snap that summit picture" (Giss 2006)? Consequently, Mr. Sharp perished on the snowy slopes of Everest. It is important to understand that during Nazi occupation, rescuing, caring for, feeding, transporting, giving false identification, or helping victims in almost any way was punishable by death, so it is understandable that many were fearful for their lives during WWII. However, on the slopes of Mt. Everest, saving the life of another is not a crime; on the contrary, it would have been viewed as an honorable act.

Our research (Oliner and Oliner 1988; Oliner 2003) has focused on the factors that motivate individuals to move from being bystanders to becoming heroes, and how to inculcate these motivations into more people. How can we bring about a more caring society? What encourages people to be engaged in altruistic behavior? We have found several traits that help explain engagement in altruistic behavior.

Empathy

Empathy is a salient motivation centered on the needs of another—on that individual's possible fate. It emerges out of a direct connection with the distressed other; empathy is feeling another's pain and not being able to ignore it. Of the Carnegie Heroes we interviewed, 62 percent reported empathy as their motivation (Oliner 2003). The word empathy is often used interchangeably with compassion, sympathy, and pity, which are its characteristic expressions. Reactions to another's pain or danger may be emotional or cognitive, frequently both.

A Carnegie Hero who is a truck driver related his successful rescue of another driver who had crashed and was stuck hanging upside down in the cab of his truck. When he saw that no one else was going to be able to save him, he decided to do his best. He relates:

> He [the victim] said, "Please don't let me burn alive in here alone. Don't leave me to burn alive in here. I have a family." At that time I saw my whole life as a young man, even through my tour in the service. I saw my family. I could see my parents [and] I said, "Listen, if I can't get you out of here, I'm going to sit right here with you and I'll hold your hand, and we'll go together." ...I didn't want to lose hope, and I guess the old boy upstairs said, "Hey, there's the button." I hit it and he fell over my shoulder . . .like a bag of potatoes, perfect. . .I said, "Just keep your head down, we're going through this thing" (Respondent 102).

The truck driver was able to place himself in the shoes of the man he saved. It was that ability, those feelings of empathy and understanding, that drove him to risk his own life in order to save the other's—and even to choose to stay and give solace to him if he were not able to save him.

Efficacy

Efficacy, which psychologists see as directly related to self-esteem, is the sense that one has the power to produce effects or achieve intended results. The importance of efficacy and the courage that it engenders can be taught to children at a very young age. Efficacy, after empathy, was the next most common motivational factor for Carnegie Heroes (38.8 percent) when the rescuers said that they took action because they felt confident that they would be able to help. Many times this sense of confidence was the result of prior life experience or training, which is why it is so important to impart this sense to our children and to remember it ourselves.

One internationally recognized martial arts instructor teaches young adults and at-risk youth to train their minds to think positively. He teaches that they can be better than who they were. His goal is to show them a better future:

> I would say that working with any of these kids who don't see options or opportunities before them, that's the goal; to show them that you're not stuck where you're at. Your past doesn't

determine your future. Your own decisions do. I tell my students and the people I work with that the thoughts you think all day, they're either pushing you forward, or they're pulling you back; one or the other. And you basically have to pay attention to the thoughts you're thinking. I tell them that when you wake up in the morning, the first thing Monday morning, and you're saying to yourself, "I don't want to get up; I'm tired; I don't want to go to school," all you're doing is setting yourself up. Whatever it is that you tell yourself in your mind, your mind is going to react to it.... So what I tell them is when you wake up in the morning, you need to say, "Okay, what do I have to look forward to today? What do I have to achieve today?" And I tell them to try to do two things every day towards whatever that goal is. And of course we go off into peer pressure, and people that you hang out with, and on, and on. I've written booklets on this, and it all has to do with going into basic human needs and what we need to feel that word "successful." (Respondent 034)

Reciprocity

Rescuers, like other people, have multiple values that overlap; any one of them might assume supremacy at any given moment. Some of the Carnegie Heroes felt that norms and expectations dictate that people help others, because they expect others to reciprocate when they are in need. Approximately 30 percent of those interviewed gave the reason for rescue as reciprocity. A 21-year-old male student who rescued another man from his fiery automobile following a crash related this story: He and a friend were just about to cross the street when they heard the noise of someone's accelerator down the road. The car proceeded extremely fast and slammed into the rear end of the car that was waiting for them to cross. After it hit this car, the speeder kept going, jumped a curb, and hit a tree at the bottom of a ditch. The car that had been rear-ended spun around into the opposite traffic lane and left in its wake a gas trail 20 feet long. The gas sparked, and the rescuer's friend froze and urged him away from the scene. The rescuer said,

> "I just kept thinking, *what if it was me? What if I got smashed?* And if nobody helped me, I would just sit there and burn. I just hope and pray that if that ever happens to me, somebody would do the same for me" (Respondent 179).

Personal Morality and Moral Goals

Many of our exemplars work toward a moral objective and goal; doing what they do simply feels morally right to them, and these moral values drive them to act in a caring way. Among all the respondents, 81 percent related that their motivation for caring and acting prosocially in their community was based on their personal morality, fulfilling personal moral goals. A local Humboldt County minister shares his reasons for helping others. He states:

> We are all living in this world together. I believe in the idea that we are all sort of moving together toward whatever it is. It is not an individual matter of salvation. It is a corporate one, a community one (Respondent 001).

An Hispanic corporate director and philanthropist defines his reasons for helping others in need:

> I think the morality is that we have to have responsibility for making sure that we do more than the minimum. So it's not just a crumb of bread, but helping people to move beyond the dependency. Anything less than nurturing the whole independence of individuals is minimal; at its best, maternalistic (Respondent 018).

A priest we interviewed feels that the whole purpose of helping is to make the world a better place, and this is what forms the foundation of his moral convictions:

> I think that the goal of being in solidarity with and supporting people who are on the outside and seeking a better life is a moral goal. And making the world a better place than I found it is a moral goal (Respondent 025).

A social worker defines her moral compass as one that stimulates positive social change to create a society where everybody has basic human rights and freedoms:

> I guess it has to do with creating; being involved with activity that creates a society that respects self-determination and the rights of human beings to live in their full capacity. Because in antiviolence work, basically the belief is that everybody has a right to be free, to walk free wherever they want, whenever they want, in their homes, outside of their homes, in every country, in every part of the world.

So having that be the agenda creates a moral and just society because it respects each person's right to freedom. It also engages individuals in a kind of societal change because it engages each person in their own moral inventory of how they act and behave with every other human being. It is a dynamic activity (Respondent 027).

Moral goals include being honest and responsible for other human beings. As this philanthropist states:

I guess I could say honesty is a moral goal. I think being a responsible human being is a moral goal. Other than the Ten Commandments...don't lie, don't cheat (Respondent 043).

Some respondents did not feel that "goal" was an accurate word to use; rather, just having the opportunity to help and hoping that some good would come from it is their *motivation*, not their goal. As this social worker states,

I would see [good results] as the moral output. I am uncomfortable with the word goal because I don't know what else I could really do. My goal really is just to be present. The hope that I have is that with my presence and the training that I've had to be helpful for them to make the choices that will better their lives. You know, I have some expertise, but the outcome is to help people improve the lots of their lives (Respondent 054).

Learned Caring Norms

Sixty-eight percent of our respondents said they learned their caring behavior from others within their cultural and social upbringing—from the family (extended or immediate), religious group, or the community at large. For example, a female cleric who volunteers her time and spiritual strength to help parishioners in need, said:

In my Presbyterian church, we're assigned a care member...someone who is an adult in the community who, because they don't have family connections or they don't have any friends, are asking to have a contact or a visit or phone calls and for people to take care of their emotional or spiritual needs (Respondent 047).

One priest reports learning from his mother the values of caring and compassion and helping anyone in need. This includes all people. He states:

> I learned from my mother openness, compassion, courage. She was one of those women who always responded to a poor man at the door and always welcomed the new and unwelcomed neighbors into the community (Respondent 025).

One woman, who teaches inmates at a prison, was raised in a culture of sharing and giving and was influenced by her family to do the right thing by helping others. She now incorporates that in her life, as she testifies:

> And so my parents have always been very caring people, I don't think they have been necessarily involved in any sort of formal volunteer work, but they have always given as much of their time and everything to other people, always had people in our home, always opened up our home, especially back in Sudan, for people who are on the street and things like that. And so remembering that as a young child I think has definitely influenced me to see that as a very normal part of someone's life (Respondent 031).

Yet another exemplar, a philanthropist who heads a foundation to assist those in need of mental health services, said:

> I think I learned how to love, how to both give love and to receive love. I learned equality of every man and woman, that none of us are better than anyone else, that life wasn't fair, there was a lot of unfairness and inequality (Respondent 033).

A Native American activist and writer of poetry credited her parents:

> In teaching me things that required enormous patience. In reading and writing and other kinds of history. In working with me to raise my brothers. They had twins and they gave me one of them. They said, "We have a well baby and a baby that is kinda sick," which was the case. They said, "The well baby is yours." So at age five, I became the baby's mother. I mean I really thought that I was now the mother of the oldest twin and then together we were the kinda co-parents of my brother's younger twin. I never really looked at them as siblings. So my parents really, they were teaching all sorts of lessons by doing that (Respondent 045).

This social worker and teacher was raised with the value of helping those in need, often not expecting anything in return. He states:

> It was at the end of the Second World War and there were lots of

single men who were riding the railroad cars all over California, and every evening there would be seven or eight of those men who would come in the nice weather. My mother and grandmother would fix them dinner, feed them, and give them a place to sleep, either in the bunk house where my uncles stayed or in a little area there that was a covered area with a little trellis over the top for them to sleep out. And when children were in trouble or anything, my mother was always the one that was there. When people in our community died, my mother would fix a family dinner for everybody, plus then the day after the funeral, she would go and they would fix a large dinner for everybody. Generally she worked with my father.

My dad ran a grocery store and he had policies that were incredible. Like when poor people would come and they didn't have money for food they would say can we charge food and pay you later. He would say, "Let's do it this way, how about I give you food and if you get money you can come and pay me later, but you never feel like you are obliged." Some people remembered years later.

I think I grew up in a family that has real respect for differences. My dad would do that for anyone who came to him whether he knew them or not, or whether they were Anglo-American or African-American or Hispano-American, he was really comfortable. He was that way with everybody. My dad grew up in Italy, and I don't think he knew a stranger. He never treated anybody like they were a stranger. If you came into the store, you were treated with the same respect as somebody he had known you for 25 or 30 years. And it made no difference (Respondent 054).

A minister who grew up in a small Midwestern town maintains that it was his upbringing and the small-town community culture that embedded in him the ethic of supporting the community. He says,

But underlying that too, in a small Midwestern rural community, you helped where there was a need. I've heard many stories of someone being sick and they couldn't get their fields planted, so the neighboring farmers would come with their tractors and planters and come and plant their field for them, or harvest it. So there was really that kind of community where you helped one another. I think that's one of the things I learned and was taught, that you're respectful, courteous, and you're helpful (Respondent 014).

A volunteer who helps with the Jewish Community Center maintains the Jewish values she learned and has adopted these into her life. She states:

> I adopt the Jewish value of caring, and I think we all have a choice to do that. And so you don't see yourself in terms of your small framework; you see yourself as a participant in the world community (Respondent 019).

Courage and Heroism

Courage is another factor involved in motivating heroic altruism. The psychoanalyst Heinz Kohut (1985) maintains that it is important to look at human behavior during crises. He defines courage as the ability to brave death and tolerate destruction rather than betray the nucleus of one's psychological being, one's ideals. Some forms of courage need no explanation—they are self-evident, like performing heroic acts to save children. Other individuals report of having no choice but to act heroically. An example is Rosa Robota, an inmate who smuggled explosives in her brassiere to help destroy one of the crematoriums at Auschwitz. She told her compatriots in her last moments of life before she was executed, "Friends, have courage and be strong."[5] John Percival, writing about courage in war, said,

> But if for any reason war becomes inevitable, courage is not just desirable, it is essential. Without courage whole armies disintegrate and flee in confusion, and lonely men die an ugly death for want of anyone brave enough to rescue them. Without courage there is no power on earth to deter an aggressor, nothing to oppose the principle that might is right (Percival 1985: xii).

There are many ways that heroism may be displayed. Franz Jaegerstaetter, an Austrian farmer, was so upset when Germany invaded Austria in 1938 that he refused to serve his required stint in the German military. Kohut (1985) explains this refusal by referencing the "nuclear self," consisting of a person's deeply felt values. These values can be based upon simply feeling that some things are evil and against the will of God, hence they must not be obeyed.

Kohut relates the story of Hans Scholl who was released from military service but subject to active service at the front from time to time. While traveling to the Russian front, his train stopped at a small station in Poland. There he noticed a line of women and young girls laboring heavily on the railroad tracks. They wore the yellow Star of David fixed to their garments. Suddenly Hans jumped from the train and walked toward the women. The first woman in the row was a young girl. He noticed her slender hands and intelligent, beautiful face, which seemed to express unspeakable sorrow. He tried to think of something that he could offer her; then he remembered his "K-rations," which consisted of a mixture of chopped up raisins and nuts. He tried to give them to the girl, but she threw them back at him with a proud gesture. He told her he had only wished to give her a little pleasure and left it at her feet along with a daisy he picked for her. As he boarded his train he saw that she had put his daisy into her hair. Scholl and his sister later formed a student resistance group at Munich University.

Kohut recognizes the courage of these resistors. He labels Jaegerstaetter and the Scholls as "martyr heroes," distinguishing them from "rational resisters." An example of rational resistors cited by Kohut is the Oster-Canaris-Stauffenberg Circle, which attempted to kill Hitler by putting a bomb in a suitcase and placing it under the table near him. The difference between the two is that Jaeggerstatter and the Scholls constructed their nuclear selves from ideals and religious teachings, including the idea that there are some things worth resisting, even worth dying for. The Oster-Canaris-Stauffenberg conspirators made their assassination attempt because they saw it as a necessary response to Hitler's efforts to destroy the world and kill millions of people. Kohut believes that martyr heroes gain their values primarily from parents and religious teachings, including basic moral precepts of right and wrong and compassion for those who are in need (Kohut 1985).

Franz Jaegerstatter's religious ideas led him to decide not to join the German army. He was given all kinds of options in the army, including not serving on the front line, but he refused them as well. In 1943 he was executed. Kohut relates Franz's dream:

> Right at the beginning I want to describe a brief experience during a summer night in 1938. First I lay awake almost until midnight, even though I was not ill; but then I must have fallen asleep for awhile, because I was shown a beautiful railroad train, which circled around a mountain. Not only the grown-ups but even the children streamed toward this train, and it was almost impossible to hold them back. I hate to tell how very few of the grown-ups there were who resisted being carried along by this occasion. But then I heard a voice, which spoke to me and said: This train is going to hell...
> (Kohut 1985: 13)

Kohut's interpretation of this dream is that the Austrian population, grown-ups and children, rushed to embrace Nazism and the terrible consequences that followed. Kohut states that Jaegerstatter felt the basic "wrongness" immediately and was quite unable—even at the cost of his own life—to join the Nazi party and the military.

When believers act as martyr heroes, the God concept is the ultimate explanation of their reality, and they find themselves with unscientific certainty in a fully intelligible universe. Some things are wrong and some things are right. On the other hand, those values motivating the rational hero may be at the core of the liberal self, which is based on the need to help the persecuted and disadvantaged, resulting from his deeply anchored personality. Kohut defines three major components resulting from this. First, rational heroes harbor an early empathic identification with the humiliated and helpless, because they experienced the same feelings in childhood. Secondly, they internalize messianic religious ideals from parents. Thirdly, they act out a partial integration of grandiose fantasies (to be their mother's protector, for example), which provided pleasure and pride in their early years.

Heroes help members of a society to focus on the difference between good and evil. Thus, Hamlet—perhaps Shakespeare's greatest character—focuses dramatically on the nature of evil. Kohut maintains that certain qualities of the nuclear self, once structured, cannot be comprehended unless the "it" is conceptualized as an independent and autonomous unit. Thus the role of the nuclear self, the core of one's being, is mutable. It may then change from simply resisting Nazism or other evils to facing death in the name of principle (Kohut 1985). In our sample, 71 percent felt that courage is a necessary factor involved in risking one's safety for another.

Religious Faith/Spirituality

In 2003, journalist Paula Zahn (2003) reported on a survey titled "Faith in America," which indicated that a majority of Americans are "church-goers." In our study, one salient motivating factor was religiosity and/or spirituality.[6] Of the 56 respondents in our general population sample, 87 percent felt a strong sense of personal spirituality or religiosity, and these respondents scored 81 percent on the religion/spirituality variable in our data. Using both qualitative and quantitative data in comparing clergy and moral exemplars, we find that 87 percent of the 60 moral exemplars, and 96 percent of the 77 clergy, felt a strong sense of personal spirituality or religiosity. Prince and File's (1994) research on philanthropists suggests that people are donating money to nonprofits for religious motives, or because they see it as God's will. They give to others in need and at the same time gain something for themselves. Gerard (1985), in a British study of 1,231 volunteers, identified religious motivation as important. Story (1992) proposes the primary nature of freedom of choice in the voluntary act, and the spiritual nature, of volunteering.

A chaplain bases his actions on his relationship with God. That spiritual relationship stretches out to all of life, nature, and humanity:

> For me my relationship with God is what connects me with spirituality. But within that spirituality, it's being able to appreciate a sunset, enjoy nature, enjoy sitting quietly, having a cup of coffee. It involves relationships, caring for people, being compassionate, forgiving, merciful (Respondent 014).

Another respondent, a philanthropist, finds that his spirituality is directly related to his positive and generous interaction with others:

> I guess I believe my spirituality is not traditionally religious spirituality. It's more of a belief in the value of the individual. It has to do with a concept of how I live my life, which is to be a person who is generous in all aspects; a sort of generosity of spirit, a positive attitude, an attitude of trusting people, an attitude of respect for myself and others, a feeling that each of us … I'm not sure exactly how to put it. Our lives are in some way influenced by the lives of others.…being a person who distributes a sense of good will and good feelings not only enhances the lives the people around me, but my own as well (Respondent 033).

One of our respondents, a minister helping the homeless population in Humboldt County, works on the spiritual community level and then carries that to the physical community:

> I believe what we do in spiritual communities is perhaps the most important thing that happens within our communities (Respondent 001).

A psychologist-turned-management consultant still believes in the all-encompassing connection between humans and other species. He states:

> I have a belief that we are all connected, that there is energy in all of us; I think there are beings on other planets. I would say that I

believe in everything, but I don't have the truth in all things. I try to treat even the smallest creatures with great respect. If I catch a fly or mouse I will throw it outside or in the garden, not kill it (Respondent 008).

A physician intertwines God and friend, so they are one to him. He says:

My whole life has been loving people. When I hear faithful people speak of their sincerity around their particular God, I hear them use the language I use for friends, so I assume my metaphor for God is friend (Respondent 050).

An environmental activist has been involved with old-growth red-wood stands in Humboldt County and has internalized her caring for the earth:

One day I just felt this immense amount of love beginning to fill me up, and I was like, wow, where is this coming from? And I realized that what I was feeling was the unconditional love of the earth (Respondent 004).

Another environmental activist from Humboldt County wants to create awareness of watersheds, not only for the community, but also for the ecosystem and wildlife dependent upon the watershed. She relates her spiritual connection with the world:

Spirituality is how you connect to the rest of the world and the people and the beings in the world. And also, long after you're gone, how will your presence here have affected what happens a long time from now? What you do here now will somehow affect that whole. And if you do really good things, then you are going to leave that whole a better thing, and add to that energy, rather than detract from it (Respondent 034).

This fifth-grade teacher defines his spiritual growth in terms of connections and relationships with others. He elaborates:

I feel the important things in life that help you to become a better person and interact with others are the things I focus on. So if spirituality involves being a part of a group of people that you feel connected with, and you want that relationship to grow with those people, then that sense of spirituality is strong (Respondent 021).

A Humboldt County volunteer, a chaplain who gives spiritual support to hospital patients, correlates spirituality with interconnectedness with everything in the world. She states:

> I'm finding myself. It's an evolving thing. I'm beginning to sense the world beyond the surface; to see interconnectedness. They talk about the luminous quality of being, to be sensitive to that presence. I'm highly aware of that synchronicity, and that when I'm on a path that feels right, things seem to flow and come to me without any effort; that making an effort usually means I'm on the wrong path, not always, but usually (Respondent 010).

A long-time activist with the League of Women Voters also addresses the spiritual connectedness with people and nature when she says:

> I believe there's a great deal that we don't understand out there that is beneficial to us.... The most important thing is the connectedness of people, and that we connect one another to the spiritual things we don't understand—to the earth, to nature, to all of those things. I believe that it's all connected, and I think that's important. If we forget our connectedness, then we miss out and we can go astray (Respondent 042).

Three male clergy speak to us on religion and spirituality:

> Spirituality is the most important thing in my life and the lives of other people. Religion only helps me to live the spirituality. The spirituality is more for seeking peace and to live in a righteous way, and to be responsible for the neighbors. And also to feel responsibility for community, nation, and family. Religion is a set of rules, a set of rituals (Respondent 064).

> To be religious means to walk the talk. It means to be accommodating to people's real needs. It means to be in prayer-contact with God. It means to forgive, to be understanding. It means to search for meaning in life. We need to develop the soul aspect of our being rather than indulge the body. We need to enhance our minds, expand our consciousness of God and truth and beauty. For example, I am open to prayer forms that are not part of my own culture. I pray in ways that the Orthodox do, that the Buddhists do, that the Jews do. Religion is our relationship with God and God's relationship with us. Spirituality is the inner life (Respondent 070).

My definition of a spiritual person is an individual who quests within the community after that which is sacred. I don't see spiritualism, as many people do today, as an issue of individualism. There is a big thing today to define someone as spiritual in a sense that's juxtaposed to organized religion. Actually, I guess I find myself too Jewish for that. I am reminded each time I hear that discussion that our prayer books have only one prayer that is in the first person. All the rest of them refer to "we" collectively. So, when I define spiritualism, I mean somebody who seeks the sacred in community with others. I see that as far more powerful. I am not denying that there is an individual element. There are certainly individual elements there, but it is a matter of questing for and yearning for that which is sacred in the universe. I don't think that the distinction between religious and spiritual is as meaningful as some people would make it out to be (Respondent 082).

One Catholic nun explains what guides her:

I think being a religious person is striving to deepen your own understanding of the reality of a divine being. On a personal level, it is trying to be authentically who you are intended to be, to seek always to grow as a human. Spirituality is more important than a religion, or adhering to a particular religion. Spirituality is a deepening sense of beauty. It is the sense of the beauty of all creation. It is a sense of wonder, a sense of awe and respect for all that is. One's choice of a denomination is just a way of living out that reality, that realization that all that is is beautiful (Respondent 067).

Another nun contrasts spirituality and religion:

Religion is more of guidelines, rules, dogma, principles, and tenets that one intellectually assents to and chooses to practice. Spirituality is for me personal rather than a set of objectives that you adhere to freely. Spirituality is one's personal response to those, and the depth to which one aspires to them, and the meaning and the purpose of the ongoing challenge to be fully human (Respondent 069).

There can be little doubt that the American public is gaining a new regard for the importance of spirituality in American life. *Newsweek*, in its September 5, 2005 issue, reported on the results of a survey dealing with spirituality in America. They surveyed 1,004 Americans about how they worship and what they believe and how that affects their lives. The results in some measure reflect our own research. One of the findings was that 79 percent of the sample describes themselves as spiritual and 64 percent as religious. When asked about the importance of spirituality in their daily lives, 66 percent of those respondents older than 60 said that it was "very important," 63 percent of those between 40 and 59 years old agreed that it was "very important," and 44 percent of those between 18 and 39 thought it "very important." Another interesting response was that 67 percent believe that when they die, their souls will go to heaven (Adler et al 2005).

ALTRUISM AND HEALTH

Recently, scientists and researchers have found that there are many physical, psychological, and emotional benefits to altruistic behavior. People actually improve their own health and well-being if they help others. Researchers at the University of Michigan found that those who make efforts to help others tend to live longer than those who do not. These findings suggest that it isn't what we *get* from relationships that makes contact with others so beneficial; it's what we *give* (Swanbrow 2002). This has caused those who work with people with serious diseases to rethink strategies of giving help to the patients. It seems more beneficial for those suffering from terminal diseases to help others than to have others help them. Recent research shows that giving to or helping others improves mental health and increases longevity. Carolyn E. Schwartz and colleagues surveyed 2000 Presbyterians; their studies have been able to confirm the health benefits for givers, and receivers. Medical doctor and researcher Esther Sternberg reports that there are many aspects to altruistic behavior that help the giver's health, and most seem to be related to reduction of stress and a balanced emotional state. "It could be the stress response is reduced or could be other beneficial pathways that are enhanced," she says. One of these beneficial pathways that may be activated releases "feel-good" hormones called endorphins (Goldberg 2003). Sternberg's review of studies indicates that the neurobiology of altruism is similar to that of simple happiness, with all the benefits that such contentment provides (Institute for Research on Unlimited Love).

Stephen Post (2007) edited the research of leading experts on ways in which altruism improves one's own well-being and found a positive association between altruism and mental, physical, and emotional health. Doug Oman (2007) found that volunteers improve their physical health in two ways: First of all, activities that improve one's psychological state may prevent or reduce maladaptive behaviors, such as smoking or the abuse of other substances. Secondly, he finds that those who exhibit altruistic behavior experience less wear and tear on their own bodies. Oman concludes that living a loving and altruistic lifestyle has immediate and long-lasting physical and emotional benefits.

Similarly, Harold Koenig writes that there is a positive correlation between altruistic love and physical health (2002) as well as a connection between religion and health (Koenig 2001). Those who display altruistic tendencies in their lives have a lower risk of cancer and generally stronger immune systems. A main reason for this might be a reduction of the negative effects of the "fight/flight" response, which takes a serious toll on the human body. He concludes:

> It is difficult to be angry, resentful, or fearful, when one is showing selfless love towards another person. Such loving acts neutralize negative emotions and stimulate physiological responses known to adversely affect immune, endocrine, and cardiovascular function (Koenig 2007: 646).

Charlotte Witvliet (2001) addressed the important question of the relationship of health and faith, finding that those who are more religious and spiritual live longer. Nicholas Bakalar reported a study recently in the New York Times that shows there is an association between religion, spirituality, and health. Researchers found that 75 percent of a sample of 1,444 doctors reported that there is a positive relationship between health and spirituality.

Altruistic Behavior and Moral Exemplars

Looking at profiles of some moral exemplars—such as priests, ministers, nuns, rabbis, political activists, and environmentalists—we find that they share a number of common attributes. These attributes developed over time as the exemplars grew, learned, experienced the world, and recognized the need for moral behavior. What started in youth was affirmed through witnessing the moral behavior of parents or other people of significance in their lives. It was through acquiring an understanding of cognitive and affective behaviors that they began their involvement in helping, choosing settings that would bring forth their personality characteristics. A. Caspi, D. J. Bem, and G. H. Elder (1989), in "Continuities and Consequences of Interactional Styles Across the Life Course," maintain that individuals sometimes channel themselves into environments that give them an opportunity for further development along the road of helping. Individual interactions with others also are involved in developing the caring personality, because they later trigger and reinforce caring and prosocial behaviors, including forgiveness.

Environmentalist moral exemplars—such as Rachel Carson, Chico Mendes, and Julia "Butterfly" Hill—want to persuade others to be better caretakers and environmentally sound stewards of the earth. Rachel Carson was a pioneer of the environmental movement (Knauer 1996). As a young girl, she had aspired to be a writer, but after taking a required biology course in college, she switched her major from English to science, even though she feared doing so would diminish her chances for a writing career. It turned out, however, that her scientific training and her passion for the natural world provided her with the content for her writing. This passion led her to write such best-selling books as *Under the Sea Wind*, and *The Sea Around Us,* and win many literary awards.

After Carson received her master's degree in biology, she gained knowledge and experience working for the U.S. Fish and Wildlife Service. While there, she became concerned about the hazards of DDT and other pesticides used in agriculture, which led her to write her most famous book, *Silent Spring*. She chose *Silent Spring* as the title because she felt that the use of chemicals would eventually "still the song of birds, and the leaping of fish in the streams," literally resulting in a silent spring. Members of the chemical industry flexed their muscles and tried to block the book's publication, while some companies attempted to sue her for slander. Others spent millions in advertisements trying to discredit Carson—their efforts failed. Carson's book contained an important message, was written in a language and style the public could grasp, and came at a time of increased interest in environmental issues.

Carson fought battles against big business, educated scientists, sexism, and even her own cancer. She wrote to a friend, "The beauty of the living world I was trying to save has always been uppermost in my mind—that, and anger at the senseless, brutish things that were being done.... Now I can believe I have at least helped a little" (Better World Heroes 2006). Helped a little indeed! Though she died six years before the first Earth Day was celebrated, she is credited with having spawned many grassroots movements for saving Mother Earth and its creatures, human and nonhuman. The plight of endangered species, as well as the importance of stopping pollution of the water and air, were made a part of the public discourse as a result of her efforts. Former vice president Al Gore has said that had it not been for her books and her desire to understand what humans were doing to humankind and the environment, the environmental movement might have been delayed or not occurred at all.

Chico Mendes, a Brazilian, had a similar environmental consciousness and died fighting for the rain forest and its vitality—not only as the vast source of oxygen for the planet, but as habitat for many diverse species and home of indigenous tribes. He was the leader of rubber-tapping *seringueiros*, an indigenous group that had lived in the rain forest for over a hundred years, sustaining themselves by tapping rubber trees, collecting Brazil nuts, and pursuing other activities that ensured a healthy lifestyle for them and their offspring. Mendes organized a union—the Xapuri Rural Workers Union, consisting of rubber-tappers and small farmers— which worked "against encroaching cattle ranchers who were incinerating the rain forest to create pasture and to profit from tax breaks and booming real estate prices" (Reykin 1990: 4). As part of his efforts, Mendes convinced the Brazilian government to preserve 61,000 acres of rubber trees for "extractive reserve," an area designated only for the purposes of sustainable harvesting of rubber, Brazil nuts, and other natural resources. The concept of the extractive reserve, invented by Mendes and the tappers, was then refined with help from environmentalists and anthropologists. With the establishment of this and three other extractive reserves, Mendes had pulled off one of the most significant feats in the history of grassroots environmental activism.

As union president, Mendes made trouble for many powerful stakeholders and businessmen, namely cattle ranchers and the owner of Brazil's largest meatpacking corporation. One rancher, Darly Alves da Silva, had established a tradition of murder in the region. Although Mendes survived many attempts on his life over the years, he may have brought about his own downfall through his successful efforts to prevent Alves from taking tracts of property and converting them into pasture for his cattle. One night in late 1989, Mendes was killed; the murderers have never been brought to justice.

Chico Mendes "was to the ranchers of the Amazon what César Chavez was to the citrus kings of California, what Lech Walesa was to the shipyard managers of Gdansk" (San Francisco Chronicle 1998: 21). Mendes' inspirational leadership is still desperately needed again, because the Brazilian government has done little to save the forests. The *San Francisco Chronicle* editorialized: "We cannot let Chico Mendes be forgotten. His struggle is everyone's struggle, because justice for the people of the Amazon can benefit everyone's future" (*San Francisco Chronicle* 1998: A21).

Julia "Butterfly" Hill spent two years sitting atop an ancient redwood tree, named Luna by activists, to protest clear-cutting by Pacific Lumber Company in Northern California (Hill 2000). These were her words when her feet touched the ground after two years:

> I understand all of us are governed by different values. I understand that to some people I'm just a dirty tree-hugging hippie. But I can't imagine being able to take a chainsaw to something like this.... I think before anyone could be allowed to cut down [a tree] like this they should be mandated to live in it for two years (Wilson 2000: 35).

By making Luna her symbol and gaining an agreement with the lumber company that it would never be cut down, she brought the plight of our forests to the world's attention. Her fight was to make the world aware of the clear-cutting of old growth forests. These old growth redwoods, having towered over the land for thousands of years, were being cut down in a matter of minutes. Clear-cutting practices indiscriminately demolish thousands of acres of forest and wildlife habitat and are viewed as an irresponsible and unsustainable effort to increase corporate profits. For Hill, the clear cutting itself was a concern, because the logging method caused the devastation of the environment around the clear-cut area. When rain falls, the slopes have nothing left to absorb it. This results in landslides, soil erosion, floods, and a chain reaction of negative consequences affecting the ecosystem. Such was the fate of the little town of Stafford, California, which was demolished by unnatural flooding due to the clear cutting of trees and the mudslides that followed heavy rains.

To Hill, these trees were God's creations and needed preserving. She continues her fight for more sustainable logging of second and third-growth trees—those trees that are replanted or sprouted from seed after an area is cut down. When we interviewed her, she said:

> I had to make a stand against the raping of the forest unnecessarily. The human species can survive without having to cut down ancient forests. We should be recycling, reusing, being less wasteful, and while I am not against cutting down old trees, it should be done with an ecological plan in mind so as not to destroy everything around. (Oliner 2000a)

The daughter of an itinerant minister, Hill considers herself to be a spiritual person, and she was taught to take care not only of herself but others. This meant caring and seeing the connection among all living things. In her book, *The Legacy of Luna* (2000), she says, "I've always felt that as long as I was able, I was supposed to give all I've got to ensure a healthy and loving legacy for those still to come, and especially for those with no voice. That is what I've done in this tree" (Oliner 2000a).

When asked if she was afraid during those two years in the tree, she responded that she had felt fear, anger, and disappointment. Initially, she was afraid to be on top of the tree. She questioned whether she was doing the right thing. She was afraid of the lumber company security guards, the lumberjacks who harassed her by cutting down nearby trees that grazed hers, by noises in the night, including horns that kept her awake, and by being buzzed by company helicopters. But she said, "I had to conquer my fears.... Through prayer and the support of many, many people, I was able to prevail.... I was able to carry on there.... Besides praying, I did a lot of singing, so much so that even some lumberjacks would sometimes stop and listen. That is how I conquered my fears" (Oliner 2000a).

After her tree-sitting experience, she was honored by *Good Housekeeping* as one of the "Most Admired Women of 1998," while *George* magazine named her "One of the 20 Most Interesting Women in Politics." She helped found the Circle of Life Foundation, created to promote sustainability and preservation of life. Hill's hope for the future is to sensitize people to what is happening to the environment due to logging practices in old growth forests. She believes that each person who becomes sensitive can make a difference—by speaking out, recycling, and "taking on corporations that are involved in the unnecessary destruction of the environment" (Oliner 2000a).

Religious moral exemplars have left their mark on the world. From Buddha to Jesus and Mohammed, from the Dalai Lama to Mother Teresa, the values and morals of the religious have changed how we think and act toward our fellow humans. In the course of his life's work, the Dalai Lama has taught the world about compassion and forgiveness, which has endeared him to millions. He maintains, "The main theme of Buddhism is altruism based on compassion" (Hevesi 1989: A6). As an approximate definition, he believes compassion is "A mental attitude based on the wish for others to be free of their suffering and is associated with a sense of commitment, responsibility, and respect toward the other" (Hevesi 1989: A6).[7] The type of attitude of which he speaks is a feeling that enables people, when faced with a choice, to choose the welfare of another over their own. The development of this type of compassion is not an easy task; nevertheless, he understands that various means for its cultivation exist. He suggests, "One could begin with the wish that oneself be free of suffering, and then take that natural feeling toward oneself and cultivate it, enhance it, and extend it out to include and embrace others" (Dalai Lama and Cutler 1998: 114).

He says that empathy, the ability to appreciate another's suffering, is an important factor for the development of compassion. The Dalai Lama maintains that once you encourage the thought of compassion in your mind, once that thought becomes active, then your attitude toward others changes automatically. If you approach others with the thought of compassion, that will automatically reduce fear and allow openness with other people.

3

MANIFESTATIONS OF ALTRUISM IN DIFFERENT RELIGIOUS TRADITIONS

There are aspects to religious traditions that have caused enormous harm to humanity. We need only look at the Hebrew Bible, in which the Israelites attacked people in Canaan as they were attempting to claim their new homeland; the Crusaders, who caused enormous mass murders against Jews and Muslims; or at Christian missionaries in the New World, who helped devastate native populations. Richard Dawkins, in his book *The God Delusion* (2006), says that belief in God is a delusion that has destructive effects. Sam Harris (2004) maintains that religion is dangerous because it is a form of ideology that has been a permanent and "perpetual source of human conflict" (Harris 2004: 236). Christopher Hitchens (2007) is a recent critic about the devastating effects of religious teachings. But we are not dealing here with the negative aspect of religion, even though we recognize it, but rather with the manifestations of altruistic inclination and behavior inspired by religion. Hitchens, Dawkins, and Harris fail to credit the positive contributions of religious faith toward the poor and neglected, whom other institutions ignore to a large extent. While some religious traditions are likely to help only their own believers, others are inclusive and help the needy of whatever faith.

In this chapter, we briefly look at the commonality of the altruistic inclinations of different traditions, supporting our view that religious tradition does in fact help those in need. What is significant in comparing these religious traditions is the commonality of all, even though they have different interpretations and explanations for the meaning of the beginning and end of life. It is only by chance that each of us is born into the culture we live in, whether it is based on Judaism, Buddhism, Christianity, or another religious tradition. We humans often think less of the religions of others simply because we do not know enough about them. According to Levine (2006) this ignorance is shown even by well-meaning Christian scholars who do not know much about Judaism or ignore its relationship to Christianity. A similar statement could be made about some Jewish scholars who do not know enough about Christian doctrine. When we are able to understand each other's religions, we see the beauty and profundity of all faiths, and this may help to break down the barriers among us. Indeed, if there is one very important point that we learn from all these traditions, it is that we are all children of the same universe.

Jacob Neusner and Bruce Chilton (2005) focus on the question of whether altruism is a useful category for the academic study of religion and whether it provides a distinctive perspective to that study. The answer seems problematic, because if one's religion tells us to act in a certain manner, does this mean that religious individuals' acts, which seem to be for the benefit of others, are actually altruistic? In other words, does helping poor people become a self-interested act? This question is further confused when salvation through works is involved, as it is in some interpretations of Catholicism. Neusner and Alan J. Avery-Peck (2005) give examples of how Judaism's adherents ought to behave, and we have seen how adherents to other religions are expected to behave within the context of their own traditions. Hence, many argue that mandated behavior cannot be properly labeled "altruistic" in this sense. They argue that altruistic behavior is not really voluntary, which is an important part of most religious traditions.

There is a problem for us with this approach, because what interests us here is the outcome of altruistic behavior. We do not see much value in discussing whether or not religion fosters altruistic behavior, because in fact it does. In fact, studies show that people who score high on religious values also are more likely to be among the selfless helpers (Batson 1991). We also do not give much weight to the discussion of whether altruistic behavior benefits the helper, that is whether it is in reality egoistic, or whether it is largely motivated by empathy. What is important is to understand the positive outcome of such behavior. Finally, it is inconceivable for us to understand how major religious traditions can advocate kindness, acts of compassion, and loving one's neighbor, and not have a profound influence on those individuals who do not know much about religious precepts, but rather have been influenced by religion's moral role models and their moral communities. We cannot help but emphasize that some religious teachings do have a positive effect on caring and helping those in need, thus bringing about a more caring world.

William Scott Green maintains, "Without question, religions are major forces for other-directed human behavior. That such a behavior operates within the transcendental or eternal framework does not diminish its impact or lessen its capacity to improve human conditions" (Green 2005: 194).

So, we must return to the question we posed earlier: namely, what kind of people act justly for the benefit of others? We have seen that there is no single explanation. However, our research (Oliner and Oliner 1988; Oliner 2003, 2004, 2005) and the studies of others (Gushee 2003; Tec 1986; Paldiel 2000; Midlarsky, Kahana, and Corley 1986; Fogelman 1995; Huneke 1986; and Baron 1986) help us piece together a list of the attributes associated with an individual's tendency toward altruism.

Altruistic people are fundamentally empathic: they feel others' pain. They tend to come from loving homes with caring role models. They were raised in a positive manner, where discipline was a process and talking about right and wrong was key. They were attached in a healthy emotional and psychological way to their families. They internalized the ethics of justice and compassion for others, as well as a universal sense of spirituality that is tolerant of other faiths and moral traditions (Roth 2005 2006). They are members of a moral community, in which individuals are encouraged to learn social responsibility. They believe in social justice, being involved in social action, and in social responsibility. They live the idea of "love thy neighbor as thyself" and realize that without love, there is no future. And those individuals who exhibit altruistic personality traits believe in the power and necessity of apology and forgiveness as the means to restoring broken relationships.

Next we examine some major religious traditions, looking for salient examples of altruistic inclination and behavior. We begin with Judaism.

JUDAISM

The basic source of Jewish belief is the Hebrew Bible, called the Old Testament by Christians, which consists of three major works: The Torah (the five books of Moses) and the First and Last Writings; together they form the Tanakh. The *Torah* was traditionally regarded as the primary revelation of God and his laws to humanity; it is considered valid for all time. Its laws were clarified and elaborated in the oral *Torah*, or the tradition of the elders, and were eventually written down in two other works, the *Mishnah* and *Talmud*. These traditions consist of legal, ethical, philosophic, mystical, and devotional issues, and they are impressive in their length.

The goal of Judaism lies in strict obedience to God. The philosophy perceived in Judaism is that humankind has two impulses: good and evil. One can alleviate the plight of the individual and of society by being compassionate, just, forgiving, and by loving and obeying God. Or, one can rebel and be influenced by Satan, who caused God's creation to go astray. To follow God's law is the highest morality, which includes—among many other good things—justice, charity, ethics and honesty, and being true to the one true God, Yahweh. The Ten Commandments propose desirable relationships with one's neighbor, one's father and mother, and God.

Judaism is the mother religion of both Christianity and Islam, and Christianity has inherited main religious ideas and ritual practices from Judaism. Jews do not belong to any one race or people in the anthropological sense. They were expelled from their homeland, ancient Palestine, and today are found in most parts of the world.

Despite dispersal, Jews have retained a sense of peoplehood, and in great part this is due to their religious practices. Jews claim a special relationship to God and believe that by receiving the Torah, which contains the Ten Commandments, that He has ordered them to be righteous. The prophet Micah made the famous declaration that God requires all humankind to do good, which means to practice loving kindness and walk humbly with God.

During Rosh Hoshanna, observant Jews recall their deeds towards other human beings over the preceding year. Ten days later on Yom Kippur, the Day of Atonement, observant Jews are encouraged to think about the harm and offenses they have committed over the past year. They are asked to apologize to neighbors, and if they do not apologize, to try to do better for their fellow human beings. Acts of loving kindness are the best means of making amends. As the rabbis have said, "whoever has sinned, let him go and do a good deed, and he or she will be forgiven" (Ross and Hills 1956: 120).

Tzedakah is the Hebrew word for charity. It means giving aid, assistance and money to the poor or to worthwhile causes, and it includes the responsibility to give a portion of one's personal substance for the common good (Degroot 2005). A *mitzvah* includes 613 commandments Jews are obligated to observe, and, more generally, refers to any good deed. One often reads of the "*mitzvah* of *tzedakah*." *Tzedakah* is more than just giving money to the poor. In the writings of Maimonides, whoever gives *tzedakah* to the poor with a sour expression and in a surly manner, even if he gives a thousand gold pieces, loses his merit. One should instead give cheerfully and joyfully, and empathize with his sorrow.

The command to love one's neighbor, found in the book of Leviticus, is central to the Jewish faith (Templeton 1999: 11). In fact, Templeton argues that in Judaism, "When one loves and cares for others, one is loving God" (1999: 11). The Bible portrays a God who loves all people: the rich and the poor, the weak and the powerful. God's love is unconditional.

One of our interviewees, a man who has helped in the Jewish community for many years, said:

> My own feeling about being spiritual is that I'm a person that other people can look up to. I consider two main qualifications: one, that you do good [in Hebrew, *tikun olan* – fix the world], that you're a constructive person in your family, in your community, and in your country. Secondly, that you have goals and beliefs and activities that are bigger than yourself. (Respondent 013)

Another, a woman who identifies herself with the culture of being Jewish and of helping:

> Just being Jewish influences a me lot.... I mean there's such an infusion of persecution throughout Jewish cultural history that there is always a sense of helping out in communities for people who don't have as much, through thick and thin; you know, helping people more.[8]

The Bible holds many references to altruism. In Leviticus: "And when you reap the harvest of your land, you shall not reap all the way to the edges of your field, or gather the gleanings of your harvest. You shall not pick the vineyard bare, or gather the fallen fruit of your vineyard; you shall leave them for the poor and the stranger; I am the Lord your God" (Leviticus 19:9–10). In Deuteronomy, God commands the faithful: "If, however, there is a needy person among you, do not harden your heart and shut your hand against your needy kinsmen. Rather, you must open your hand and lend him sufficient for whatever he needs" (Deuteronomy 15:7–8).

It is considered more credible by some to develop a habit of giving regularly rather than giving large sums infrequently. Placing a *pushke*—a tin can where coins may be donated—in the house represents one way people express a commitment to helping their communities philanthropically. By collecting money in one's home regularly, whether for a specific cause or the community's general good, one is fulfilling an obligation to help neighbors. The use of a *pushke* is meant to further the spirit of philanthropy and righteousness in the home and in the community.

Charity has been defined in many ways. It may consist of offering help to the poor, or almsgiving. It may be a general benevolence or generosity toward others or toward humanity, or indulgence or forbearance in judging others.

Helping your neighbor can manifest itself in many ways. One such way for Jews is through MAZON, a citizens' movement, which is the outgrowth of tens of thousands of American Jews who have stepped forward to try to solve hunger, one of the world's most devastating—and most preventable—problems. With their support, MAZON works around the globe to bring critical relief to millions of hungry families. MAZON also funds emergency food providers, food banks, multi-service organizations and advocacy groups both in the country and abroad.

Like all other religions, Judaism teaches about the importance of ethics, love, kindness, caring, and social responsibility. Yet it is important to realize that the faiths that we discuss in this chapter have an ideal level and a real level. By *ideal level,* we mean they preach these things; however, they fail to live up to the ideals in their sacred books.

Chief Rabbi Jonathan Sacks, a major Jewish scholar who represents an ecumenical spirit in his writings, emphasizes the importance of responsibility. In his book *To Heal a Fractured World* (2005), he speaks about responsibility as one of the major ethical virtues. He speaks about charity as justice and the importance of love that must translate into compassionate deeds. He feels that human beings are capable of repairing the world now. He addresses the universality of all human beings and emphasizes strongly the importance of kindness towards strangers and society.

Rabbi Sacks maintains that Judaism is a complex faith, but that Jewish ethics are down to earth and practical. It is not enough to speak about help, caring, and compassion: it matters to the Jewish God only when he sees action on the part of one to another. Sacks stresses the concept of inclusiveness among human beings. He cites Rabbi Abraham Kook (1865-1935), who said, "The narrow-mindedness that leads one to see whatever is outside the bounds of one's people ... is ugly and defiled, is a terrible darkness that causes general destruction to the entire edifice of spiritual good, the light of which every refined soul hopes for" (Sacks 2005: 10). Judaism also stresses the importance of righteousness.

Deuteronomy 16:18 tells people, "Do not stand by idly by the blood of your neighbor." In other words, don't be a bystander to murder or injustice. Jewish writings have much to say about justice. Isaiah 1:17 says "Learn to do good, seek justice, aid the oppressed, uphold the rights of the orphan, defend the cause of the widow." Dr. Sacks disagrees strongly with Karl Marx, who famously called religion "the opium of the people." Rather, he maintains that religion, in its most authentic form, is actually quite practical and helpful, because it includes, among other deeds, helping others to obtain justice. Within Judaism, justice is a form of caring or altruism; it is considered a form of charity. A *Tzedaka* is a kind of deed, intended not to humiliate the recipient, but to render him aid and return him to a condition in which he can stand on his own two feet. Charity as loving kindness has many manifestations in Judaism. For example, when King Alfonso V of Portugal captured 250 African Jews and sold them as slaves throughout the Kingdom of Portugal, Portuguese Jews formed a representative committee of 12 members and traveled throughout the country redeeming the Jewish slaves, often at a very high price. These ransomed Jews were clothed, lodged, and maintained until they had learned the language of the country and were able to support themselves (Sacks 2005).

Jews believe, at least at the ideal level, that the world is reparable by loving thy neighbor. Using a vast body of literature and learning, Rabbi Sacks speaks about the singleness of the human soul—and it is not simply a Jewish soul but inclusive. Great emphasis is stressed on the treatment of strangers. Rabbi Sacks concludes that even the smallest good deed can change someone's life, and that religions reach their highest level when they stop worrying about other people's souls and care instead for the needs of their bodies. The ability to give to others is a gift. Judaism, like other religious traditions, has great and lofty teachings in its sacred texts, although not all Jews live up to those ideals.

CHRISTIANITY

Christianity is based on the teachings of Jesus of Nazareth some 2,000 years ago. It is the world's largest religion, followed by Islam. Scriptures in the Christian Bible consist of the Old Testament (39 books of the Hebrew Bible) and the New Testament. There are three major sects of Christianity: Catholicism, Eastern Orthodox, and Protestantism, which has splintered into many denominations. Like Judaism and Islam, Christianity is mono-theistic. The goal of Christians is to gain eternal life with God in heaven, which is considered a perfect existence of bliss. The path of attainment is obedience to God. As in some other major religions, Christians believe that man is born a sinner and can receive salvation only from God. For them, this salvation comes through belief in Jesus Christ as savior. Some Christians have an unshakable belief that Christianity is the only true religion, the only path to salvation, and that only "good Christians" will be saved, which is somewhat problematic; but the other side of Christian-ity emphasizes love, compassion, and caring. Christianity, like Judaism, adheres to the Ten Commandments. Also, as in Judaism, Christianity teaches the Golden Rule: "Do unto others as you would have them do unto you."

Jesus is the central figure of the Christian religion. Stories about Jesus are numerous; probably the best known come from the first four books of the New Testament, known as the Gospels. Each of the books is separately written and presents Jesus's life in a way that would appeal to a wide group of people. The main point emphasized in Christianity is that Jesus was born to the Virgin Mary, is the Son of God, and that God loved humankind so much that he sacrificed his own son, Jesus, in order to absolve humanity from its sins. Though Jesus was a Jew and some of the teachings of the two religions overlap, Jesus's teachings were never accepted by the Jews. Even though Jesus's disciple Peter insisted upon keeping the movement exclusively Jewish, Paul was able to persuade Peter and others to admit non-Jews into the group (Ross and Hills 1956: 137). It was not long before non-Jews outnumbered Jews in the Christian movement.

Christianity, like other faiths, strongly emphasizes that its believers should clothe the naked and feed the poor, but to Christians, caring for other human beings reflects the essence of the love of Christ for humanity. Christianity preaches love for one's fellow human beings and peace and justice for all. It also teaches that there is no greater love for a man than to give up his life for another man. Christians manifest caring and altruism on a global scale through establishing charities that assist the needy around the world. In fact, there is a worldwide Catholic charitable institution called *Caritas*, which stands for altruism, charity, and compassion for others.

A recent example of Christian charity was manifested in Mother Teresa of Calcutta, who dedicated her life to helping the poor and afflicted in India. In Macedonia, where she grew up, statues and shrines of the

Madonna and Child impressed her, moving her to become increasingly involved with the activities of the local Sacred Heart Church. One of the most influential priests in her life was Franjo Jambernkovic, a Croatian who encouraged her; it was he who pushed her toward missionary work in India.

In 1928 she traveled to Ireland and entered the Order of the Sisters of Our Lady of Loretto and was subsequently sent to Darjeeling, India for her training. She then studied for a teaching certificate at Loretto Entally in Calcutta, taking her final religious vows in 1937. Every time she left the convent and ventured out into the city, she was moved by the plight of the sick and the dying, always to be found on the streets.

In 1946, on a train trip to Darjeeling, she received the call from God that transformed her life, thus beginning her quest for permission to minister to the sick and dying. In 1948 she was allowed by the Vatican to leave her post at the convent. She founded the Missionaries of Charity in 1950, and a number of nuns trained and worked with her. During the day the nuns taught, and during the evening they cared for the poor in the slums of Calcutta. Their creed and purpose was:

> To fulfill our mission of compassion and love to the poorest of the poor we go: seeking out in towns and villages all over the world even amid squalid surroundings the poorest, the abandoned, the sick, the infirm, the leprosy patients, the dying, the desperate, the lost, the outcasts; taking care of them; rendering help to them; visiting them assiduously; living Christ's love for them; and awakening their response to His great love. [9]

In 1952, Mother Teresa opened the *Nirmal Hriday* (or "Pure Heart") Home for Dying Destitutes in Calcutta and subsequently extended her work onto five continents. In recognition of her efforts, she was awarded the Nobel Peace Prize in 1979. In presenting the prize, Chairperson John Sanness said of her: "Can any political, social, or intellectual feat of engineering, on the international or on the national plane, however effective and rational, however idealistic and principled its protagonists may be, give us anything but a house built on a foundation of sand, unless the spirit of Mother Teresa inspires the builders and takes its dwelling in their building?" [10]

In 1990 Mother Teresa became ill and was forced to scale down her activities; in 1997, after a long and selfless life, she died. Mother Teresa represents the ultimate example of how altruism is exhibited through

Christian love and caring, although recently Hitchens (1995) has pointed out that she has not been a perfect human being.

Just as all Jews do not subscribe to *Mazon* or practice *Tzedaka*, not all Catholics support Caritas, and not all Christians dedicate their lives to the poor and dying. But many do involve themselves in this faith-based form of helping others. There are common themes in Judaism and Christianity: the Golden Rule, loving one's neighbor, clothing the naked, and feeding the hungry. This similarity can be traced back to the Abrahamic roots of both religions.

ISLAM

Moslems believe that their religion, founded in the early seventh century, is the restoration of the original religion of Abraham (Judaism) through the Prophet Mohammed. It is the second largest religion after Christianity with approximately one billion believers, primarily in the Middle East, Pakistan, Bangladesh, Africa, China, Indonesia, Central Asia, and India, although many adherents can be found in Europe and the Western Hemisphere as well. There are two main divisions within Islam: The Sunnis are followers of the political successors of Mohammed. The Shiites are followers of Mohammed's family successors, Iman Ali and others, all of whom were martyred at an early age. The major scripture is the Koran.

The primary goal of Islam is to enjoy eternal spiritual life in heaven with Allah (God). Heaven is a paradise in which all the joys and pleasures abound, and man is the noblest creation of God, ranking above the angels. To attain this state, Muslims believe that they must observe the virtues of truthfulness, temperance, and humility before God, and that the practices of fasting, pilgrimage, prayer, charity, and acts of altruism to the Moslem community—and other creatures of God—are most necessary to please Allah.

In the Koran, it was explained that while Judaism and Christianity also had prophets who revealed the truth, Mohammed was the latest prophet who proclaimed the truth to humanity. One of Mohammed's major biblical functions was to try to convince other tribes that there was but one God, Allah, and that Mohammed was God's prophet. He drew up a constitution for his people, who were trying hard to unite, and made them into a close-knit fellowship. The people had to protect each other against enemies and help with other difficulties. Mohammed expected that the Jews and the Christians would accept him as the next prophet because of all they hold in common. He was prepared to be very patient with his Jewish followers. In Medina, he asked his followers to pray facing Jerusalem as Jews do currently, and emphasized the common elements of their traditions. When it became clear that the majority of the Jews had no intention of calling Mohammed their prophet, and some of the Jews violated the terms of the agreement they had with Mohammed, he demanded that they convert to Islam or leave.

In Islam there is a Day of Judgment, such as in Judaism and Christianity, when Allah judges everyone for their deeds and for having followed the precepts of Islam. Islam's contribution to altruism is its belief that Allah is goodness and its central teaching is that men should help each other. One of the five pillars of Islamic faith is the obligation of charity, *zalat;* that is, the admonition to aid the less fortunate. The Koran instructs those who would follow God not only to do for others what they would have others do for them but to "give in full what is due from you, whether you expect or wish to receive full consideration from the other side or not" (Templeton 1999: 37). The emphasis on giving and helping within the Abrahamic religions is a primary reason prosocial behavior is considered a social norm and a moral imperative in Western culture.

The Koran is filled with messages ordering people to behave ethically. Mohammed forbade gambling and intoxication. Donations and alms to the poor are strong precepts, as are kindness, compassion, and caring for one's neighbors.

"What is the purpose of being good?" asked Islam scholar Aminah Assilmi. "As a Muslim, I believe that there is a God, Creator of the universe. We should judge what is good by what the Creator has said. Good is something that changes with time. Islam goes through the relationships between parents and children, brothers and sisters, and so on; and these guidelines will never change or be outdated. However, the understanding of Islam by different people may change." Assilmi noted the unique nature of the basic value structure of Islam. "If we could just learn more about these guidelines, we could make the world a better place." She notes the differences in the concept of altruism from Islam to other religions. "Every religion requires you to be kind, but Islam goes down to the minutest details. For example, Muslims are supposed to know their neighbors well enough to be able to help them out with their problems" (Khan 2003). Koran, Sura al-Hashr (The Gathering 59:9), "But those who, before them, had homes [in Medina] and had adopted the Faith, show their affection to such as came to them for refuge, and entertain no desire in their hearts for things given to them, but give them preference over themselves, even though poverty was their own lot. And those saved from the covetousness of their own souls; they are the ones who achieve prosperity."[11]

In Islam it is not considered enough to have noble beliefs and principles. One must work for the economic upliftment of the less fortunate and needy. The Koran states (The Gathering 59:9) "Those saved from the covetousness of their own souls; they are the ones that achieve prosperity."[12] The Koran also says (The Gathering 39): "So give the kinsman his due, and to the needy, and to the wayfarer. That is best for those who seek the favor of Allah, and it is they who prosper." In this verse the Koran uses the Arabic word which means "present" instead of "give," indicating that when a Muslim gives charity to his poor brother, he is not doing a favor but rather discharging the obligation he owes him—returning to him what is his due. According to the Prophet Muhammad, if the right hand gives charity, the left hand should not know to whom he gives. Islam requires that not only should the material needs of the poor be fulfilled, but also that their dignity be maintained.

Kindness is another very important attribute of the Islamic religion. Muhammad said, "God is kind and loves kindness in all things." He also said, "God is kind and loves kindness, and grants kindness but is most granted to harshness, and what is not granted to anything else." He also said, "Anything is beautiful by the inclusion of kindness and is marred by its lack" (Cleary 2001: 130).

BUDDHISM

Buddhism is about 2,500 years old and is based on the teachings of Guatama Siddhartha Buddha. The main goal of Buddhism is to attain nirvana, which is defined as the end of change and the end of birth and rebirth. One can reach Nirvana through various practices, including meditation, leading a moral life, and detaching oneself from possessions and the struggle for wealth.

Buddha adapted the Vedic and Brahmanic concepts of rebirth and dependent origination. According to these theories, the next life is dependent upon the good and bad that one does in the present. In order to leave behind the cycle of death and rebirth, and thus also leave behind suffering, one must follow the precepts of Buddhism. In Buddhism the causes of suffering include the force of desire. Cessation of suffering comes from completely giving up the desires that lead to suffering; only after detaching ourselves from desire can we end the cycle of birth, pain, and rebirth. There are eight paths that one can follow to end suffering: right thought/aim; right speech; right action; right livelihood/occupation; right effort/endeavor; right mindfulness—which includes caring, love, and right meditation. Another very important step is to give love and show compassion toward other creatures.

There are at least two major sects in Buddhism: Mahayana and Hinayama. Mahayana Buddhists emphasize the ideal of the unselfish *bodhisattva*, a living being committed to awakening. The bodhisattvas, because of their compassion for suffering beings, have delayed entering Nirvana even though they are capable of reaching enlightenment. The bodhisattva remains instead in this world to help others attain enlightenment.

Buddhism views altruism as an expression of one's awakening to one's true self and explains that it stems from compassion, appreciation, and a sense of interconnection. Buddhism encourages a holistic view of self, a view that transcends selfishness. Robert Ruffner Chilton (1992) notes that the essence of Buddhism, according to the Dalai Lama, consists of loving kindness and compassion; these are the two cornerstones upon which all of Buddhism rests. The core of Buddhist doctrine is to practice altruism: one should refrain from harming others and help others whenever possible. The most important practice is the *lojong* tradition (mind training), which implies ethical behavior on psychological grounds and accounts for why bodhisattvas act for the benefit of others and abstain from self-cherishing.

In Tibet, an Indian known as Atisa (980–1054) was involved in lojong instruction. Atisa traveled through parts of Southeast Asia including Sumatra, where Mahayana Buddhism—under the patronage of the Sailindra Empire—was introduced. Much of the teachings of Atisa focused on generating *bodhicitta*, which means an equal exchange of oneself in others. Atisa said, "Whenever I meet a person of bad nature who is overwhelmed by the negative energy and intense suffering, I will hold such a rare one dear and as if I found a precious treasure" (Geshe Tsultrim Gyeltsam quoted in Chilton 1992: 12).

The practice of bodhicitta is simply letting go of the feeling of indifference toward others and maintaining a sincere and loving mind towards all (Chilton 1992: 14). His Holiness the Dalai Lama said the bodhicitta is the ultimate state of mind that will allow us to accomplish our own welfare as well as the welfare of all other sentient beings (Chilton 1992: 15).

According to Chilton, there are five steps in generating *bodhicitta* by way of practices that equalize the exchange:

1. Viewing the equality between oneself and others

2. Contemplating the faults of self-cherishing

3. Contemplating the advantage of cherishing others

4. Exchanging oneself for others

5. Engaging in the practice of giving and taking

Thus, the essential spirit of altruism in these *lojong* teachings can be summarized as recognizing that self-concern is a true enemy of others' happiness and that others are true friends, worthy of our concern (Chilton 1992: 34).

Self-cherishing is one of the problems in the world today, by which we mean that a person looks out for "number one" and is not concerned with "the other." By cherishing another you are benefiting from it, and that may result in being cherished yourself. Having perceived emptiness, as compassion arises, there is no self or other. When there is no self or other, you will bring about the well being of all living beings (Chilton 1992: 24).

The Buddha, as he was about to die, was questioned by some of his students. They were concerned that after the master's death, people might begin propounding doctrines that had not been spoken by the Buddha himself, and these people might tell others that these doctrines were the actual words of Buddha. In reply, the Buddha told them "Whatever is well spoken is the word of the Buddha." If teaching results in greater peace, compassion, and happiness, and if it leads to a lessening of negative emotions, then it can be safely adopted and practiced as *dharma*, no matter who originally propounded it.

The Dalai Lama's contribution toward the promotion of global peace was formally recognized in 1989, when he won the Nobel Peace Prize. According to the Nobel Committee, he "consistently has opposed the use of violence…and advocated peaceful solutions based upon tolerance and mutual respect in order to preserve the historical and cultural heritage of his people" (Dalai Lama 1989). The Dalai Lama exhibits his love of humanity and warmth. He does not speak bitterly against the Chinese who continue to oppress Tibet, his homeland. Instead, he stresses a positive focus on human rights and the preservation of Tibetan cultural values. He has a great desire and need not only to hold onto faith and spirituality but also to seek truth. He believes that truth leads to understanding, inspiration, and a full liberation from ignorance and the suffering that we impose upon each other; these in turn will help bring about world peace. Buddhists believe that suffering can then cease and that lasting peace can be achieved—both peace of mind and peace in the world. "The path to such peace," the Dalai Lama says, "begins with the development of a calm abiding." He believes people need to have faith that they can achieve a more enlightened state of existence, even when the material world seems to deny such a possibility. There must be an ongoing interaction between reason and faith, between analysis and the growing conviction that one can find ways to live for the betterment of all human beings.

The Dalai Lama also maintains that there is another aspect of spiritual wholeness—compassionate action. Just as reason and faith interact to enhance conviction, so too do reflection and action interact to determine our spiritual faith. He further maintains that *all* religious thought points toward loving kindness and compassionate action. We must not believe that we are isolated, totally independent actors in this world. Rather, it is important that we keep our interdependence in mind, and remember that we are woven together by spiritual life. If we can maintain faith and conviction that such an understanding is the foundation on which we build our lives, then we must treat all human beings and other living things with respect and love. We may not succeed, but it is important to try our best. Then we will have at least made an attempt to form a better human society.

The Dalai Lama says that all the religious faiths, despite their philosophical differences, share an emphasis on human improvement, love and respect for others, and compassion. Prejudice and intolerance are afflictions of human society. When altruism is practiced, we are not angry at our enemies but are kind to them. When we are altruistic, we not only have inner happiness but can work toward social understanding, cooperation, unity, and harmony. Buddhism has historically sought a solution to suffering in inner transformation and a corresponding commitment to the highest ethical ideals, unlike science, which has sought a solution through knowledge (Davidson and Harrington 2002).

Kenneth Liberman (1985) concludes that the Tibetan people have developed a cultural praxis for the generation of altruism which operates on a mass scale and which is soundly based on a philosophical logic. In the Tibetan system of bodhicitta thought training, epistemology interacts with ethical practices: "method" and "wisdom" mutually affect each other.

Just as one is said to be incapable of achieving enlightenment through altruistic compassion alone, it is held to be impossible to attain Buddhahood with only wisdom. Compassion and wisdom are mutually influential consciousnesses. Each augments, activates, and sets the tone for the other at every stage of the path. Bodhicitta is the seed for all higher mental and spiritual development. In this fashion, the Tibetans undertake ethical training that is philosophical, and conduct philosophical investigations that are ethical, in their orientation and their consequences (Liberman 1985: 125). Meditation is another attribute of Buddhism. Some perceive that meditation is a form of self-absorption, an Eastern relaxation technique. But some scholars feel that meditation is "better considered as a powerful means of engaging a universal psychological process, that of shifting one's preoccupation with self to a sense of interconnectedness with others." Jean Kristeller and Thomas Johnson (in press) compare the Buddhist tradition of loving kindness meditation, Judeo-Christian means of cultivating compassion and altruistic behavior, and the resurgent Catholic interest in contemplative prayer; all stress this idea of interconnectedness (Kristeller and Johnson, in press: 18–19). In effect, all religious traditions seek to encourage what Kristeller and Johnson term "a universal capacity for altruistic experience, love, and compassion" (2).

However, Catholic scholar Mathew Fox sees some differences between Buddhism and the Judeo-Christian traditions:

> Buddhism is explicit about compassion, for example, although I think that the Jewish and Christian traditions are more explicit about justice—but justice is a part of compassion. The Western prophets bring a kind of moral outrage, what I call "holy impatience," whereas the East brings serenity and an emphasis on patience. I think there's a time for both, but I think we are in a time now of holy impatience. (Van Gelder 2006: 22)

HINDUISM

Hinduism is considered to be the oldest organized religion in the world. Hindus accept other religions with respect and do not look down upon them. Hinduism teaches that all reality is ultimately one, in being and in function. Thus, if all are one, then the only way to treat others is with *agape*, respect, kindness, justice, and compassion. In a Hindu context, agape is the byproduct of *bhakti yogi*, which is the realization of God through love—compassionate love is the highest vehicle to union with

God. Agape follows as a natural expression of purifying one's motives and being of service. In pursuing God, one becomes more like God, and agape follows as a natural result.

There are a number of gods in Hinduism; the supreme one being Brahman, creator of the world. Unlike Christianity or Judaism, many of the gods are personalized and have human characteristics. The largest percentage of Hindus worship three main gods: Brahman; Vishnu, the savior; and Shiva, the destroyer and restorer.

Hindus believe that the creation of the world is a continuous process and is not finished. The world is a living entity with human beings reincarnated into various stages in life, depending upon their deeds in previous lives. A complex religion, Hinduism seeks answers to questions about the meaning of life and about aspects of living a moral and ethical life. Hindus seeking to live a good life have several goals. They should participate in the good life—and material goods can be important—but while one is making a living, one should not strive to accumulate wealth for its own sake. Each person has an important obligation to himself and to society to help all living things. Hindu teachings emphasize the idea of moral duty; selfishness is frowned upon, while selflessness is perhaps the most important moral precept.

The ideas of justice, caring, and nonviolence were added to the Hindu religion by Rama Krishna (Ross and Hills 1956: 42), who is considered by some to be the reincarnation of the supreme Lord Vishnu (Ross and Hills 1956: 44). Rama Krishna attempted to combine the great spiritual values of Buddhism, Islam, and Christianity. He is remembered as one who sought the unity of all religions. One of the main values of Hinduism is peace, and its most famous representative among Hindus is Mahatma Gandhi, who was known worldwide as an advocate of peace and nonviolence. In fact, in the areas of human rights and social activism, there is no greater moral exemplar than Mahatma Gandhi. Gandhi's persistent passive resistance helped liberate India from years of oppression, and his *Satyagraha* ("truth-force") acts of nonviolent resistance in the service of moral truth were among the most influential events of the twentieth century. In 1948, India gained its independence largely through nonviolent resistance. Gandhi's ideology of nonviolent resistance on behalf of freedom and human dignity is his most durable legacy. Martin Luther King, Jr., employed Gandhi's techniques to change the face of a segregated nation. Likewise, Nelson Mandela inspired South Africans to work persistently against centuries of racism, terrorism, and oppression in that country and on the African continent. Both of these men saved lives and gained freedom for their oppressed people. Gandhi's philosophy has been planted in the minds of people all over the world and is perhaps the most powerful and inspirational force in modern history. The following statement by Gandhi offers us deep insight into his worldview: "Mankind is one, seeing that all are equally subject to the moral law. All men are equal in God's eyes. There are, of course, differences of race and status and the like, but the higher the status of a man, the greater is his responsibility" (Brinkley 1999).

Gandhi did not believe in the doctrine of the greatest good for the greatest number. He felt that the only real, dignified, human doctrine is the greatest good for all (Shepard 1987). When all his arguments in favor of the moral path proved futile, his answer was to voluntarily invite suffering in his own body to open the eyes of those determined not to see the light. Gandhi's perseverance and influence have been far reaching, and his life and death have touched and inspired some of the world's most influential spiritual leaders who continue to spread messages of nonviolent disobedience, affecting social change through empathy, compassion, inspiration, and love.

Theodore M. Ludwig (1996) notes that Hinduism, unlike Christianity and Islam, does not appear to be a missionary religion. The fundamental belief of Hinduism is that there are many spiritual paths appropriate to different people, dependent upon their own path, past karma, and spiritual perfection, and the idea of converting others to Hinduism does not fit this concept at all.

Hindu sages classify their values into four groups: physical, economic, moral, and spiritual. The final destiny of Hinduism is, as in Buddhism, union with the supreme god. Hindus believe in reincarnation, being held accountable for one's deeds (karma), and depending on those deeds; that is, if they are moral, just, and compassionate, their reward is a higher status upon rebirth. Thus, altruistic behavior is directly rewarded.

TAOISM

Taoism began about 2,500 years ago in China. The *Tao Te Ching* (or *Book of Reason and Virtue*) is the shortest of all scriptures, containing only 5,000 words. The primary goal of Taoism may be described as realizing the mystical intuition of the Tao, which is the way, the undivided unity, and the ultimate reality. Tao is the natural way of all things, the nameless beginning of heaven and earth, and the mother of all things. All things depend upon the Tao, and all things return to it. Yet it lies hidden, transmitting its power and perfection to all things. He who has realized the Tao has arrived at pure consciousness and sees the inner truth of everything. Only one who is free of desire can apprehend the Tao, thereafter leading a life of "actionless activity." There is no personal god in Taoism and thus no union with a god. This is a strong ethic of caring for others.

According to Ross and Hills, Lao Tse, founder of Taoism, lived in China about 600 BCE, and the world would be poorer without him. He taught that "the world moves according to a divine pattern, which is reflected in the rhythmic and orderly movements of nature. The sum of wisdom and of happiness for man is that he adjust himself to this order and himself reflect the way the world moves. You seek wisdom, goodness, and contentment. In the ways you are trying to attain them, you are blind and foolish. Can you not see that wisdom is trust, goodness is acceptance, and contentment is simplicity? This is the way of the world" (Ross and Hills 1956: 76).

"Tao" means "way" or "way to go," or possibly as "nature" or "way of nature." The Tao is the source of all created things, even the Chinese gods. It existed before there was any universe. Rise and fall, flow and ebb, existence and decay, the Tao simply operates. The early Taoists frequently referred to a past "Golden Age," when men lived in peace and harmony, because they were free from artificiality and were simple. The "Man of Tao" is described by them:

> He is cautious, like one who crosses a stream in winter;
> He is hesitating, like one who fears his neighbors;
> He is modest, like one who is a guest;
> He is yielding, like ice that is going to melt.
> (Ross and Hills 1956: 80)

It is this person who sees that his true welfare is good for all men. The good for all men is his good, too. This is what Lao-tse meant by loving. The man of Tao trusts the world, and the world can be entrusted to him.

Taoism is the indigenous religion of China and may be defined as the Chinese philosophical and religious tradition dedicated to achieving harmony with salutary forces inherent in the cosmos. Taoism teaches how to live life wisely, have a quiet mind, and detach oneself from self-serving motives and senseless activity. The avoidance of conflict allows actions of agape and charity to spontaneously flow through believers. The hope of attaining immortality for the masses not adept in the practices of Taoism lies in merit—doing good works such as building roads, performing acts of charity, and extending compassion to living things.

In some ways Taoism is the opposite of Confucianism. Confucianism seeks to perfect men and women in the world. Taoism tries to turn away from society to the contemplation of nature, seeking fulfillment in the spontaneous. The Tao, metaphysical absolute, appears to have been a philosophical transformation of an earlier personal God. Taoism is not just a passive contemplation, rather it serves a later generation of religious-minded thinkers anxious to transcend the limited conditions of human existence. "Their ambition was to 'steal the secret of Heaven and Earth,' to wrench from it the mystery of life itself, in order to fulfill their desire for immortality" (Beaver et al 1982: 251). Taoism can be distinguished from Confucianism in that its goal is the quest for freedom. For some it was freedom from political and social constraints of the emerging Confucian state, while for others it was a more profound search for immortality. The Tao was the sum total of all things, which are and which change, for change itself was a very important part of the Taoist view of reality. "The Tao is complete, all embracing, the whole; these are different names for the same reality denoting the One" (Beaver et al. 1982: 252). Lao Tse says, "The ways of men are conditioned by those of Heaven, the ways of Heaven by those of the Tao, and the Tao came into being by itself. The Tao is therefore the principle of the universe and is also a pattern for human behavior, often called uncontrived action" (Beaver et al 1982: 252).

Because as the Taoist tradition values self-perfection as an imperative, many critics thought it was useless when trying to help others. But Lao Tse counseled against just such an attitude, warning "One who cultivates himself while neglecting others has lost sight" of the path. He said, "The sage is always adept at saving others, so that no one is rejected, and is always adept at saving things, so that nothing is abandoned" (Kirkland 1986: 22). Taoists had lived in the hope of a savior who would come to redress the evils of the world. However, as noted by Russell Kirkland, Taoists soon realized that "if one waits for someone else to save the world, the task will never be accomplished. Hence the Taoist religion enjoined its adherents to take aiding others and assisting in edification as their ambition" (Kirkland 1986: 22).

CONFUCIANISM

Confucius, the founding sage of Confucianism, was born in 551 BCE and died in 479 BCE. He was a contemporary of Lao Tse, the founder of Taoism. One important source of its major beliefs is the Analects (ca. 500

BCE) compiled by the students of Confucius after his death (Confucius c. 500 BCE). Because it was not written as a philosophy, it contains frequent contradictions and is therefore somewhat ambiguous. Besides the Analects, there is the Doctrine of Means, Great Learning, and the writings of Mencious, all of which are regarded as sacred texts.

The primary goal of Confucianism is to create true mobility through proper education and the inculcation of the Confucian virtues. It attempts to formulate an expanded definition of self "until it encompasses all others." (Czíkszentmihályi 2005: 184). Confucianism is described as a return to the ways of one's ancestors; the classics are studied to discover the ancient ways of virtues. Ethics are important, as is social propriety, especially the principle of reciprocal propriety in the five relationships; that is, in the relationships between ruler and subject, father and son, husband and wife, older brother and younger brother, and friend and friend. These reciprocal relationships are important because they help sustain the moral order of the society. There is a belief in the supreme ruler in Heaven as the ethical principle, whose law is order, impersonal and yet interested in all humankind. Confucianism offers the "Silver Rule": "What you do not want done to yourself, do not do to others" (Hume 1959: 121). Similar statements in Judaism and Christianity tend to take the positive, or "Golden Rule" form.

Confucianism's ethical teachings include *Li* (ritual, propriety, etiquette), *Hsiao* (love within the family; parent for children, children for parents, siblings), *Yi* (righteousness), *Xin* (honesty and trustworthiness), *Jen* (benevolence, humanity towards others; the highest Confucian virtue), and *Chung* (loyalty to the state). Confucian morality emphasizes the hierarchical structure of social relationships. As such the social context determines what is morally proper. Discipline in the Chinese classroom does not come downward from a harsh teacher to submissive students but rather goes upward from respectful students to an admired teacher. There is a combination of high motivation and a strong sense of cooperation that exists in the absence of any externally imposed constraints. Education flowers easily in such an environment. This is possibly one of the chief differences between East and West: in the West we struggle for freedom and individual expression, which inevitably results in competition and feelings of alienation.

In traditional China, the struggle for selfless consideration of others (Confucian humanism) and collective achievement often results in strong feelings of identity at home, at work, and in the classroom. The Confucian principles are best exemplified by the concepts of Yi, the principle of reciprocity, and *Chung-shu*, conscientious altruism expressed by empathy and moderation (Ziniewicz 1996). The Confucian concepts of virtue, goodness, charity, and love are integrated into an ideal of love that finds that all forms of love are one and the same; the more we love one another, the more we are capable of loving one another.

As one major distinction between Western and Eastern religions is the difference in defining self, so is there a major distinction in addressing the concept of altruism. In Confucianism, the concept of altruism can be described as "impartial caring." As Czíkszentmihályi describes it, "goodness is defined at the level of the society as a whole, not in terms of the individual or the clan…[and] the moral rightness of an act is determined solely by the goodness of the act's consequences" (Czíkszentmihályi 2005: 181). Czíkszentmihályi introduces Mozi, a Chinese philosopher (470 BCE–390 BCE), whose ideology displayed a clear preference for altruistic behavior. The collective good underlies it all, and there is not much separating the idea that, "One must treat one's friend's parent as if he or she were one's own; one must treat one's friend's body as if it were one's own." Mozi continues, "If it were truly the case that the people of the world cared for each other impartially, then one would care for others *(ren)* as one cares about one's own self *(shen)*" (Czíkszentmihályi 2005: 182).

Confucianist thought on altruism points out the tension between intention and consequence. Some Confucianist thinking focuses on consequence, other passages focus on intentions. This raises the question: Should an action that has good consequences for others, but is undertaken for the wrong reasons, be considered good? It is easy to get tied up in philosophical knots when we address altruism, considering the subjectivity that such an examination inevitably involves.

NATIVE AMERICAN TRADITIONS

The native people of the North American continent, although composed of hundreds of tribes, celebrate a religion based on the One Great Spirit. Native people seek harmony and eschew conflict. Their traditions are not a religion in the Western sense (Jack Forbes, quoted in Weaver 1998: ix-x), but it has been observed that for the indigenous people of the Americas, religion is

> …in reality, living. Our religion is not what we profess, or what we
> say or what we proclaim; our religion is what we do, what we desire,
> what we seek, what we dream about, what we fantasize, what we

think—all of these things—24 hours a day. One's religion, then, is one's life, not merely the ideal life, but life as it is actually lived. Religion is not a prayer, it is not a church, it is not theistic, it is not atheistic; it has little to do with what white people call "religion." It is our every act. If we tromp on a bug, that is our religion; if we experiment on living animals, that is our religion; if we cheat at cards, that is our religion; if we dream of being famous, that is our religion; if we gossip maliciously, that is our religion; if we are rude and aggressive, that is our religion. All that we do, and are, is our religion.

The Native American religious tradition is not similar to Christianity or Islam. There is no belief in proselytizing. Rather, one tribe has its instruction from the Creator and respects the fact that other tribes have their instructions as well. There is no need for one group to convert another group, thus Native American religious traditions are pluralistic. There is no religious conflict among tribes. But what is found to be almost universal among the many hundreds of Northern American tribes is a common belief in something that is termed *Usen,* which loosely translates to "holy spirit" or "creator." Chief Seattle of the Suwamish Tribe tried to explain this in a letter to President Franklin Pierce in 1854: "Whatever befalls the earth befalls the sons of the earth. Man did not weave the web of life; he is merely a strand in it. Whatever he does to the web, he does to himself."

Joseph Marshall (2001) explains that life demands much from Native Americans. "We are all called upon to make sacrifices for ourselves and more often for others" (Marshall 2001: 105). In Native American traditions, acts are equally important, whether small or large:

> We may not wake up to a war in our residential neighborhood, or find ourselves caught up in social or political upheaval, but some measure of sacrifice is often necessary nonetheless; such as parents working two jobs to enable their children's dreams, whether it's a college education or a pair of Nikes for basketball....The acts are the gift of self (Marshall 2001: 106).

Native Americans find altruistic acts important. Courage and sacrifice and everyday examples of thoughtfulness are signs of being in balance, and those acts serve as examples for the rest of us:

> Sacrifices come in all shapes and for every reason under the sun, and there are times when we can be unaware that someone has

made one for us or because of us. Tough and extraordinary circumstances will always bring extraordinary individuals to the top with their acts of selfless courage and sacrifice. History has its crazy horses, spotted tails, and buffalo calf roads. We will never forget their deeds or their sacrifices. Ordinary, everyday people also make sacrifices and remind us that it is within human nature to do so. We stand and offer our seats on the bus or the subway, or we step back to let someone ahead of us in line. We help the elderly travelers near us in line carry their bags....These are simple acts, but they can give us all a sense of dignity and an example to follow. (Marshall 2001: 108–9)

Native American Studies scholar Martin Brokenleg (1999) says that altruism is inborn and that the rudiments of empathy are apparent even in a newborn. An apology to one we have offended can be a form of generosity, because such an act places the offender in a position of humility. More powerful is the generosity of forgiveness extended to those who have hurt us. The less the offender deserves it, the greater the gift. Such generosity heals hurts and hatred. *Mitakuye oyasin* means "for all my relations" in Lakota Sioux. It is a prayer of harmony with all forms of life: other people, animals, trees and plants, and even rocks. Most Indians hear this phrase thousands of times a year in native ceremonies, and for many the phrase seems to be a liturgical blessing that includes all other forms of life in human ceremonial activities.

Dennis McPherson cites the observations of Christopher Columbus in 1492:

> [The native people] are so ingenuous and free with all they have, that no one would believe it who has not seen it; of anything that they possess, if it be asked of them, they never say no; on the contrary, they invite you to share it and show as much love as if their hearts went with it, and they are content with whatever trifle be given them, whether it be a thing of value or of petty worth. I forbade that they be given things so worthless as broken crockery and of green glass and lacepoints, although when they could get them, they thought they had the best jewel in the world. (McPherson 1998: 79–80)

Another foreigner, Jesuit Paul LeJeune, writing a report in 1632, refers to the Huron people in what is now Quebec as "savages," but still notes that they do have some "rather noble moral virtues." Their selfless hospitality particularly struck LeJeune:

> …their hospitality toward all kinds of strangers is remarkable; they present to them, in their feasts, the best of what they have prepared, and, as I have already said, I do not know if anything similar, in this regard, is to be found anywhere. They never close the door upon a stranger, and once having received him into their houses, they share with him the best they have; they never send him away, and when he goes away of his own accord, he repays them with a simple "thank you" (quoted in McPherson 1998: 80).

Historian Robert Bremner noted that the first American "philanthropists" came from Native American tribes. Although there are only Western records of early contact between Europeans and Native Americans, they describe the interconnectedness of tribal members. The Blackfeet tribe based their religion and philosophy on sharing, giving, and receiving. Some tribes engaged in a regular philanthropic ceremony where individuals gave away their possessions to others. Although only a few tribes had specific philanthropic ceremonies, the underlying values of giving and sharing are universal to America's native peoples (Bowden 2006).

As the contemporary Native American poet Chrystos (1991) sums up in her poem, "Shame On":

> *… We've been polite for five hundred years*
> *and you still don't get it*
> *Take nothing you cannot return*
> *Give to others, give more*
> *Walk quietly*
> *Do what needs to be done*
> *Give thanks for your life*
> *Respect all beings*
> *Simple*
> *And it doesn't cost a penny…*

COMMONALITY AMONG WORLD RELIGIONS

"Truth is One—Paths are Many"

Of the several religious traditions, two of the oldest are Hinduism and Judaism, both approximately 4,000 years old. During thousands of years of human history, people searched for God for many reasons, resulting in a great diversity of religious expressions. Most of the religious prophets and philosophers reached the same truth—often it is only the language in which it is uttered that differs. All the major traditions teach morality, reverence for truth, honesty, justice, dignity, freedom, and brotherhood. The fact that religions teach peace remains true despite the many wars and the terrible cruelty committed at times in our history among and between religious groups. There is no doubt that much blood has been shed in the name of religion.

Most religions contain three basic elements: philosophy, mythology, and rituals. Reviewing the various religious traditions, we find that they have in common a basic ethical behavior in the brotherhood of all people and in the idea of love for others. It is also true that sometimes these ethical ideals are not practical. The major differences are found mainly in rituals, and these differences may be due to the fact that religions developed in different places, within different cultural settings. Thus you have some religions that question birth control, how many wives a man should have, whether divorce should be permissible, and so forth. Robert E. Hume, in his book *The World's Living Religions* (1959), looks at the major religious traditions in the world and makes some notable comparisons. Hume sees many similarities between Christianity, Buddhism, and other faiths. All emphasize a moral and ethical life. Christianity emphasizes morality, linking it to the character of God. Buddhism also links its moral framework to a universal god. Both Christianity and Buddhism condemn selfishness, which seems to be responsible for so much human misery. Christianity says that the cure for human misery is positive love for others. Both religions teach the possibility and importance of salvation, and both have produced monastic institutions. Although many religious traditions stress the underlying equality of all human beings in their teachings, Hume sees a particular focus on equality in Buddhism. It puts emphasis on a person's inner attitude, as well as containing a certain noble earnestness in its ethics. Renunciation, conditional salvation, successful repudiation of the caste system, a major attribute of the Hindu tradition, differentiate Buddhism from Hinduism.

Within Confucianism one must compensate injury with justice, just as kindness repays kindness. On the other hand, in Taoism, as in Christianity, one forgives the harm-doer, implying that we must treat others better than they deserve. There is no *quid pro quo* in human relations. Other similarities include the fact that there is a Supreme Being and a claim of divine incarnation. There is also a claim of the supernatural origin of the founder, as well as a belief in divine revelation. Hume writes that within Hinduism, we find "the immanence of the divine in the world; human society, a divinely ordained structure; union with the divine, the goal of existence." In Buddhism, we see "selfishness as the root of misery; salvation through inner purity and self-discipline. Confucianism sees "the essential goodness of human nature as divinely implanted; religion as exercised in proper social relationships." In Taoism, religion is "exercised in humbly following the serene divine 'Way'." In Judaism, "Superlative satisfaction [is] to be obtained through obedience to a God of righteousness," while in Islam, that satisfaction "is to be obtained through submission to an omnipotent God, who is not only a sovereign, but also a judge and a rewarder" (Hume 1959: 273-274).

All of these traditions make claims to being based upon divinely inspired scriptures. In Hinduism there are the *Vedas* or "Books of Knowledge." In Buddhism, there is the *Tripitaka* or "Three Baskets" of teachings. Confucianism has *The Five Classics* and *The Four Books*. Judaism claims a divinely inspired "Law," "Prophets," and the "Sacred Writings." Islam has the *Koran* or "The Reading" or "The Recital." Christianity claims the *Bible* or "The Book" (Hume 1959: 275). In many of the traditional faiths, there are reports of miracles appearing, and the Golden Rule prevails.

Shah (1994) compares Indian and western religions; western religions tend to see the universe as a creation, but while Indians look at the universe as an ongoing, cyclical process. Western religions have one absolute God, and the existence of God is proved through direct communication with Him. Indian religions tend to think in terms of receiving liberation or God's grace through experience on many paths, according to their understanding, temperament, and maturity; God is pure love and consciousness. In the West, there tends to be one true path to God; in Indian religions, man is on a progressive path that leads from ignorance to knowledge, from death to immortality. For Western religions, evil is a real, living force opposed to God's will, but in Indian religions there is no intrinsic evil.

Human values and conduct are viewed similarly in some ways. Western religions tend to be based on ethical and moral conduct, for the opposite leads one away from God. Indian religions also stress moral living, and in both the virtuous life is upheld as central. Salvation in the West comes at the end of the world, at the end of time, and has nothing to do with enlightenment. For the Indian religions, the goals of enlightenment and liberation are to be found in this life, within the context of time and within man himself. Saintly behavior in the West is based on good works, but in the East, it is based on moral ideals.

We should note here that not only religious background motivates altruistic behavior; altruistic behaviors found in cultures around the world are also motivated by identification with a definite moral community. According to Yablo (1980), there is a clear difference in the manner that Thais and Americans approach altruism; Thais showed a greater altruistic orientation than people in the United States. Thai behaviors were associated with charity and service work, and helping in ways that do not necessarily require wealth, yet require some degree of constant commitment over time. American subjects appear to most often offer help in ways associated with wealth or possessions. Thais also seem to donate more frequently to charities than American subjects. Although Thais reported that their helping behavior was influenced by Buddhism to some extent, it was due more to the collective nature of Thai culture than specifically to religion. There seemed to be much greater concern among the Thais for matters related to the heart, to such emotions as compassion, empathy, and a desire that others suffer less and experience happiness—all of which share roots in Thai culture, as well as in the Buddhist doctrine. American subjects rarely mentioned religion as a motivating factor for their responses, and their responses were very individual. Among American subjects, there seemed to be little sense of belonging to a whole. A sense of alienation is highlighted when comparing the United States to other cultures. There is a pervasive sense of alienation from society in Americans compared to Thais. American society's focus on an individualistic, "looking out for number one" attitude toward others may have short-circuited the likelihood of altruistic helping behavior (Yablo 1980: 139).

4

APOLOGY

> True confession consists of telling our deed in such a way
> that our soul is changed in the telling of it.
>
> —*Maude Petre*

In the previous chapters, we looked at the various manifestations of altruism, the first of three conditions—altruism, apology, and forgiveness—that ultimately lead to reconciliation. In this chapter we examine the nature of apology and make distinctions between interpersonal and intergroup apology. We follow with examples of how world leaders have used apologies to attempt to redress and reconcile the polarization of groups. We also look at why some apologies are effective in laying the groundwork for a real reconciliation while others fall flat.

Nicholas Tavuchis (1991) maintains that apology has four different configurations. The first is interpersonal apology from one individual to another or *one-to-one*; for example, a father apologizing to a daughter for sexual abuse. A second configuration is apology from an individual to a collectivity, or *one-to-many*; for example, a Klansman apologizing to black people for his racism and violence against them. The third is an apology from a group to an individual, or *many-to-one*, such as those who stood by as Kitty Genovese was murdered in Queens, New York, and then later, as a community, apologized to Kitty's family. The fourth configuration of apology is apology from one group to another, or *many-to-many*; for example, a nation represented by leaders, such as Germany apologizing to the world for committing genocide, or the American people, represented by its government, apologizing to Japanese Americans for placing them in internment camps during World War II. In our research we have found some important similarities between *interpersonal* and *intergroup* apologies.

Whatever type it is, apology is more than just saying "I'm sorry." When we talk about apology, we refer to a harm-doer genuinely feeling that he has harmed somebody and trying to make amends to that person. His apology involves not only expressing sorrow and contrition through words but also taking responsibility, promising to change, trying to make amends through reparations, and in general, conveying a sincere intent to reconcile a relationship. For us, apology reflects an interest and a capability on the part of the apologizer to show respect for the other. The ability to apologize shows that we care about the feelings of others and is an indication of empathy. By apologizing to another, one *disarms* the other person. The other person no longer feels the harm-doer a threat, and it quiets the other person's anger. Apology also entails recognizing the pain that has been caused. Chapman and Thomas identify five stages to apology: expressing regret, accepting responsibility, making restitution, showing genuine repentance, and requesting forgiveness (Chapman and Thomas 2006). There are negative results for *not* apologizing: those who have been harmed will tend to carry grudges, and close relations may never be reestablished.

It is clear that humanity, throughout history, has been hurt; and it is hard to think of a nation or group that does not register a grievance against another group that has hurt them. People who have been hurt in some serious way may carry a burden of resentment, an urge for vengeance, and the longing to unburden themselves. Gandhi, referring to vengeance, said, "An eye for an eye makes us blind."

When the moral order has been broken or ruptured, and when values and norms have been violated within families and communities, there is a sociological basis for apology and forgiveness. Human survival is often based upon the need of group interaction; forgiveness, apologies, and social norms serve to facilitate the maintenance and integrity of these groups (Gold and Davis 2005). Apology may restore the moral order. Through genuine apology and forgiveness, harmony may be restored.

INTERPERSONAL APOLOGY

In her book *The Power of Apology* (2001), Beverly Engel relates the story of a family whose home was burglarized. Barbara, Lyle, and their young daughter came home to find their house in shambles. Their belongings had been ransacked and strewn throughout the house, and jewelry and other valuable items were missing. The family members were upset for weeks afterward. Barbara said, "I was angry because my daughter was traumatized by the situation...[and] I lived in constant fear that that the person would come back, and this time he would harm us" (Engel 2001: 25). Soon, the culprit was caught, and it turned out to be a local boy of 15. The town in which they lived offered a special program for youthful offenders that allowed for alternative resolution in nonviolent crimes. What Barbara and Lyle found was that the boy's subsequent act of apology changed everyone's feelings about the incident. After the boy apologized, Lyle said, "I believed he was genuinely sorry, and this made me see him as a mixed-up kid instead of as a monster" (Engel 2001: 26).

Engel places both apology and forgiveness into the language of gifts, with harm-doer and harmed exchanging the gifts of apology and forgiveness. When the one is offered, the other is given. She maintains that apology to another person is one of the healthiest, most positive actions for ourselves and also for others. The debilitating effect of remorse and shame on harm-doers can eat away at them until they become emotionally and physically ill. She says, "By apologizing and taking responsibility for our actions, we help rid ourselves of esteem-robbing shame and guilt" (Engel 2001: 13).

Apology has not received the attention that forgiveness has, as an almost ubiquitous theme in spirituality, recovery philosophies, and New Age philosophy. Until recently, apology has been conspicuously absent. Engel takes it up as "a cause," claiming that apology can prevent divorces, family estrangements, and lawsuits. Failing to admit error and express regret "adds insult to injury" and "is one of the most blatant ways of showing disrespect," she says. Engel provides detailed information on how to make "meaningful apologies...that will be heard and believed," citing the "three Rs: regret, responsibility, and remedy." She also is unusually conscious of the gray areas, where apologizing or forgiving may be inappropriate or impossible, and where overapologizing may reflect low self-esteem. Unfortunately, Engel devotes little attention to the difficult task of asking for apologies, after declaring that "it is your responsibility" to do so if you feel injured.

The importance of apology and forgiveness was first advanced by Saint Augustine in the early fifth century in *The City of God* (1984), but was virtually ignored by social scientists until the mid 1980s, when it was rediscovered by a group of social scientists. Since then, we have viewed altruistic behavior and forgiveness as important topics to research.

There are many types of apology and forgiveness, and many traditions upon which they may be based. There is religious-based apology and forgiveness; for example, we saw in Chapter 3 that apology in general is very important in the Jewish faith and that apologizing to people that one has hurt or harmed throughout the year is in an integral part of the religion. When we stop to acknowledge our actions, take responsibility for them, and then apologize to those we have harmed—and are in turn forgiven by them—we know we are forgiven by God. It is not uncommon in the synagogues of Eastern Europe to see people turn to fellow congregates and friends and quietly ask for forgiveness" (Engel 2001: 24).

We have seen that apology and forgiveness are central to other religious practices as well. In Christianity it is important to ask for forgiveness. Apology reflects the commandment from James in the New Testament: "Confess your sins to one another." Even as Jesus was on the cross, he forgave those who were torturing and tormenting him. Acts of confession within the Catholic Church are an "apology to God" and have all the components of personal apology: a statement of regret, acceptance of responsibility for one's actions, a promise not to repeat the offense, and the request for forgiveness. Apology is universal and vitally important in interpersonal relationships in all cultures and religions. Engel quotes Ingrid Bengis, who says, "Words are a form of action, capable of influencing change" (Engel 2001: 22), and she recounts many stories illustrating the importance and power of apology. We find such stories throughout the world.

Expressions of apology and forgiveness are culturally differentiated and varied. In Japan, interpersonal apology is much more frequent and likely to be accepted than in the West. *Sumanai* usually includes a plea for the good will of the offended party, and the same is true of *moshiwake-mai*, which literally means, "I have no excuse for what I have done." It is the expression of the desire to be forgiven even though the relationship as such is not one where *amae*, meaning self-indulgence, would normally apply. Tavuchis explains the paradox of how in the West apology is viewed as essentially a childlike plea to the other party. In making an apology, we leave ourselves defenseless, and at the mercy of the other. It is "the fact that this attitude is always received sympathetically [by the offended party] that gives [Japanese] apology its magical efficacy in foreign eyes," he says (Tavuchis 1991: 41).

Indeed, apology is crucial to the social structure in Japan. John O. Haley (1998) studied Japanese culture to understand why crime has decreased there over recent years in comparison to the United States. He attributes this change to the fundamental importance of apology and pardon. Despite the apparently unique role of repentance in Japanese culture, the author argues that these concepts, although perhaps more readily evident in Japan, are also present to a degree in American communities. He believes the United States can learn to incorporate the Japanese approach into the American criminal justice system.

Japanese society tends to view offenders in a more lenient way than does American society and is therefore much more likely to look to rehabilitate offenders and reincorporate them into the community. Criminal justice systems in the United States, however, tend to treat offenders much more retributively. Because of cultural differences, conflict resolution will be different in different societies. For example, more American participants in Haley's study included accounts of their offenses in their messages, while Japanese participants were more likely to employ strategies such as statements of remorse, reparation, or compensation, promises not to repeat the offense, and requests for forgiveness. Therefore, it may not be sufficient to merely set up the Japanese process in the United States in an effort to improve the likelihood of apology serving as a substantial part of a reconciliation process. The effectiveness of apology will depend on the social fabric that envelops the institutions and the perceptions of harm that are held by both the offender and the society at large.

Citing studies of Japanese jurisprudence, Schneider (2004) states that apology in Japan helps avoid litigation. Some people who are hurt want simply to have an acknowledgement of their pain. In Japan, people tend to apologize even if they do not acknowledge fault or any responsibility for the act, say Yoko Hosoi and Haruo Nishimura (1999). This is expected of everyone from childhood on, and usually the injured party will forgive the offender. "The behavior pattern of 'apology–forgiveness' seems to be an ingrained cultural heritage (*habitus*), which serves to make a harmonious, peace-oriented society," they write. "Many foreign scholars have already pointed out in their writings that we Japanese have long emphasized the principle of *wa* as the main ethos of our society" (Hosoi and Nishimura 1999: 2–3).

In America, on the other hand, people fear that if they admit to some act, or apologize to someone for a grievance, they are accepting legal culpability, making it easy for lawyers to use the apology as a basis for litigation.

But refusing to apologize can backfire. Schneider offers an example:

> An apology was at the heart of a civil lawsuit brought against the Catholic Diocese of Dallas. Eleven plaintiffs claimed that the diocese failed to protect them from Rudolph Kos, a priest in the diocese, who was accused of sexual molestation of the altar boys between 1981 and 1992. In the summer of 1997, a civil jury awarded the plaintiffs $119.6 million, the largest judgment ever against a diocese. A final attorney-negotiated settlement of $23.4 million dollars stalled over the plaintiff's demand for an apology, even after the sides had agreed on the damages to be paid (Schneider 2004: 274).

Admission of guilt and apology might have obviated lawsuits, but Americans avoid admission of guilt.

Sugimoto's (1997) findings question some of the previously held presuppositions regarding American and Japanese communicative patterns, but the cultural differences in delivery and acceptance of apology remain stark. Japanese people seem to apologize less often than Americans. In most situations, the Japanese employ more elaborate types of remorse. Americans' statements of remorse tend to be more simplistic—such as, "Sorry about that"—while Japanese apologies tend to be more specific and therefore appear more genuine. Haley, too, found differences in delivery. American participants in his study included accounts of their offense in their messages, while Japanese participants were more likely to employ strategies such as statements of remorse, reparation, compensation, promises not to repeat the same offense, and requests for forgiveness.

Despite cultural differences, the social-psychological basis for apology is consistent throughout the world. We harm and hurt and offend each other every day, which causes us to feel alienated from each other. We carry burdens of shame as we hold on to resentments from being offended and guilt from offending. Some hurts may cause us to consider vengeance, even against the ones we love. This is frequently found with couples. The harmony of the relationship is broken, and there is recrimination. Marriage counselors find it important to open the process of taking responsibility for actions and beginning the process of apology as a means of reconciliation between the partners.

Charles Klein (1995), a rabbi who holds an advanced degree in social work, deals with apology and forgiveness on a daily basis. As a counselor to his congregates, he has seen the power of apology and forgiveness save marriages and heal ruptured relationships. His book *How to Forgive When You Can't Forget* (1995) cites the Jewish Bible's example of Joseph, son of Jacob, who was sold into slavery by his brothers. Many years later his brothers, suffering from drought in the country of Canaan, came to Egypt seeking help from the Pharaoh. Joseph, who had become a powerful official in Egypt, did not forget that his brothers had treated him badly, but he clearly forgave them. Rabbi Klein sees the Jewish Bible and Christian New Testament as featuring forgiveness and reconciliation. He maintains that in this "throwaway age" we must awaken in ourselves the capacity for compassionate forgiveness. It is necessary to take stock of our own faults and behaviors and to avoid shifting the blame to others. At the same time, we must accept genuine apologies from others.

Beverly Engel maintains that the world can be changed "one apology at a time." She writes:

> An apology can have a great impact on someone. If the person you apologized to was touched by your apology, it can make him think about the power that apology has to heal wounds. It may even cause him to think about the people he needs to apologize to and may motivate him to follow through with the apologies. (Engel 2001: 233)

The person to whom you apologize may be so touched by your apology that it gives her the courage to apologize to someone she has wronged, Engel continues (Engel 2001: 233). "If someone apologizes to you and you are able to accept her apology, she may begin thinking of other people she has wronged and about how good it would feel to apologize to them. You may even become the catalyst for a turning point in her life. She may adapt an entirely new attitude about acknowledging her wrongs and seeking the forgiveness of others" (Engel 2001: 234).

We asked respondents in our sample: "How important is apology?" They answered as follows:

> People will not be able to live in nurturing, sustaining, and trusting relationships without an avenue for apology and forgiveness (Respondent 207).

> Apology is crucial between groups and individuals. [It] is demonstrated that attitude change and repair can occur (Respondent 112).

Apology is, in my mind, less important than acknowledgement and change. It is part of this whole process. Forgiveness need not be automatic. Some hurts cannot be mended. That too needs to be acknowledged and admitted (Respondent 96).

I think it is the one thing that fosters a good relationship, and it is the healing ointment that can mend wounded relationships. It is the antidote to division (Respondent 63).

EFFECTIVE AND INEFFECTIVE APOLOGIES

The ability to apologize or forgive is not necessarily innate. It must be learned and encouraged. There is a right way and a wrong way to apologize. Apologies must be sincere to be effective, and apologies without remorse—including bitter and premature apologies—will not be effective. We have all experienced false or insincere apologies. We recall President Clinton's half-hearted apology for his actions with Monica Lewinsky. These kinds of apologies are generally recognized as efforts to evade punishment or disfavor and are less likely to be taken as a serious effort to make amends for a wrong.

True and effective apology must reflect a real need on the part of the apologizer to find forgiveness; otherwise it is simply a "political" apology. The same is true of angry or bumbled apologies, mistimed apologies, and those in which the apologizer trivializes the damage caused. It is often worse to apologize poorly than not to apologize at all. The key to effective apologizing is to allow the other to feel and exhibit empathy for the apologizer.

Greesh Sharma (2000) says there is an art to apologizing; it takes skill to keep the apology from being lost in translation. Sharma argues that we should choose the right time to make our apologies. It may be better to wait until the other person has calmed down; otherwise the apology may be ignored. We should be relaxed and look the other person straight in the eye (in Western culture), speak clearly and calmly, take responsibility for our actions, and clearly state that it was our fault. Also, we should consider the other person's point of view by stating that "I understand how this has affected you." We could also explain how the mistakes occurred. We may wish to follow the apology with a special gift to demonstrate our sincerity. Sharma says there is also a right way to receive an apology. We should listen to the explanation, thank the person for apologizing, and respond positively. Let the person apologizing know how good the apology makes us feel, and try to work out a solution that is in everyone's interest.

Sharma also suggests there are certain things that we should not do. These include muttering a shame-faced, inaudible apology while gazing away from the person and accusing the other person of being partly or mostly to blame. He also cautions us to avoid referring to mistakes that the other has made in the past. When receiving an apology, we should not look away; remain silent, and be careful not to minimize the importance of the apology by saying "Forget it, it's okay" or "It doesn't bother me anyway" (Sharma 2000).

Apology fosters reconciliation. Once we feel compassion for the person who offended us, it is easier to forgive. Apology, compassion, and empathy work hand in hand. When someone hurts us, most of us try to defend ourselves. An alternative is to forgive by letting go of our resentment, anger, and spite; instead, feel compassion for those who hurt us. The difficulty is that defensive responses are almost reflexive, but both apology and forgiveness take effort. Forgiveness also takes time. We should not accept an apology simply to make another person feel better, nor should we accept what we perceive to be an insincere apology.

In recent studies, Michael McCullough and his colleagues (1997, 1998) examined whether the relationship between apology and the capacity to forgive is due to our increased empathy for an apologetic offender. They found that sincere apology and the compassion it produces in the offended person make it much easier for the victim to forgive a wrongdoer. When victims can empathize with their offenders, their ability to forgive is vastly improved.

McCullough studied whether people who forgave were "more conciliatory toward, and subsequently less likely to avoid their offenders" (McCullough, Rachal, Chris, Sandage, Worthington, Brown, Hight 1998: 1595). Participants in these studies completed questionnaires describing an event in which someone had hurt them, how they were hurt, how wrong the offender was, and the extent to which the offender apologized. The researchers found that apology leads directly to empathy, and empathy facilitates forgiveness. People who forgave were less spiteful and less likely to avoid the person who had hurt them. "One seminar promoted empathy as a precursor to forgiving, and the other encouraged forgiving but did not foster empathy. Seminars met for a total of eight hours over two days. Participants in the empathy seminar reported more empathy for their offenders than participants in the nonempathy seminar or those on the waiting list" (McCullough, Worthington, and Rachal 1997: 337).

Engel suggests furthering this movement on a global scale. She explains that we can institute an apology night, devoting one evening a month to apologize to one another for hurts and slights; form apology circles made up of family, business associates, school children, or others as a way of resolving issues and airing differences, thus promoting trust and respect between people; help to mediate apology; or post an internet apology to someone you cannot locate but wish to apologize to. If the other person sees it, she can contact you.[13] Engel suggests applying apology strategies to the business environment, in employee relations, and employee conflict resolution. She also suggests we could help lower the crime rate if we make it easier for criminals to admit their crimes and ask for help by supporting and becoming involved with movements such as restorative justice (Engel 2001: 235–36).

INTERGROUP APOLOGY

On May 4, 2001, a group of Northern California clergy and community members apologized to local Native American tribes for the injustices white settlers had inflicted upon the native people. These injuries included a massacre on February 25, 1860, on Indian Island in Humboldt Bay. The group met with the Wiyot tribe and its council to apologize for racism, oppression, and specifically for the massacre. The clergy whom we interviewed signed the statement of apology, which said:

> Recognizing that the land upon which we gather was once Wiyot tribal land, as was this whole Arcata/Eureka area, we consider it a supreme honor to have you here tonight as Native hosts to this conference. We have become increasingly aware in recent years of the history between our peoples. To say "We are sorry" for the past injustices and atrocities, including the Indian Island Massacre, seems so little to offer, so miniscule when compared with the horrific nature of what your people suffered. But sorry we are indeed. We choose not to hide behind the excuse that "These were sins of prior generations." We recognize that the community and Church leaders of our race, though they did not all agree with the wickedness involved, did precious little, if anything, to find the guilty parties or bring them to justice. Little if anything was done to make amends or restitution.
>
> Although we cannot represent our entire race, we of the Christian Churches in our community acknowledge to you our

guilt and humbly ask for your forgiveness. We empathize with you and your desire to own Indian Island again and to build a center of remembrance for the lives of your people that were so brutally destroyed. Tonight we present to you the first fruits of our commitment to partner with you in buying the land and building that center. With hearts full of love for you and desire for your full restoration as a people, we present this gift of $1,000.00. And we pledge our ongoing intention to pray for you and to work with you in this endeavor until its completion.

The apology, while not resolving all the problems, laid the basic foundation for a reconciliation between local Indian tribes and the non-Indian population. The apology—from "many to many" (Tavuchis 1991)—was perceived as sincere by tribal leaders and has been backed up by action. Churches and other local groups raised funds to help the Wiyot tribe purchase Indian Island. We are seeing this kind of intergroup apology more and more as a means of reconciling groups who have had grievances against each other.

At this writing, more than 100 intergroup apologies have been made in various parts of the world. For example, British Prime Minister Tony Blair recently apologized to the Irish people for British responsibility for aspects of the Irish Famine of the nineteenth century, and President George H. W. Bush apologized for wrongful treatment of the Japanese-Americans during World War II. We are beginning to see such apologies in areas ravaged by war in our own times, such as in Bosnia (between Moslems and Christians), Northern Ireland (between Protestants and Catholics), and in Asia (from Japan to the Chinese for its atrocities in World War II). At first the Japanese authorities denied the existence of the use of "comfort women" in its military; however, very recently they did admit that in fact there was the use of "comfort women." We see the Truth and Reconciliation Commissions in South Africa and the political reconciliation process in Germany involving the *Stasi,* the East German secret police. The recent apology to Bosnians for Serbian atrocities during the 1992–1995 war also may be an encouraging sign.

There have been many apologies made in recent years by groups. Business leaders, such as Yoichiro Okazaki, the CEO of Mitsubishi, apologized for the company's failure to disclose defects in its cars that were sold to the public. In a church service in Alaska, Bishop Michael H. Kinney of the Roman Catholic diocese in Juneau, asked for forgiveness from natives for the way "missionaries had sometimes mistreated or disregarded them." An Inuit was reported to have said, with tears in his eyes, that he had been waiting all his life to hear a priest or a bishop say those words, not so much for himself, but for his grandparents, especially his grandfather.

Intergroup apologies can be a successful means of reconciliation when the harm-doers genuinely understand and regret their actions, and when those who were harmed are willing to throw off old resentments. Effective apology and forgiveness, then, require that we first of all recognize the existence of a problem and its seriousness. It is only then that those who were harmed may abandon vengeance and even begin to empathize with the victimizer. This central aspect of forgiveness aims to mend and renew fractured relations. Between 1974 and the present day, there have been at least two dozen "truth telling" commissions established in various parts of the world, including Africa, Latin America, and Eastern Europe. One aspect of these truth commissions is simply to tell the truth about what happened. In East Germany, for example, they looked at the Stasi files and saw how they had mistreated and oppressed people.

Nicolaus Mills (2001) claims that because apology and forgiveness had a negative connotation in the past, generals and political heads of states were not eager to apologize. Many perceived apologizing as a sign of weakness. Today, Mills argues, the new culture of forgiveness has many positive connotations. Intergroup apology is an important component of this new understanding of forgiveness and reconciliation, and it is responsible for the substantial number of political, religious, and other group leaders who apologize to those they have harmed historically or recently. Apology in more recent usage acknowledges an expressed regret for a fault without defense by way of reparation to the victim.

Opinions vary about these intergroup apologies. In our research, we found that approximately 87 percent of our sample felt that apology played an extremely important role in healing hurt between both individuals and groups. One respondent said:

> An apology may soften the heart of the offending party. This opens up further conversation, which leads to better understanding between the two parties and may lead to mutual forgiveness (Respondent 105).

Nicholas Tavuchis (1991) claims that apology has important implications for society. Harmful offenses violate societal norms, and these transgressions are responsible for destabilizing the basic equilibrium of our society and often lead to violence. Apology has the power to rehabilitate and restore the balance of social order. Apology is not only an act to heal the community, but it is also symbolically necessary for the welfare of society. As we shall see below, there are different types of apologies, and some apologies are not forgiven. One example is that of Albert Speer, who was the only Nazi in the Nuremberg war crime trials in 1945–46 to openly admit his guilt. This is interesting because the other defendants did not, saying that they were only "obeying orders" and therefore could not be guilty of a crime. Tavuchis tells us that many critics praised Speer for his candor and for taking responsibility for Nazi crimes. Speer stated:

> My moral failure is not a matter of this item or that, it resides in my acted association with the whole course of events. I have participated in a war, which as we of the intimate circle should never have doubted was aimed at world domination. What is more, by my ability to manage these, I prolonged the war by many months (Albert Speer, quoted in Tavuchis 1991: 21).

Speer also dealt with the excuse that he knew little or nothing about death camps. "Whether I knew or did not know, or how much or how little I knew, is totally unimportant. When I consider the horrors that would have been natural to draw from the little I did know, no apologies are possible" (Tavuchis 1991: 21). As we may conclude from the reactions to Speer's confession, some apologies are not acceptable, nor are they forgivable. The offenses committed may be understood or explained, but some people or groups do not find themselves ready to forgive.

In the past several years, we have seen the emergence of the potential for a full-fledged global movement toward apology and forgiveness in the hope of reconciliation. In 1995, the Million Man March in Washington, D.C. was organized to apologize and make restitution to women and children for not protecting and providing for them. In 1998, in South Central Los Angeles, the Grace Church began what is now referred to as the "Sister, I'm Sorry movement" through which male congregants are apologizing for wrongs done to female church members, such as abandonment, rape, and sexual abuse. This process is now spreading to other churches.

Justice systems in some parts of the world have discovered the benefits of restorative, as opposed to retributive, justice. Restorative justice places emphasis on offenders apologizing directly to their victims and making restitution as part of, or in lieu of, prison time. Even some political figures have apologized for past mistakes, not for political advantage ,but because it was the right thing to do. For example, George Wallace, the famous southern racist, confessed his wrongs to the woman he had attempted to keep out of school in the "stand in the schoolhouse door" incident in 1963. Following the lead of the late Pope, Cardinal Keeler, Cardinal Mahony of Los Angeles and Cardinal Law of Boston recently apologized on behalf of the Catholic Church for sexual abuse, racism, antisemitism, and the mistreatment of women and homosexuals. Bishops in Colorado and Oakland, as well as the Archbishop of Santa Fe, sought pardon from American Indians for the cruel actions of some missionaries during colonization. These apologies were all part of the Church's observance of a Jubilee Year, coinciding with the two-thousandth anniversary of the birth of Christ.[14] The Church admitted to not having led the way to restorative justice at times when the United States government sanctioned slavery, segregation, and gender inequality. These events are part of an effort toward the building of interreligious and ecumenical relationships in many parts of the world. Some apologies were too little, some too late, but others were welcomed and viewed as positive steps toward gradual and desirable social change.

Some critics feel that apology and forgiveness are a "sell-out." Others claim that it takes time for wounds to heal and for people to understand what actually transpired. There have to be certain preconditions and preparations for apology and forgiveness to succeed, and a free and active participation among the victims and victimizers is important. The first step is for the victimizers to determine whether the victims are willing to meet with them so that apology can take place. As stated above, some events are not easily forgiven.

Ed Cairns and Michael D. Roe (2003) maintain that memory plays an important part in conflict resolution and that conflict between groups was a fact of life at the beginning of the millennium. They claim that when the Cold War ended, most expected a New World Order—a more stable, less conflict-ridden world. However, this has not proved to be the case. Major conflict and violence exist all over the world—in Georgia, East Timor, Lebanon, Rwanda, Darfur, Northern Ireland, Afghanistan, Iraq, and in various parts of Russia and the USSR's spin-off Asian republics. The result of conflict is qualitatively different today than it was in the nineteenth century or even the twentieth. Civilians represent 80 percent of the casualties in current wars and ethnic conflicts, as opposed to making up only 10 percent of the casualties in World War I (Summerfield 1995).

Rampant nationalism seems to be a major culprit. Ambitious leaders employ real or contrived grievances that their groups have been suffering and stress a need for secession or liberation from their oppressors. Events during the recent collapse of the Soviet Union and in Yugoslavia illustrate these tendencies.

Conflict today often invites collective vengeance or revenge, and ambitious leaders resurrect historically valid or false social memories. David Mellor and Di Bretherton (2003) address the historical experiences of violence, dislocation, and cultural denigration of Australian aboriginal peoples that are ever present in their social memories. These aboriginal memories are distinct from what the dominant White Australia presents as history. Another example of historical relativity is the violence between Palestinians and Israelis and how the members of both groups select their social memories, which then underlie and perpetuate the conflict between groups. The Jews look to the Hebrew Bible for their claim to the Holy Land, while Arabs point to the Dome of the Rock, their holiest Mosque in Jerusalem.

Younger generations are surprisingly more likely to feel anger towards an outside "enemy." Dutch young people harbor stronger anti-German attitudes and feelings than older citizens who actually lived through the German occupation. Social memories change according to the times. The older generation has tried to forget the past traumas, while the younger generation feels that Germany was unjust and violated Dutch sovereignty during the war. The issue of ethnic conflict is currently especially important: there are now 185 sovereign states in the world, and few of them are ethnically homogeneous; almost all have substantial ethnic-minority populations, and approximately 40 percent of those nations contain five or more ethnic groups. In all these countries, there is a potential danger of ethnic reconstruction of social memory and conflict.

Patrick Devine-Wright (2002) speaks about several sources of memory and distinguishes between individual and collective memory. He refers to Emile Durkheim, who introduced the concept of collective representation, "which referred to the set of beliefs and sentiments common to the average members of a single society, which form a determinate system that has a life of its own" (Devine-Wright 2002: 11).

Collective memory is socially constructed, reconstructed over time, and intimately related to people's sense of identity in its present context. Slobodan Milosovic of Yugoslavia emphasized the 400-year-old conquest of the Serbs by Muslim Turks. Though this event occurred four centuries ago, it was made current and relevant, and it helped to propel the violence that Serbs committed against the Kosovars and other Muslims within the borders of Yugoslavia. This led directly to the disintegration of the Yugoslavian federation.

Group commemorations are one of the processes that help keep collective memory alive. These commemorations are often simply social occasions in which group members get together to focus on past events and communicate a sense of social identification with a specific historical event they want to reconstruct. This is a form of social control when politicians emphasize and remember events that suit them politically, while forgetting others.

Victimization is another form of commemoration, the adaptation of a social memory about victimization of ingroup members by members of the outgroup. For Jews, an example is Masada, a fortress in modern-day Israel. Realizing that they could not defeat the Roman legions, and not wanting to be taken as slaves, the Jews decided to commit mass suicide. This kind of historical event, which occurred nearly two millennia ago, has become a permanent part of the Jewish collective memory. There is a tendency also to remember a group's victimization when it has a moral dimension. Thus the Holocaust serves as an example that morality, justice, and compassion had vanished at the time when it was most needed.

Devine-Wright has argued that "ethnomyths," ethnic histories, and territorial associations underlie the present global system of nation states (Devine-Wright 2002: 20) and refers to Claude Lévi-Strauss on the structural approach to myths, "the claim that myths function as a device that mediates and overcomes present contradictions or oppositions." Lévi-Strauss continues: "The myths set up a set of irreconcilable contradictions in ideas and, through their structural characteristics, mediate them. As narrative, myths typically possess a beginning ,or moment of origin, and a temporal diachronic sequence from the remote path in which later events are embedded and anchored to the immediate present context" (Lévi-Strauss, cited in Devine-Wright 2002: 20)[15]

Social psychology deals with forms of social memory. Social identity theory (Tajfel and Turner 1986) addresses ingroup identity and self-worth and implies the existence of an outgroup. A collective narrative is developed by the ingroup regarding the relationship between the groups. But what of conflicting myths?

Is it necessary for the social memories of the two parties to a dispute to be "symmetrical" for the apology to be effective? If the sides have drastically different understandings of the conflict, apology and forgiveness are difficult, and reconciliation remains out of reach.

CASE STUDIES OF GROUP APOLOGY

The Pope's Apology

Pope John Paul II has made the most noted of all intergroup apologies. A look at his background provides insight into how this came about. The Pope, known as "Lolek" in his youth, from an early age tried to help heal the pain among groups. As a young man, Lolek had a Jewish friend, Jerzy Kluger, "Jurek." These two boys went through elementary and high school together and participated in many activities together. They visited each other's homes and studied together.

Lolek experienced some tragedies in his early life. His mother, brother, and father died when he was young. He was an outgoing young man who went to study at a seminary in the 1930s, when antisemitism was becoming active again in Poland. In 1939 the Nazis occupied most of Poland. Lolek studied in the seminary and belonged to a Polish underground organization. He also studied acting in a secret, underground university that was prohibited by the Nazis during their occupation of Poland. He was angry and upset about antisemitism and the mass extermination of Jews in concentration camps such as Auschwitz, located only 60 kilometers from his home town of Wadowice. Lolek completed his seminary studies, became a priest, then a bishop in Krakow, and eventually became pope in 1978 (O'Brien 1998, The Holy See 2006).

During the war, Jurek and his father escaped to Russia, served with the Polish army in the Soviet Union, and survived the war, eventually settling in Rome. The rest of their family was destroyed in the Wadowice ghetto. Thirty years after the war, Lolek and Jurek renewed their friendship in Rome. Pope John Paul II established a memorial in Wadowice, and Jurek was invited for the dedication. The fact that these two men remained friends may well have influenced later events.

It was John Paul II who finally officially recognized the state of Israel. In 2000, the Pope offered a concert in the Vatican commemorating the *Shoah,* the Holocaust, to which the Chief Rabbi of Rome and a number of Jewish congregates were invited. The 200 Holocaust survivors in attendance wore special scarves made from the uniforms of Holocaust prisoners. Chief Rabbi Toaff of Rome and the Pope embraced each other, and the event was emotional and cathartic.

John Paul II was the first pope in history to set foot in a synagogue in Rome. During the visit, Pope John Paul II called the Jews his elder brothers and subsequently wrote a number of letters condemning antisemitism. When the Pope visited Poland, he went to the execution wall at Auschwitz and knelt, praying for the victims. He was able to intervene in an ugly dispute between the Carmelite nuns, who wanted to establish a convent in the Auschwitz camp, and the Jewish community, who protested because they considered the camp to be their holy ground. The Pope convinced the nuns to move their convent several hundred yards away from the camp. Finally, when he visited the state of Israel, he apologized to Jews for 2000 years of Christian persecution and to Moslems for the Crusades and other abuses. He also apologized to Africans for slavery and colonization.

The Pope's apologies were certainly motivated by Christian teachings of love. He believed that Christianity, especially Catholicism, had harmed other peoples and faiths. Pope John Paul's background helps explain how he could come to make such a public apology on behalf of the faith he guided (Svidercoschi 1994, Weigel 1999, O'Brien 1998, Flynn 2001, Ontario 2001).

On a more personal level, in January 1984, Pope John Paul went to the Roman prison holding Moslem Turk Ali Agca, who shot him in May 1981 (Morrow 1984). Agca had been sentenced to life in prison for the attempted assassination of the Pope. For 21 minutes Pope John Paul sat with Agca and tenderly held the hand that had held the gun that was meant to kill him. The two talked softly. Once or twice, Agca laughed. Pope John Paul II forgave him for the shooting. At the end of the meeting, Agca kissed the Pope's ring in a gesture of respect. It was a startling example of forgiveness and reconciliation. On one level, it was an intensely intimate transaction between two men. On the other hand, the Pope, though he spoke in whispers, also meant to proclaim a message to the world. The Pope brought a Vatican photographer and a television crew to the prison in hopes that the images of forgiveness portrayed in the prison cell would be viewed around a world filled with nuclear arsenals and unforgivable hatreds, hostile superpowers and smaller, implacable fanaticisms (Morrow 1984).

In our recent research on apology, we found that 89 percent of respondents reacted positively to the Pope's apology to Jews and others harmed by the Catholic Church. A typical response came from one of our Polish study respondents:

> I am sure that Pope John Paul II's apology to the Jewish people was the right thing to do, on behalf of Christian persecution of

Jews. It is important to correct historical hurts and grievances. The institution of the Church is influential, and the Pope's apology was the right thing to do (Respondent 55).

We also interviewed a sample of rabbis, soliciting their response to the Pope's apology. More than 80 percent responded that Jewish-Catholic relations have never been better than they are now.

In Pope John Paul II's apology to Jews for their persecution over the centuries by Catholics, we can see the major outlines of an effective group-to-group apology. The Pope took responsibility for specific acts committed by a specific group that he represents. He did not try to gloss over the horrible nature of the crimes, did not look to place blame on others, and did not try to bring in extenuating or mitigating factors to diminish responsibility. Along with apologizing, the facts were represented fairly, and details of the events were either already known or were made public. Lastly, the Pope's sincerity was generally accepted; there were seen to be no material benefits to be gained by a papal apology other than to reconcile with groups Catholics had harmed over the years.

We find that even under the best circumstances, apologies are not the final step in the reconciliation process. But when all of the facets of an effective apology come together in this manner, it is possible to lay the groundwork for a real reconciliation. At the same time, we find that even under the best circumstances, apologies are not the final step in the reconciliation process.

Christian apologies to Jews have resulted in eight statements, offered by Jewish scholars, on how Jews and Christians can better relate to each other. These statements consist of the following:

1) Both worship the same God.

2) Both seek authority from the same book.

3) Christians should respect the claim of Jewish people upon the land of Israel.

4) Jews and Christians need to accept the moral principles of the Torah.

5) Nazism was not a Christian phenomenon.

6) Differences between Jews and Christians will not be settled until God redeems the world.

7)   New relationships between Jews and Christians will not weaken Jewish practice.

8)   Jews and Christians must work together for justice and peace.

Germany and the Holocaust

The Holocaust stands alone as a terrible crime committed by one group on other groups. A large percentage of the German people bear responsibility for a wide spectrum of complicity in the killings of millions of Jews, Gypsies, homosexuals, and other "undesirables" during the Hitler years. The Nazi ideology of racial purity dictated a total annihilation of these groups, especially of Jews, and most Germans were willing participants. After the war, one of the first orders of business for the German people was to come to grips with their collective guilt and responsibility for these crimes and to form the basis for Germany's reintegration into the international fabric of nations. Germans were horrified at what "they" had done and felt morally compelled to make amends. German support of Israel, monetary reparations, symbolic and public blame taking, and repeated public and ceremonial apologies by a wide spectrum of German leaders to a wide variety of (especially Jewish) victims have paved the way for the possibility of a reconciliation of the German people with Jews. Although there will always be those who cannot bear to hear the German language spoken, and cannot find it in their individual natures to forgive the Germans for what they did, there seems to be progress down the path of reconciliation.

Willi Brandt was the first German chancellor to apologize to Jewish people, as well as to others, who were taken as slave laborers to German factories during the war. The apologies expressed by a succession of German chancellors have resulted in a general German acknowledgment of guilt and agreement to monetary compensation for the victims and their heirs. President Richard von Weizsacker recognized the unspeakable tragedy of the Holocaust and maintains that it will always be a part of German history. In a speech to a conference on the Holocaust in 1985, he stressed the importance of memory, maintaining that all Germans, "guilty" or not, whether old or young, must accept the past, because all are affected by its consequences and can be held responsible for it (Bindenagel 2002). This conference in remembrance of the Holocaust was not only for Germans. It was crucial for the entire international community to learn about and remember the historical facts of the Holocaust.

Charles Hauss (2003) tells of the roles played by apology and forgiveness in postwar Germany. Every German government since the creation of the Federal Republic in 1949 has sought to establish good working relations with Israel. Not only has the German government apologized to Israel for the Holocaust, but German nongovernmental organizations (NGOs) are actively involved with Israel as well. For example, while in Israel to play an international match, the German national soccer team visited the Israel Holocaust memorial. Hauss believes that the Germans have dug deep into their own souls to try to figure out how their country could have produced the Third Reich.

The many German apologies and requests for forgiveness are examples of what can be regarded as a model for religious and political groups to attempt to improve relations between the harmed and their offspring and the harm-doers and their offspring. Yehudith Auerbach (2005) states that German apologies to Jews and to Israel have led to a normalization of relations between the nations of Israel and Germany, because they "wish to free their relations from the heavy chains of the past" (Auerbach 2005: 58).

The German apologies to the Jewish victims of the Holocaust have been effective because the Germans have taken responsibility for their actions, apologized on numerous occasions in various forums to many different representative groups, and manifested their remorse in the form of tangible reparations. The German reparations program, *Wiedergutmachung*, offers restitution in the form of cash if victims can prove that they were forced into ghettoes, concentration camps, or were forced to labor in German factories or farms. This program is not limited to Jews but includes Slavs, homosexuals, Gypsies, and other victims of Hitler's reign. So far, the program has paid about $70 billion directly to victims of slave labor.

Berlin and other German cities have monuments and memorials that commemorate German involvement in the Holocaust, and Germans are now producing films that portray the Holocaust years. The German educational system has included accurate coverage of the events of the Hitler years in its curricula, and the German public generally understands and acknowledges German responsibility for the terrible deeds of those years.[16] Recently, President Johannes Rau said, "I pay tribute to all those who were subjected to slave and forced labor under German rule, and in the name of the German people, beg for forgiveness. We will not forget their suffering"(Bindenagel 2002).[17]

Germany and the Hereros

Germany not only apologized to most of its victims but initiated genuine efforts toward reconciliation and reparation. As a participant in the European colonizing of Africa, where the "great" European powers literally divvied up the continent, Germany obtained a part of Southwest Africa now known as Namibia. Among the colonized peoples of Southwest Africa lived the Hereros. When the Hereros rebelled against German rule in 1904, the Germans killed between 35,000 and 105,000 people. Commanding General Bon Trotha stated, "Any Herero found within the German borders, with or without a gun or with or without cattle, will be shot" (BBC 2004). Not only were many of the Hereros massacred, but the Germans poisoned their wells. On August 14, 2004, Germany's Development Aid Minister Heidemarie Wieczorek-Zeul offered the first formal apology to the Hereros for the colonial-era massacre. News sources had reported just months before that the German government resisted making reparations (Kuteeue 2004), but Wieczorek-Zeul said that "Germany has learnt the bitter lessons of the past" (BBC 2004).

Recently Wolfgang Massing, German Ambassador to Namibia, observed that, history could not be undone, but "we can give back to the victims and descendants the dignity and honor of which they were robbed, and we Germans wished to express how deeply we regret this unfortunate past."

The leader of the Hereros, Paramount Chief Kuaima Riruako, accepted the German apology but insisted that compensation be paid to the Herero people to heal past wounds. He maintained that reparations were necessary not only to Herero dignity but also to restore what had been wrongfully taken away from them. He wants the German government to accept some responsibility for the genocide and to engage with issues of mutual interest. While the Herero case has not yet been resolved, it is clear that Germany, more than other colonial powers, has tried to make amends and to take responsibility for the people they have oppressed and murdered and whose property they stole (BBC 2004).

Japan and War Crimes

The Japanese, whom we have seen as models for personal and even corporate apologies, are surprisingly inept at political *mea culpas*. Japan committed its own list of unspeakable crimes as a result of Japanese militarism in the 1930s and 1940s. The Japanese record of apologizing, however, leaves much to be desired, especially when compared to how the Germans have approached their responsibilities. Japanese efforts to ethnically cleanse various countries they occupied during the war, their use of concentration and prison camps, and the brutalities they inflicted on civilians in occupied areas are similar in many ways to crimes committed by Germany. People in many Asian countries, including the Philippines, China, and Indonesia, suffered terribly during the war years. Yet Japan has never offered an unconditional, unambiguous apology for its wartime actions. The Japanese, while seemingly effective in apologizing in their interpersonal relationships, are reluctant to assume responsibility for their wartime atrocities or to apologize for them. The apologies they have made for individual crimes, or to specific groups that were victimized, generally have been ineffective and have often served to intensify the anger of victims, rather than to offer a step on the road to reconciliation. It is not surprising that Japanese apologies are often perceived as self-serving, insincere, and meaningless, because many Japanese do not admit to the various atrocities committed during the World War II years. Even Japanese textbooks avoid taking responsibility for atrocities and to this day portray Japan as having been backed into a corner and almost forced to go to war. This inability to bring the ugly truths of that period out into the open prevents Japan's victims from appreciating Japanese efforts at apology.

Many Chinese people are still angry for the occupying Japanese Army's "Rape of Nanking" in 1937–38, when there was widespread rape and violence and an estimated 300,000 men, women, and children were killed (Chang 1998). In 1995, when Japanese Prime Minister Tomiichi Murayama tried to apologize to various people for these events, the Japanese Diet defeated the measure by a two-to-one margin. Widespread public antipathy to such an apology was indicated by a national campaign organized by a former education minister that gathered 4.5 million signatures opposed to the apology resolution. Even Murayama's apologies have been less than perfectly remorseful. In his statement on the occasion of the fiftieth anniversary of the war's end, Murayama consistently included the suffering of the Japanese people themselves in discussing the victims of Japanese wartime atrocities. He blamed a "mistaken national policy" for "ensnar[ing] the Japanese people in a fateful crisis...and caus[ing] tremendous damage and suffering to the people of many countries, particularly to those of Asian nations." Similarly, when he expressed his "feelings of profound mourning," it was for "all victims, both at home and abroad," of "that history" (Murayama 1995). He never said, "As Prime Minister of Japan, I apologize for all the harmful actions our country committed during the war years," which might have been received as a starting point for reconciliation by other Asian people victimized by his country.

Upon the sixtieth anniversary of the end of the war, Japanese Prime Minister Junichiro Koizumi echoed Murayama's comments when he said he offered condolences to "the victims of the war at home and abroad." Koizumi compounded the effects of his half-hearted apology with a visit to a Shinto shrine to honor Japanese war dead immediately afterward. In response, China's official news agency remarked that, "Actions speak louder than words....His words appeared faint and his sincerity is also in doubt" (Standing 2005).

Japan's reluctance to acknowledge its role and to apologize to those it harmed has translated into outright animosity toward the country by those hurt by its actions. In 2005 we saw riots in China decrying the lack of a real apology from the Japanese for its war crimes. Even now, almost 70 years after the atrocities, there is still discontent among some Asian-Americans for Japanese wartime actions. The "Rape of Nanking Redress Coalition" (RNRC) recently organized a conference addressing Japan's actions in China. The resolution from the RNRC's Berkeley conference outlined several main demands: first, a Japanese apology that includes a clear acknowledgement for atrocities committed in China and other Asian countries during the Pacific war; second, legislation that authorizes disclosure and preservation of documents related to the war; third, the removal of all statutes of limitation under Japanese law that prevent victims of World War II war crimes and crimes against humanity from seeking due redress in the courts of Japan; fourth, education of the Japanese people. Japanese students at all levels should learn about the Asian-Pacific war and the crimes and atrocities committed. Japan should provide funds for a memorial museum in Tokyo dedicated to the commemoration and remembrance of the victims of World War II, as well as for research and publication of material related to all facets of the war. Japan should also establish a day of remembrance for victims of the Pacific war and outlaw the denial of war crimes committed by the Japanese Imperial forces. In addition, it should—must—return all looted national prizes, including cultural and historical relics; and, finally, provide just compensation for the victims and their families who suffered and whose property was looted and destroyed as reported by RNRC (2001). So far, the Japanese government has refused all of these measures.

One may conclude that Japan, unlike Germany, has not genuinely apologized to the people it deprived of life, dignity, and property, particularly the "comfort women" used as sex slaves during World War II, as well as the prisoners on whom medical experiments were performed. Japanese leaders may have spoken similar words and followed a similar process to that of German leaders, but their apologies have not been well received, because they have not carried the legitimacy of a true backing of the people or even of the legislature. BBC news reports that Japanese Prime Minister Shinzo Abe apologized only after Asian neighbors criticized Japan's previous comments, which cast doubt on their role in coercing the women, and after the U.S. Congress began considering an unequivocal apology through a non-binding resolution.[18] The Japanese were reluctant to apologize, because they perceived the draft resolution as not including the efforts made to compensate the comfort women on behalf of Japan. Even after the apology, the Chinese and South Koreans still have criticisms of the apology and compensation efforts. An Article published by Norimitsu Onishi on April 25, 2007 in the *New York Times*, titled "Japan's Atonement to Former Sex Slaves Stirs Anger,"[19] states that the comfort women have by and large rejected the offer of compensation from a private fund set up by the government on behalf of the Japanese population; they advocate a government fund and a meaningful Japanese apology that takes responsibility for the coercion. Many Japanese rejected the idea that Japan and its Prime Minister should be told to apologize from oversees. The victims perceive a continued refusal of responsibility and guilt on the part of the Japanese government. This refusal of guilt is partly because conservatives in Japan maintain that the comfort women were compensated, and abuses were carried out by private contractors not the military. In any case the country's apologies are perceived as ineffective and have made matters worse.

Ireland—Protestants and Catholics

Northern Ireland has been embroiled in conflict for centuries, but the conflict has been further exacerbated in the last 30 years, known as the "the time of troubles." The social conflict in Ireland arises directly from identity-group membership and the grievances those groups have against each other. It is based largely on historic reconstructions of grievances, both perceived and real, that have been passed on from generation to generation. Both Protestants and Catholics see themselves as victims of aggressive and hurtful actions by the other party. Hurts are remembered and often are commemorated. In spite of the fact that both sides in the battle are Christian, albeit split into Protestants and Catholics, the teachings of Jesus seem to get lost in the recurring revenge process. The cycle of violence and retaliation has been rekindled by brutal killings committed by both sides since the 1970s. The role of apology has not been readily recognized or accepted by those involved; because of the historical nature of the conflict, it is imperative that the apology and forgiveness process be truly heartfelt, or it will only make matters worse. If forgiveness is not genuine, or if the harms experienced by either side are trivialized in this process, apology may serve to exacerbate pain and may result in yet more violence.

A recent study examined the role of apology and forgiveness among people directly affected by the violence (McLernon, Cairns, and Hewstone 2002). The authors worked with eight focus groups, each composed of 12 people. These groups consisted of participants from all sides of the Irish conflict, including victims, loyalists, and the Republican paramilitary. The groups focused on several topics, including the role played by remorse in the forgiveness process, the definition and nature of forgiveness, the relationship between justice and public acknowledgements of wrongs, and the components of what actually constitutes apology and forgiveness among individuals and groups. Focus group discussions tended to dwell on what participants felt forgiveness really was. There was general agreement that one cannot deny the right of another to resentment for being hurt. One of the suggestions that came forth is that those who have been harmed must "endeavor to view the wrongdoer with compassion, benevolence, and love" (McLernon, Cairns, and Hewstone 2002: 286).

The authors point out the difficulty of this kind of apology and forgiveness. For example, they found that some relatives had forgiven the murders of their wives and children because they felt that doing so might make reprisals less likely. Still, the groups have learned the importance of promoting self-respect by enabling the injured parties to refuse to let their lives be dominated by harmful thoughts, memories, and negative feelings. Some of the participants referred to the teachings of Jesus Christ in discussing the importance of forgiveness. Focus group participants considered the idea of time and that pain becomes less hurtful as time goes by. The passage of time, then, might make it easier for some to forgive. Some things are not easily forgotten, or forgiven, such as physical injury. One of the most important factors addressed was public acknowledgment of wrongdoing inflicted on the group. This, as we have stated elsewhere, is important, because harmed people want to have their hurt recognized and acknowledged publicly. Discussion distinguished between group and individual forgiveness, which is more easily accomplished. Group forgiveness is more difficult, because members see themselves as "victims by association." Groups of people may feel that any violence committed by their own side is justified because of the way that they as a nation or community have been treated. They discussed trust and how crucial it is to the forgiveness process to develop trust between the harmed and the harm-doers. Researchers found that sincere apology can provide the first step toward rebuilding trust and laying the groundwork for reconciliation.

Trust, the cornerstone of friendship, is an important aspect of practically all relationships. Another group of researchers in Northern Ireland dealt with 341 students in a representative sample of Catholics and Protestants (Paolini, Hewstone, Cairns, and Voci 2004). The authors were interested in testing whether direct or indirect friendship between the two groups had generalized effects on prejudice and perceived outgroup variability, and whether reduced anxiety about future contact with outgroup members mediated such relationships. The research confirmed that in both direct and indirect samples, group friendship between Catholics and Protestants were associated with reduced prejudice towards the religious outgroup.

The authors conclude that religious denomination is not a barrier to personal friendship. Beliefs about the other group influences friendship and social understanding, and contact between the groups can help reduce friction and polarization. They claim that personal friendship can help reduce prejudice and increase perceived outgroup variability, even when contact takes place against a background of intergroup conflict, as in the case of cross-cultural community relations in Northern Ireland. Such an influence is partly mediated by anxiety-reduction mechanisms. Having friends among outgroup members, and among ingroup members who have outgroup friends, can contribute positively to improve intergroup relations by virtue of reducing anxiety associated with outgroup encoun-ters. The authors add that even though these findings might be considered optimistic, having outgroup friends is not, unfortunately, a vaccination against group conflict. They compare the conflicts in Ireland, Yugoslavia, and Rwanda and find examples of perpetrators betraying or killing former friends who belong to other groups. Even though friendship contacts may be an insufficient bulwark against norms of outgroup segregation or aggression, the authors maintain nonetheless that such contact is, in many cases, a powerful antidote to intergroup bias.

McLernon, Cairns, Hewstone, and Smith (2004) studied intergroup forgiveness in Northern Ireland. Their intent was to study the relation-ships between and among forgiveness and three factors: the type of injury incurred, whether it is verbal, physical, or bereavement; the length of time since the injury occurred; and the degree of perceived hurt following the injury. They used a sample of 340 participants, aged 25 and under, who had been hurt in some way as a result of the violence in Northern Ireland. They found that the severity of the injury inflicted was not an accurate predictor of forgiveness. The individual's *perception* of the severity of the injury was the more important factor.

Hewstone, Cairns, Voci, Hamberger, and Niens (2006) recently compared two studies examining the correlation between contact and forgiveness. They found that the "contact hypothesis" proposed by Gordon W. Allport can be effective, "that bringing together individuals from opposing groups can reduce intergroup conflict 'under optimal conditions'" (Allport 1954: 102). Allport states that reducing intergroup conflict was most likely if four conditions were met: First, majority and minority group members must have an equal status. Second, a common goal should be pursued. Third, contact between the groups should be sanctioned by institutional supports. And last, contact between the two groups should be perceived as reflecting common interests and recognizing the humanity of the two groups.

According to the literature, in Northern Ireland "both primary and secondary education are highly segregated…with support [for segregation] coming from both communities." However, research has found that "total residential segregation [in Northern Ireland] does not exist."[20] Therefore, it is assumed that contact between members of the two groups exists in many areas. However, the author maintains that "even though segregation is not thought to be the *cause* of the intergroup conflict[s], it is believed to play a major role in establishing and maintaining conflict between two communities" (Hewstone, Cairns, Voci, Hamberger, and Niens 2006). "Consistent with the contact hypothesis, [the] first study showed that respondents with previous experience of outgroup contact had more positive attitudes toward mixing with members of the outgroup." Despite the inherent weaknesses of secondary analysis, "even when prior schooling, education level, and social class were controlled, the positive effect of contact was evident" (Hewstone, Cairns, Voci, Hamberger, and Niens (2006: 114).[21]

The authors conclude that intergroup contact can make a difference, because exclusion and segregation sustains conflict by creating a social climate that fosters mutual ignorance and suspicion. It should be noted that there is safety in segregation, and things are unlikely to improve dramatically until people feel safer. Therefore, planned intergroup contact schemes are still badly needed. This study also reported that segregation was associated with perceived rejection of outgroup members. According to the researchers, societal solutions must achieve some kind of trade-off between the benefits and costs of segregation (Hewstone, Cairns, Voci, Hamberger, and Niens 2006: 115).

The study by Hewstone and colleagues revealed less forgiveness and trust among those who had suffered most, yet found that contact with friends was significantly correlated with forgiveness in both groups. The researchers believe that exposure to violence feeds the conflict, and that in both communities, exposure to violence is associated with public support for paramilitary groups; thus violence breeds violence. According to their findings, contact in the midst of intergroup conflict is an essential part of any solution, and positive experience of cross-community contact also translates into better ways of dealing with the past, and the authors maintain it is a more positive strategy for dealing with the future.

Ongoing apology and forgiveness processes in Ireland highlight the importance of contact between members of groups that are in conflict as a prerequisite to reconciliation. When individuals see the humanity of the other, empathy is strengthened and allowed to guide behaviors. When similarities and commonalities are seen, instead of differences and divisions, healing becomes possible. There are currently hopeful signs that reconciliation between Protestants and Catholics will be effective.

Ukraine/Poland—Ethnic Massacres and Persecutions During World War II

In 2003 Ukraine and Poland commemorated the sixtieth anniversary of the massacre of Poles and Ukrainians by their respective rightist underground armies in the region of Volyn. Historically, that region—now incorporated into Ukraine—had been a part of Poland, even though ethnic Poles were a minority there. For generations, Ukrainians blamed Polish expansionism and imperialism for the oppression of their people. Ukrainians were relegated to second-class citizenship. The massacres, visited on both sides, one upon the other, took place from 1941 to 1943, during the German occupation. The Ukrainian motivation was to drive out the Polish citizens from that area. The Ukrainian underground (known as the Ukrainian Insurgent Army, or UPA) killed between 50,000 and 60,000 men, women, and children. Estimates vary, and Poles claim a much higher figure. The true numbers will never be known. Retaliating for these killings, the Polish

Underground Army (known as the *Armija Krajowa,* or AK) took part in the slaughter of approximately 15,000 to 17,000 ethnic Ukrainians. Toward the end of the war, another tragedy occurred, which was particularly gruesome for Ukrainians. In March 1945, a detachment of Polish anti-Nazi guerillas killed hundreds of Ukrainian inhabitants of Pawlokoma. The Ukrainians were herded into a local Greek Catholic church, interrogated and tortured, and then executed in a local cemetery.

After the war ended in 1945, the animosity remained. Communist authorities of Poland expelled Ukrainians or relocated them in the western part of the country, which had been recaptured from the Germans. These resettlements were collectively known as the "Vistula Action" and were explained as a defensive reaction by the Polish government to the outrageous murders committed by Ukrainian nationalists in Southeastern Poland. The resentment felt by people of both nations prevented the neighboring countries from enjoying normal relations for decades.

The sixtieth anniversary of the events at Volyn was a turning point in the relations between the two countries. President Kwaśniewski of Poland and President Kujchma of Ukraine, after securing the approval of their respective parliaments, met in the region where the tragedies took place to commemorate them and offer apologies to each other, hoping to lay the groundwork for reconciliation. Both presidents admitted that their people had committed unspeakable crimes against the other. Although some continue to refer to the crimes as genocide, neither government used that term in the discussion, instead substituting the term "tragedy." During the ceremony, President Kwaśniewski said that the Ukrainian nation is not to be blamed for the massacre of Polish civilians. He maintains that there is no national culprit and that specific individuals are guilty of the crimes and wrongdoings.

Both Ukranian and Polish historiographers have their own interpretations of the facts. One Ukrainian, E. Misilo, claims that the expulsion of Ukrainians from their homelands in Poland in the Vistula Action was really instigated by Polish communists and their Soviet counterparts, who were equal partners. He maintains that the Polish communist government decided upon the total and obligatory expulsion of all Ukrainians, including the Lemko, an ethnic group related to Ukranians. The Polish government used force to accomplish this expulsion and humiliation of the Lemko and Ukrainians. Polish historians have explained that Poland was upset with the Ukrainians and Lemkos for their nationalistic agitation, as well as the perception that these non-Poles had sided with the Nazi occupiers during the war years. These back-and-forth accusations have now subsided as a result of the apologies between the countries' presidents, and a push for reconciliation, and the opening of the borders.

Zbigniew Wojciechowski, one of the leaders of Lublin, Poland, was authorized by the city board to make every effort to intensify Lublin's role in the Polish–Ukrainian relations (CBOS 2001). He says that he "met a lot of wonderful people, including mayors and governors of Ukrainian partner cities. My friends from Lvov, Luck, Tarnopol, Kiev, and other cities have gladly joined the initiative to build cooperation." In 1999, Lublin opened a permanent economic mission in Lugansk. Wojciechowski considers the mission "a great success, since no one, nowhere, had ever initiated such an undertaking before. I am the patron of establishing missions together with Ukrainian mayors." The Polish businessmen who made investments in Ukraine adapted easily to the new conditions, and both sides mutually benefited from them. These instances of cross-border cooperation suggest that the seeds of reconciliation have been sown. Polish-Ukrainian cultural festivals have introduced the peoples to each other's cultures, and 64 percent of Poles feel that contact and cooperation among these groups is possible and desirable (CBOS 2001).

In 2005, Lubomyr Husar, head of the Ukrainian Greek Catholic Church, and Archbishop Jozef Michalik of Przemysl, head of the Polish Bishops' Conference, conducted an explicit act of reconciliation between the Polish and Ukrainian people, prompted by the teachings of Pope John Paul II. Five hundred representatives of both church hierarchies and more than 100,000 people participated in a solemn liturgy headed by Cardinal Lubomyr Husar to close the Eucharistic Congress. Six people from both the Ukraine and Poland, chosen to symbolically represent the entirety of the two peoples—a bishop, a priest, a married couple, a boy, and a girl—performed the act of reconciliation. This monumental act reaffirms the hope that reconciliation between peoples is always possible (Kowal, Tomashek, and Zurowski n.d.).

In May 2006, new presidents of Poland and Ukraine, Lech Kaczynski and Victor Yushchenko, joined in prayers conducted by leaders of Poland's Roman Catholic Church and Ukraine's Greek Catholic church at the recently built memorial commemorating the Ukrainian victims in Pawlokoma. President Kaczynski said, "A strong and lasting reconciliation can only be built upon the truth. We cannot change the past but can ensure that it doesn't determine our future" (Kaczynski 2006). In turn, President Yushchenko referred to the event as a salient step toward consolidating good Polish-Ukrainian neighborly relations and the two peoples' historical reconciliation.

Since the sixtieth commemoration of the massacres in 2003, there have been greatly improved relations between Ukraine and Poland. Travel between the countries is easier, and tourism is increasing. Cultural exchange is taking place, including festivals celebrating each other's cultures, and there is increased cross-border commerce. These examples are good signs that the seeds of reconciliation have taken root. According to the most recent research, mutual trust and good feelings between the people of the two countries have developed significantly during the last decade (CBOS 2005).

Poland—Lemko Ethnic Cleansing

The troublesome postwar history of one Polish ethnic group has strong parallels with the drama of Polish—Ukrainian relations. In Karpathia, a mountainous region in southern Poland, lives an indigenous ethnic group known as the Lemko.[22] Related ethnically to the Ukrainians, the Lemko were a homogeneous cultural people who kept themselves separate from the greater Polish culture. In 1945 more than half of them were deported to the territory of the current nation of Ukraine. In 1947, as part of the above-mentioned Vistula Action, the communist government of Poland forcefully relocated the rest of the Lemko population to the newly acquired Northern and Western Territories of Poland that had previously belonged to Germany. Some of the Lemko leaders, including their religious leaders, were imprisoned. The purpose of the removal of the Lemko population was what we today know as "ethnic cleansing" and was intended to solve the "Ukrainian problem" once and for all. These people lost their individual property, land, and buildings; but more importantly, the Lemko as a group lost their communal property, such as schools and churches—the homes for the institutions that preserved Lemko culture.

It seemed as if the Lemko were headed for extinction by forceful diminution of their culture, but a resurgence has been seen since the fall of communism. No large-scale reconciliation has taken place between the Poles and the Lemko, probably because of the Lemko's small numbers, even though the Polish people seem to sympathize with their plight. The Lemko are still struggling to regain their churches, cemeteries, and land plundered by the communist government. So far, there has been no apology expressed by the Polish government, although those Lemkos who wanted to return were allowed to do so.

Poland, Antisemitism, and the Jedwabne Massacre

Poland has had a substantial Jewish population for more than 800 years, and of the 36 million Poles in 1939, three and a half million were Jews. For centuries, Poland was a shelter for European Jews. Many national and regional rulers in Poland granted Jews rights and privileges unavailable to them in the rest of Europe. In some areas, such as Krakow in southern Poland, Jews enjoyed relative freedom, and Jewish culture and religious life flourished. However, their existence in Poland has always been overshadowed by antisemitism, if perhaps less at times than in other European nations. This antisemitism is mostly rooted in religious origins. Catholics and Protestants in Poland often share the belief that Jews are responsible for the suffering and death of Jesus. These sentiments, although not usually supported by the official doctrine of the churches, are very deep-seated. Anti-Jewish feeling has been so pervasive that one may still find Poles today, especially among the poor and uneducated, who deny Jesus's Jewish origins.

The situation of the Jews in Poland began to seriously deteriorate at the end of the eighteenth century, when Poland lost its independence and was divided up among the three major powers of the age: Germany, Austria, and Czarist Russia. The conditions for Jews worsened when the Nazis invaded in 1939. Sometimes at the instigation of the Nazis, and sometimes independent of German involvement, Polish right-wing parties organized pogroms against the Jews in dozens of Polish towns. The most notorious of these was the massacre in Jedwabne.

On July 10, 1941, shortly after the region was occupied by the Germans, almost the entire Jewish community in the small town of Jedwabne was wiped out. After some were beaten and murdered in the streets, the survivors—including some Jews who had escaped from pogroms in other towns—were driven into a barn and locked inside, while their Christian neighbors burned it to the ground. Those trying to escape from the inferno were killed. Originally, the German occupiers were blamed, but years later, the publication of Jan Gross's *Neighbors* (2001), which describes the events, aroused great debate. *Neighbors* laid the blame for the tragedy at the feet of the townspeople. Recently, Polish historians responded to the Jedwabne tragedy and analyzed the events from their perspective, shedding additional light on this intense debate (Aleksiun 2007). A thorough investigation by Poland's Institute of National Remembrance (Institute of National Remembrance 2002) found that the Germans had played only a minor role, and that it was the local Catholic townspeople who carried out the atrocities. In response, government officials removed the monument in Jedwabne that had attributed this heinous incident to the Nazi occupiers. The President of Poland, Alexander Kwaśniewski, performed an official act of penance during the sixtieth anniversary of the massacre. While some members of the Catholic Church, including high-ranking clergy, expressed horror that the Polish people committed such atrocities, others disagreed with the need for apology (Gruber 2001). Some blamed the Jews. "I think it is the Jews that ought to apologize to the Poles for being communist under the Soviet occupation," said the town priest, Father Orlowski. He and others declared the supposed massacre "all lies" and claimed only Germans were responsible for the killings (Gruber 2001).

Although many Poles were victims of Nazi occupation, a small percentage of Catholic Poles were evildoers during the war. Given the long history of Polish antisemitism, one could hardly expect it to be otherwise. Some Poles tried to argue the facts of the case. In his speech at the memorial, President Kwaśniewski sought to clarify the issues for Poles, addressing this directly by saying:

> We know with all certainty that Poles were among the oppressors and assassins....We cannot have any doubts—here in Jedwabne citizens of the Republic of Poland died from the hands of other citizens of the Republic of Poland. It is people to people, neighbors to neighbors, who forged such destiny....For this crime we should beg the souls of the dead and their families for forgiveness. This is why today, as the President of the Republic of Poland, I beg pardon. I beg pardon in my own name and in the name of those Poles whose conscience is shattered by that crime (Kwaśniewski 2001).

He continued, saying that this was a particularly cruel crime, because there was no justification, and it was committed against helpless and defenseless victims. Many of the people present were moved to tears. President Kwaśniewski, while acknowledging that the tragedy could not be undone, hoped that the clear statement of the facts and the sincere apology offered would "turn the wrong into the right" (Kwaśniewski 2001).

The local priest of Jedwabne advised his parishioners not to be present at the ceremonies. Father Orlowski told the townspeople, "Do not take part in these lies" that imply a need for Poles to apologize to Jews, because it was not their fault. On the other hand, a substantial number of Poles learned the truth about the massacres and realized that Poles were to blame.

It is clear that the simple act of acknowledging culpability in the massacre was a learning experience for many Poles who learned of the event through the apology process itself and would otherwise have had no idea of the facts surrounding them. Some are saying that if relations between Jews and Poles are to improve, this kind of public teaching and sincere compassion is important. The first step in the process must be public acknowledgement of the facts.[23]

Jewish–Polish relations have a sad history. After World War II, some Jews who had survived the German extermination camps, or who had been in hiding, returned to their homes. They were greeted with great resentment, and several pogroms ensued. I remember a near-pogrom in my own small town of Gorlice, which, fortunately, was avoided. The most famous of these was the Kielce pogrom on July 4, 1946, which was instigated by the police chief and other authorities in the town, or at least tacitly approved by them. The story began when nine-year-old Henryk Blszczek left home without informing his parents. He stayed away for two nights, and, upon his return, he concocted a far-fetched story about an unknown gentleman who kidnapped him. Because of the traditional beliefs of some ignorant Polish peasants, the townspeople suspected that Jews were kidnapping local children for use in barbaric Passover rituals. The boy identified a local Jewish home, where he allegedly had been imprisoned. What followed was a tragedy. More than 40 Jews were massacred that day with no police or official interference. The event had a profound effect on the remaining Jews, who soon left not only the town but the country. Bozena Szaynok wrote an article titled "Kielce Pogrom," reconstructing the indifference of the authorities and how the violent mobs coalesced to murder these people. This pogrom was set in the context of the political struggle; people had started to say that Jews were the leaders of the Communists in Poland.

Most Poles still do not recognize that they and the Jews were unequal victims during the Nazi occupation of Poland. While the previous President Kwaśniewski has apologized for the Jedwabne massacre, the current government, headed by President Lech Kaczynski and his twin brother Jaroslaw, chief of the Law and Justice Party, have caused Poland to take steps backwards in terms of tolerance of minorities and ethnic groups. There is strong bias against homosexuals in Poland, as well as rising antisemitism, generated by the conservative coalition that rules the country. The Law and Justice Party took power by means of a coalition with fringe conservative groups: Self Defense, which openly admires the dictator of Belarus, and the League of Polish Families. This program is supported by Radio Maryja, a Catholic radio station with millions of listeners, which is openly nationalistic, antisemitic, and antiforeign. Although Pope Benedict has asked them to stop broadcasting bigotry, the station continues. In late May, Poland's chief Rabbi, Michael Schudrich, was punched in the chest and sprayed with pepper spray by a young man who shouted "Poland for the Poles!" Although President Kaczynski personally apologized to the rabbi, the actions of the government seem to give an official wink to bigotry.

While relations between Poles and Jews may have improved, the old canards and fears still apply. I still am hopeful, because a free press has the power to counter these trends, there is hope for the relationships between Poles and the ethnic minorities to become more amiable. It must be added to this discussion that there were Poles who risked their lives to save Jews, including me, from certain death. This too must be part of the history books. See Chapter 7, which deals with collective guilt and the Jedwabne massacre.

United States—Hawaiians

On November 23, 1993, the Congress passed Resolution 19, which offered an apology to native Hawaiian people on behalf of the United States government. The resolution acknowledged the 100th anniversary of the January 17, 1893 overthrow of the Kingdom of Hawaii and the replacement of Hawaiian laws and customs with American ones. The Congressional resolution expressed deep regret to the native people, and to the State of Hawaii, and expressed the hope of fostering better relations between mainland Americans and native Hawaiians. The apology included an admission that the overthrow was illegal and specified that it resulted in the humiliation of the Hawaiian population and the deprivation of the rights of the native people to self-determination.

Unfortunately, a disclaimer was added stating, "Nothing in this joint resolution is intended to serve as a settlement of any claims against the United States." The effectiveness of the Congressional Resolution was thereby greatly reduced, though at this point we do not know the real outcome. Parenthetically, aside from this apology to the native people of Hawaii, we are not aware of an official U.S. government apology for massacres of Native Americans.

United States—Internment of Japanese Americans

The United States government interned 110,000 Americans of Japanese descent during World War II, because officials feared they would assist Japanese forces in an invasion. Under the internment order, signed on February 19, 1942 by President Franklin D. Roosevelt as Executive Order 9066, the western states of California, Oregon, and Washington were deemed military zones. West Coast residents of Japanese heritage were rounded up and kept in internment camps throughout the war years, causing them to lose their houses, businesses, and other possessions. They were detained for up to four years and held in spite of their legal right to due process. Their only crime was being of Japanese ancestry—being "enemy aliens". The camps were fenced with barbed wire, and those interned were kept under constant surveillance by armed guards. In some cases, family members were separated.

The camps were officially referred to as "relocation centers." There were 10 located in California, Idaho, Utah, Arizona, Wyoming, Colorado, and Arkansas. The farmers' lobby played a key role in the internment because they were in direct competition with Japanese labor at the time. According to a report conducted by the War Relocation Authority, conditions were poor with "tar-paper covered barracks of simple frame construction without plumbing or cooking facilities." Eventually, internees were allowed to leave the camps only if they enlisted in the U.S. Army. Following the closing of the internment camps, 5,766 *Nisei*—second-generation, American-born Japanese—renounced their American citizenship (National Park Service 2000).

This humiliating act of the United States government was a blight on American democracy. Only a couple of Japanese Americans were found to have aided the Japanese war effort against the United States, but ten Caucasians were convicted for aiding Japan (Burton, Lord, and Lord 2000). Japanese Americans' service to the United States during the war is well documented. Young men of Japanese ancestry volunteered in high numbers for military service, and their regiment, the 442nd, was the most decorated regiment in the history of the United States Army.

The relocation camps were dismantled and the internees freed within a few months of the end of hostilities in 1945. Within a year, the last of the camps were closed. The Evacuation Claims Act of 1948 authorized payment to Japanese Americans who could prove they suffered economic loss during the imprisonment; 10 cents was returned for every dollar lost (Iritani 1995). This futile attempt to compensate the Japanese-American people seemed to serve more as an insult than an apology. No responsibility was taken for the racial basis of the internment, and the economic and emotional hardships it caused are incalculable; but it took more than 30 years for the American government to address it. President Gerald Ford, in 1976, offered a proclamation deploring the internment.

In Proclamation 4417, Ford outlined some of the harm done to what he termed "loyal American citizens" and declared that Americans had "learned from the tragedy of that long ago experience forever to treasure liberty and justice for each individual American, and resolve that this kind of action shall never again be repeated." He ended the proclamation by officially terminating the executive order. What President Ford did not offer, however, was an apology. He acknowledged:

> In this Bicentennial Year, we are commemorating the anniversary dates of many of the great events in American history. An honest reckoning, however, must include a recognition of our national mistakes as well as our national achievements. Learning from our mistakes is not pleasant, but as a great philosopher once admonished, we must do so if we want to avoid repeating them (Ford 1976).

Twelve years later Japanese Americans received their apology from President Ronald Reagan. With the passage of the Civil Liberties Act of 1988, the American government offered an apology—and reparations of about $20,000—to each surviving internee. At the signing ceremony on August 10, 1988, Reagan said:

> The legislation that I am about to sign provides for a restitution payment to each of the 60,000 surviving Japanese-Americans of the 120,000 who were relocated or detained. Yet no payment can make up for those lost years. So, what is most important in this bill has less to do with property than with honor. For here we admit a wrong; here we reaffirm our commitment as a nation to equal justice under the law (Reagan 1988).

Reagan's apology admitted that the relocation and internment was based on "race prejudice, war hysteria, and a failure of political leadership," and beginning in 1990, the United States government began paying reparations to the surviving internees (Reagan 1988).

United States—Tuskegee Experiment

In May 1997, President Clinton apologized on behalf of the nation to survivors of the Tuskegee Syphilis Experiment, a secret study of black men in Macon County, Alabama, whose cases of syphilis were deliberately left untreated to see what would happen (Mathias 1997). Americans were shocked to find that their own government had sponsored such a study. The experiments were conducted between 1932 and 1972, when it became public knowledge that more than 400 black men went untreated for syphilis after the government offered them "free medical care." The men were never told they were to be part of a study, which was clinically titled *Tuskegee Study of Untreated Syphilis in Negro Males*. The government doctors failed to offer any treatment. Twenty-eight men died of syphilis during the years of the study, and 100 others died of related illnesses and complications. Forty wives and 19 newborns were subsequently infected with syphilis by their untreated husbands and fathers. A few years after news of the study came out, the government paid the survivors and relatives $10 million for damages but without offering a formal apology. Herman Shaw, a Tuskegee survivor, was 95 years old when Clinton made the apology. He stated that this ceremony was important because the damage done by the Tuskegee study was "much deeper than the [physical] wounds any of us may have suffered. It speaks to our faith in government and the ability for medical science to serve as a force for good." The few survivors were gathered amid the opulence of the White House to hear the simple words: I am sorry. President Clinton stated that what is done cannot be undone, but we should stop turning our heads away. Speaking to the audience of survivors and their families, he said, "We can stop turning our heads away, we can look you in the eye and finally say, on behalf of the American people, what the United States government did was shameful, and I am sorry" (Mathis 1997: 1). This apology received standing ovations from those in attendance, and it showed that the survivors of these experiments sincerely appreciated such an apology.

In the speech, Clinton committed the American government to strengthening training in research ethics for scientists, creating new post-graduate fellowships for bioethicists, especially African Americans, and extending the life of the National Bioethics Advisory Commission through October 1999. The President also ordered his Health and Human Services Secretary, Donna Shalala, to report to him in 180 days on how to increase minority participation in legitimate health care research. The President concluded, to the already tearful audience at the White House, "Today all we can do is apologize...but you have the power to forgive. Your presence here shows us that you have chosen a better path than our government did so long ago. You have not withheld the power to forgive" (Mathis 1997).

The Three Sister Communities of Kentucky

In 2001, as part of a wider effort by Catholics worldwide to repent for the mistreatment of others, the Sisters of Charity of Nazareth, Sisters of Loretto, and the Dominicans of Saint Catherine, decided to look at the past to confront "the enduring sin of racism." Slaves had cleared the land and built the Church in the early 1800's, and these communities, prior to 1806, had sisters come to the convent with slaves as dowries. The Sisters regret that their communities did not do more to oppose the system of slavery, and they struggled to understand the role that slavery played in their past. The nuns also acknowledged that racial segregation has existed in their orders. The apology took place at a Church in Bardstown, Kentucky, in 2001 and was attended by nearly 400 people. The Dominicans of Saint Catherine also apologized for the burning of African American churches in the South by issuing a statement in 1996 "to promote the dignity of persons...transform unjust structures...and work against the violence that alienates and marginalizes."

Some African Americans we interviewed in Kentucky accepted the apology of the three religious communities. Elaine Riley, an African-American nun, said, "We hear you, we have listened to your stories, and we humbly accept your apology." She cautioned that there are steps to be taken in the healing process and that a close connection must be established with the African-American community. Deacon James Turner accepted the apology, stating, "May God of all understanding forgive you and grant you peace." A communal promise to continue fighting against racism was pledged by sister communities. Other African-Americans rejoiced in the power of the apology, offered forgiveness, and commented on how all of their ancestors, black and white, were "crying tears of joy in heaven." The three orders have established scholarships for minorities in their high schools and colleges, and they continue to make efforts to bring racial diversity to their boards, especially on the local level. Those African-Americans that we interviewed in the Kentucky area reported that race relations have improved some in their communities (Smith 2000).

United States—Racism and Lynching of African Americans

Although Clinton did apologize explicitly for the racism inherent in the Tuskegee study, it was not a blanket apology for racism and slavery *per se*. However, Congressman Tony Hall introduced a resolution in which Congress specifically apologized for the slavery imposed on Africans and

African-Americans in the United States. The resolution explained that the apology itself would help heal interracial rifts. It was crucial for Congress to recognize the cruelty of the actions of past white Americans against blacks, Hall argued. In discussing the resolution, Hall said:

> Americans have tried to heal race problems many times before today, but perhaps we can find a lasting solution if we change our approach. We have started new programs, invested money, written countless reports. But, I say with respect this has not been enough; we need to acknowledge the past, recognize the present, and hope for the future (Hall 2000).

Many African-American congressmen supported Hall's resolution, but they were overruled. Journalist Naomi Wolf (1998) emphasized that without apology for slavery, blacks and whites will have problems getting along. On May 25, 2004, during his own attempt to pursue an apology to Native Americans for past crimes and abuses, Senator Sam Brownback recalled

> ...vitriolic phone calls a few years ago that blocked a similar attempt by former representative Tony Hall, a Democrat from Ohio, to obtain an official apology for the descendants of the former slaves. Circumstances are different now, because we have matured further, and therefore he is asking the American government to apologize for the oppression, slaughter, humiliation, and other ills that the American government has perpetrated on native peoples. It is too early to say whether it is going to be successful or whether this resolution will be also rejected" (Cox News Service 2004).

Although the resolutions apologizing for slavery of African-Americans and mistreatment of Native Americans has yet to pass, an apology was offered in June 2005 for failure of the United States Senate to pass anti-lynching legislation. Some 4,742 lynchings have been documented in the United States. Senator Mary Landrieu of Lousiana, co-sponsor of the bill, lamented the fact that past Senates had not enacted legislation to protect African-Americans from lynchings. Ninety-one-year-old Jim Cameron, the one known survivor of a lynching, was present at the celebration of the resolution's passage. It had been adopted by voice vote, indicating that some senators may have been reluctant to sign on publicly to such an apology. Senator John Kerry maintained that "It's a statement in itself that there aren't 100 cosponsors" of the bill (Stolberg 2005). There is, however, an important beginning by some states to recognize that slavery was evil. In February 2007, the state of Virginia expressed "profound regret" for slavery. Other states—Georgia, Maryland, Alabama, Delaware, New York, Missouri, Massachusetts, and Vermont—are considering taking measures that recognize the evils of slavery as well.[24] This is a symbolic gesture and recognition that the institution of slavery had an important effect on African-Americans as well as American society in general.

Australia and Its Indigenous Peoples

The Australian government has grappled for decades with the consequences of past injustices done to its indigenous people. Aborigines in Australia suffered from the taking of their tribal lands over many years. In 1788, colonizers applied the legal doctrine of *terra nullius* (meaning "land of no one") to the Australian continent. This became the basis of European settlement. The loss of their lands and autonomy, and the resultant cultural erosion and welfare dependency—all as a result of terra nullius—led to a startling decline in the health and well-being of many indigenous groups. In April 1979, a treaty was proposed in an attempt to right the wrongs of the past and to reexamine fundamental assumptions such as terra nullius. A proper settlement was considered necessary to address the legacy of past injustices, which continued to tarnish the relationship between aboriginal people and mainstream society, but the treaty pushed the indigenous people to assimilate. Critics argue that Australian reconciliation should not promote the single unifying moral vision implicit in the "one nation" strategy. It should seek to achieve a simple cessation of hostilities and address the harm that flowed from internal colonization (Short 2003a).

The Australian *Roadmap for Reconciliation* contains four national strategies. The first is understanding the oppression of the native people of Australia since the occupation by the British began. The second is to build on achievements toward a genuine reconciliation. These achievements indicate considerable improvement in the treatment of Australian aborigines since the sixties. In recent years the civil rights of indigenous peoples have been recognized through the extension of voting rights, the 1967 Referendum, and the Racial Discrimination Act of 1975. In 1991, the Commonwealth Parliament established the Council for Aboriginal Reconciliation to promote a process of reconciliation between aboriginal and Torres Strait Islander peoples and the wider community for the benefit of the nation. The third strategy on the roadmap was the first Corroboree 2000—Towards Reconciliation, which included the declaration of a "commitment to an ongoing reconciliation process and equality of opportunity for all Australians." The last part of the Roadmap to Reconciliation consists of actually translating the first three into reality (Reconciliation Australia 2000).

The Australian Roadmap Commission conducted research and held hearings for a number of years and submitted its final report to the Parliament in December 2000. This report recommends actions for advancing reconciliation between the aboriginal and Torres Strait Islanders and the larger society. Suggestions were made for improving leadership and education. An important first step was to celebrate significant dates and events and take joint action to achieve reconciliation goals. Another was that certain protocols and ceremonies should be observed with the aboriginal and Torres Strait Islanders and their elders. Governments, organizations, and communities were called upon to negotiate to establish and promote symbols of reconciliation and formally give their support to reconciliation. Governments should also ensure and encourage education about reconciliation, legislation, changes in the constitution, partnership work arrangements, effective business practices—such as securing loans—and other practical means of extending reconciliation.

These ideas sound very good, but some analysts are critical of the actual progress. Gillian Cowlishaw (2003) sees disappointing results and claims that efforts to apologize to or reconcile with the aboriginal people have been minimal and unsuccessful. Despite expressions of disdain for racism against aboriginal people, and the enthusiasm for diversity that seems to prevail in the media, Cowlishaw states:

> Everyday urban lives are distanced from foreign practices, unless they are domesticated in food we ingest, dances we mimic, or the healing techniques we employ. However, mundane conversational forms of approval and disapproval reveal automatic judgments around which everyday identities are constructed. While sophisticated citizens take pride in the appreciation of elements of exotic culture, and deference to difference is automatic among cosmopolitan urbanites, it is always understood that some things are beyond the pale (Cowlishaw 2003: 106).

Damien Short (2003a, 2003b) relates the Australian government's attempts to "address progressively" colonial injustice and its legacy. All parties agree that an apology is in order, but Short demonstrates that restrictive policy framing and a lack of political will have severely hindered the progress of the reconciliation process. Short argues that the passage of the 1991 Council for Aboriginal Reconciliation Act by the Australian Parliament constitutes the real beginning of attempts at reconciliation. However, so far, he maintains that not much has been accomplished. Unlike the United States, Canada, and New Zealand, Australian colonization did not entail settlements involving dialogue and treaties between the European invaders and the indigenous people. He says that over the last 200 years, the indigenous people of Australia have been victims of appalling injustice and racism that was compounded and legitimized by the colonizers' conviction that the indigenous peoples did not deserve a negotiated settlement. The concept of terra nullius, declaring that Australia was an empty land without people, in essence prevented negotiations or reconciliation. The government does not like the idea of treaties that would also mean the recognition of the rights of the native peoples; and it would prefer to say that justice for all is necessary, and Australia should be a unified nation, without any separatisms: "A united Australia, which respects this land of ours, values the aboriginal and the Torres Strait Islanders' heritage and provides equity for all" (Short 2003b: 293).

The native peoples of Australia resist the label of "minority." They emphasize the uniqueness of their culture and express pride in their heritage; they are pushing, not yet successfully, for autonomy as a moral claim. They do not like the status of being a dispossessed people and maintain that there is doubletalk by the government. Moana Jackson, a Maori lawyer, says, " The colonial mind is always inventive, and its final resort is always a political reality that neither permits nor denies the rights of self-determination. But reality, like law, is changing human constructs" (Short 2003b: 297). Other aboriginal leaders say that there can be no reconciliation without justice that recognizes continued aboriginal sovereignty and brings meaningful self-determination to aboriginal people (2001: 299). There is collusion between huge landowners—including Rupert Murdoch, owner of Fox Network and other media outlets—and Prime Minister Howard. For these giant landowners, reconciliation would mean they would have to return land to their original owners, and this is against their self-interest.

Short maintains that negotiations and bargaining are still going on and finds optimism in public forms of apology. For example, a private plane trailing a sign that read "Sorry" flew over about 400,000 native people marching on the Harbor Bridge in Sidney in commemoration of the injustices that whites have committed against the native Australian people.

Efforts toward reconciliation are continuing in Australia. Many white Australians are now aware of the injustices done to native peoples, and the government has made a very public and seemingly sincere effort to take responsibility. Although the first steps have been taken on what could turn into a substantive process of reconciliation, there are serious issues that seem insoluble. For just one thorny example, how is compensation possible for expropriated land? Awareness of the issue has been raised for further discussion and remediation.

Our impression is that while apology and public pronouncements have occurred in Australia, there are still "repugnant practices" towards aboriginal people. Violence still exists not only between whites and blacks, but racism and racist policies also have spawned violence within aboriginal communities. Thus the nature of reconciliation in Australia has not been optimal because of the current extent of racism and interracial polarization exacerbated by poverty among the indigenous people. One small step forward has been taken in the area of reconciliation, apology, and forgiveness.

Canada and Its Indigenous Peoples

In 1998 the federal government of Canada offered a formal expression of regret, together with an assistance package worth approximately $245 million, to native people who suffered physical and sexual abuses in the residential schools that operated across Canada until the 1970s. The apology forms a central part of the government response to a penetrating Royal Commission report that presented a devastating account of everyday conditions facing Canada's aboriginal peoples. The report was particularly critical of the officially sanctioned schools run by the Catholic, Methodist, and Anglican churches for over a century. Like the infamous boarding schools for Native Americans in the United States, these schools took children out of their tribal communities and subjected them to the often brutal pressures of cultural assimilation.

The Canadian government apologized on behalf of "all Canadians" for this treatment. The apology's aim was to recognize the mistakes of the past and to work to incorporate the full participation of the aboriginal peoples into the economic, political, social, and cultural life of Canada ,while preserving collective identities of indigenous tribes.

> The Government of Canada acknowledges the role it played in
> the development and administration of these schools. Particularly
> to those individuals who experienced the tragedy of sexual and

physical abuse at residential schools, and who have carried this
burden believing that in some way they must be responsible, we
wish to emphasize that what you experienced was not your fault
and should never have happened. To those of you who suffered
this tragedy at residential schools, we are deeply sorry (Indian and
Northern Affairs Canada 1998).

This apology and reconciliation project is designed to offer a new start in
relations between white Canadians and the more than 600 tribes and bands
of Canadian Indians. The terrible treatment and deprivation of native people
was enumerated by the Royal Commission's 1996 report as sadly representative of the history of native peoples since the founding of Canada. The
commission proposed an ambitious twenty-year, multibillion dollar program
of economic aid to help counter native unemployment and impoverishment
and to improve housing and health conditions. The official apology, given
in a formal ceremony by Indian Affairs Minister Jane Steward, expressed the
hope that the statement of reconciliation would establish a new partnership
between the government and the First Nation. National chief of the Assembly
of First Nations, Phil Fontaine, accepted the apology and called it the beginning of a new era, although some native groups stated that the apology and
financial support did not go nearly far enough (BBC 1998).

Guatemala

Guatemala has experienced numerous periods of violence, often with
American fingerprints left behind. It is a very poor country, and, because
of the lack of tax revenue and widespread corruption, the state's ability to
provide basic services—such as law enforcement and medical support—
have been undermined. The country suffered through a decades-long civil
war between various (generally right-wing) government administrations
and a leftist popular movement. The violence was horrific, with one writer
referring to Guatemala as "America's Rwanda" (Reding 1999).

The army and its paramilitary allies carried out at least 626 massacres, many of entire villages. Security forces slaughtered civilians
without regard for age or sex. They impaled and shot children.
They raped women, slashed open the wombs of pregnant women.
They skinned, amputated, and burned victims alive. They forced
townsfolk to watch as they disemboweled still-living relatives and
neighbors. At gunpoint, they forced Mayans to kill fellow villagers
or even their own kin (Reding 1999).

One Mayan leader said it was virtually impossible to find a Mayan girl between the ages of 11 and 15 who had not been raped. This terror was the work of a small elite, allied with the army, waging an undeclared war against the people, especially leftists, intellectuals, and indigenous peoples. Conservative estimates put the death toll at more than 200,000 men, women, and children killed by the Guatemalan government.

But it is more than just the killings that created the continuing sense of fear felt by Guatemalans. There has been no resolution to these atrocities. People disappear, clues lead to this military figure or that member of a right-wing death squad, but no prosecution follows. Often, those involved in the killings have risen in the ranks of the security forces and exert political power. Those who have been victimized or family members of victims are left with nothing but questions and alienation. One girl, the 13-year-old daughter of an abducted law student, talked about how she and her friends used to look at the boys at the country's military academy and say, "This one is cute, this one is ugly." Now she feels that these people are her "enemies" (Simon 1988).

Paul Jeffrey (1999) describes the new impetus toward openness and a lasting peace in Guatemala and outlines the necessary steps, beginning with a clearing of the air about past injustices and atrocities. Under the Project to Recover Historical Memory, funded and organized by the Catholic Church in the 1980s, more than 600 Guatemalans affiliated with the Church were trained in interviewing techniques, given tape recorders, and sent into the countryside to record evidence of the killings and disappearances. The 6,500 stories of these interviewers formed the backbone of a 1,400-page report blaming the government for the violence.

A second issue facing Guatemalans is the corrupt justice and police systems. Two days after the Church released its report, the bishop was murdered by unknown assailants who crushed his head with a concrete block. Eight years later, in spite of some evidence pointing to the military, the perpetrators of this crime remain at large. Each successive government failed to initiate a real investigation, and this crime seems destined to remain unsolved like so many others.

It is ironic that the bishop may have been the best chance for an understanding to be reached. A few weeks before his death, he told Jeffrey that forgiveness was the key to reconciliation. "The person who forgets or who pretends to forget doesn't do away with what happened," he said. "To pardon really means to create new attitudes, to provoke change inside people and between people—not just to palliate the hurt that remains" (Jeffrey 1999).

President Alvaro Azru attempted to apologize to the people when he delivered a speech in 1999 to a crowd of mostly indigenous people. He asked for forgiveness for the government's role in the violence committed against the Guatemalan people. But the government has steadfastly refused to accept blame for specific incidents, making the apology so general as to be insulting. One indigenous leader, Rosario Pu, called the speech "a sham…The wounds will remain open until the government specifically admits it was the army that [did the killing]. To talk about forgiveness is easy, but moral and economic reparations are necessary if we are to begin to forget these sad histories" (Jeffrey 1999).

Eventually, the government allowed a U.N.-supervised truth commission to operate which generated a 3,600 page report detailing government acts of genocide against Mayan people and others. Government leaders sat "stony-faced" in the audience when the report was publicly delivered. Books and publications have memorialized the events, and there is an understanding that the government was behind them. There has not been a reconciliation between the government and the people.

The United States must shoulder much of the responsibility for the worst crimes in Guatemalan history. In 1954 the U.S. government orchestrated the overthrow of a democratically elected government and in its place installed an oppressive military regime that governed the country for the next 30 years. Successive U. S. administrations supported these governments as they engaged in widespread human rights violations. Two weeks after release of the Truth Commission report, President Clinton visited Guatemala and said, "United States support for the military forces and intelligence units which engaged in violence and widespread repression was wrong, and the United States must not repeat that mistake" (Jeffrey 1999). Clinton's words did not really constitute an apology, because he did not outline specific complicity or even include the words "apologize" or "sorry." But Clinton's words were taken as a positive step. Unfortunately, the good intentions of Clinton's speech are somewhat muted by the release of official documents detailing the extent of the US government's knowledge of Guatemalan security forces involvement in the death squads. In one memo, an American diplomat bemoans American involvement in "atrocities and torture…This leads me to an aspect that I find most disturbing of all—that we have not been honest with ourselves" (Jeffrey 1999).

The Guatemalan victims of violence have waited long for any governmental action. Guatemalan humans rights chief Frank LaRue announced recently that a commission was to be launched to investigate the tens of thousands who were "disappeared." As in other areas where violence caused the deaths of loved ones, the victims' families are left with a terrible uncertainty. "Uncertainty is a kind of permanent torture for the survivors," said LaRue in his speech announcing the formation of the investigative commission. That commission seems to be oriented more towards retributive justice than an airing of facts and steps toward reconciliation. Victims' families are encouraged, however, by the prospect of a national registry, with information about those who disappeared, and about the prosecution of the soldiers, policemen, and paramilitaries involved in the abductions and killings (Rosenberg 2006).

It will take time to see if the retributive course of the current initiative is effective, or if it loses steam as powerful figures feel threatened by prosecution, or if it transforms into a more restorative process, as we see in the South African government's efforts to reconcile its peoples.

South Africa

South Africa has only in recent decades come to terms with its longstanding discriminatory practices, known as *apartheid*, and begun a national effort of reconciliation among racial and ethnic groups. Many atrocities were perpetrated during the years of white rule and during the struggle for equality, and details have only recently become available about many of these crimes. M. B. Ramose refers to South Africa between 1949 and 1993 as "a festival of arbitrary detention and arrest, torture and callous murder in the name of ideology, which earned itself the disrepute of being a crime against humanity" (Ramose 1999).

Having long been rent by strife along racial and ethnic lines, South Africans have realized that their country's only hope is to help its citizens unite as South Africans, rather than to perpetuate divisions based upon traditional ethnic, racial, and tribal status. According to Ramose, "National unity means the protection and promotion of human dignity and the continuous active protection and promotion of human rights. This is why the Act established the Truth and Reconciliation Commission (TRC) and has made provisions for a committee to investigate human rights violations" and to air the truth about them in an effort to reconcile the various groups. Reconciliation as a concept is a potentially powerful tool for the construction and realization of justice and peace. However, Ramose notes that it is vitiated by the widespread human fear of honesty and truthfulness. One of the underlying aims of the TRC at the psychological and moral levels is to assist human beings to overcome this fear. But most human beings would rather live in fear of honesty and truthfulness. Self-preservation is the reason given for this preference (Ramose 1999).

Established in 1995, the TRC process in South Africa was responsible for investigating human rights violations occurring between 1960 and 1994. Perpetrators guilty of violations were offered amnesty in exchange for disclosure of their past crimes. The goal was to document, as completely as possible, the atrocities of that period in order to facilitate the collective healing of the nation and a smooth transition from apartheid to democracy. Reconciliation in South Africa was "built ideally on a perpetrator's repentance and a victim's forgiveness" (Graybill and Lanegran 2004).

The Truth and Reconciliation Commission functioned under two separate committees; the Human Rights Violations Committee and the Amnesty Committee. At the Human Rights Violations Committee, a small number of people testified publicly—about 2,000 of the population of 43 million. But anecdotal evidence shows that even with such a small number giving testimony, the process did contribute to healing and reconciliation.

At the Amnesty Committee hearings, about 7,000 people applied for amnesty. Many were simply common criminals attempting to convince the committee that their crimes were politically motivated. Few were leaders of the apartheid system, responsible for the majority of the atrocities, and nearly half were from the African National Congress. Contrition was not a requirement for amnesty, and many amnesty seekers did not apologize for their actions. Of the 7,000 amnesty applicants, only about one out of seven acknowledged responsibility or participation, thus earning amnesty and reintegration.

After analyzing the South African TRC outcome, Tristan Borer (2003) maintained there needs to be a clear definition of reconciliation to test the argument that truth leads to reconciliation, rather than simply asserting it before any further analysis can be attempted. Borer argues that because of the lack of a clear objective for the TRC, and the lack of a clear definition of reconciliation, the TRC is most likely to be judged in a way that makes it least likely to appear successful (Borer 2003).

Psychologists and psychiatrists have investigated the effectiveness of the TRC among victims. They found that participants who displayed low forgiveness had higher rates of depression and anxiety disorders than those with high forgiveness scores. If justice is perceived done, psychological healing may be facilitated. A lack of forgiveness is related to poor psychiatric adjustment and increases the risk of psychiatric morbidity. Survivors who gave public testimony tended to be either more forgiving or unforgiving. The process of giving public testimony may facilitate a high level of forgiveness when effective but a low level of forgiveness when ineffective (Kaminer, Stein, Mbanga, and Zungu-Dirwayi 2001).

The authors note that the effectiveness of the public process may depend on the respondent's gender; there was a tendency for men to be highly forgiving and women unforgiving. Further research on this is suggested to come to more conclusive results (Kaminer, Stein, Mbanga, and Zungu-Dirwayi 2001). The authors conclude that the TRC approach can be highly effective in encouraging reconciliation among people in human rights cases, but individual mental health counseling and treatment for depression are also necessary.

The Truth and Reconciliation Commissions in South Africa made an impressive beginning toward reconciliation.

Rwanda

Hitler once said, "Who remembers the Turkish genocide of 1915?" The implication here is that no one cares about one group of people destroying another group. Most people are bystanders, which is true in the case of the Rwandan genocide of 1994, where an estimated one million people were massacred.

Rwanda, a Belgian colony until 1962, was considered the "Switzerland of Africa." It is a small nation composed of two major ethnic groups; the Hutus make up the majority of the population at 85 percent, while the Tutsis represent 14 percent. For 600 years, the groups had, for the most part, coexisted peacefully, even though the Tutsi were politically favored by the Belgian colonizers and often possessed power disproportionate to their percentage of the population. When Belgium gave Rwanda its freedom, the Tutsis were given substantial advantage in the areas of government, bureaucracy, and desirable jobs. This fostered enormous resentment among the Hutus. When the Tutsis eventually took political power in Rwanda, this resentment exploded into ethnic violence directed against the Tutsis. The perception—and perhaps the reality—was that the Hutus were oppressed by the Tutsis, who dominated the Rwandan government and military. The situation was exacerbated when in April 1994, the Rwandan president Habyalimana and Burundi's president Ntaryamira, while returning from a meeting in Tanzania, were killed when their small jet was shot down by shoulder-fired missiles on approach to Rwanda's main airport in Kigali. That gave Hutu extremists the opportunity to stoke the simmering violence by spreading news that Tutsis had shot down the plane. It is now assumed that it was actually the rightist forces themselves that killed the leaders who were seeking peace in the region.

This incident culminated in outright genocide. Between April and July 1994—about 100 days—approximately 800,000 people were massacred. They were mostly Tutsis, but the toll also included many Hutus who were sympathetic to their Tutsi neighbors. The Hutu government explicitly encouraged this genocide and organized a group called the *Interhamwe*, an informal militia, to methodically kill Tutsis. The government-controlled radio called for the continuance of mass killings, urging Hutus to act against Tutsi "vermin." One radio broadcast exhorted slaughter of the Tutsi, saying, "We have to kill the Tutsi. They are cockroaches. All those who are listening, rise, so we can fight for our Rwanda, fight with weapons that you have at your disposal, call on those who have arrows to use arrows, those who have spears to use their spears, we must fight. We must finish them, exterminate them, sweep them from our whole country, there must be no refuge for them. They must be exterminated, there is no other way."

There was plenty of evidence that genocidal massacres were being perpetrated. Leaders and observers appealed to the United Nations several times to try to stop the killing. The U.N. dispatched a woefully inadequate multinational peacekeeping force of 2,500 soldiers to stop the massacre, but the small peacekeeping force was hopelessly outnumbered and unable to effect any sense of order. The U.N. Security Council voted unanimously to abandon Rwanda and immediately withdraw the small force. Without opposition, the Hutus embarked on an orgy of mass destruction. Not only did they kill innocent Tutsi men, women, and children, but also any Hutus who opposed the slaughter or who tried to rescue Tutsis from danger. Many Hutus claimed they were forced to join the *Interhamwe* gangs, because the military threatened their lives if they did not kill their Tutsi neighbors. Eyewitnesses have reported horrors that are seemingly beyond human comprehension, such as bodies tossed into rivers and floating down to Lake Victoria. The genocide was stopped largely by the Rwandan Patriotic Front, an armed Tutsi force that attacked the killers and protected the surviving Tutsis.

The U.N. has finally publicly admitted that their leadership failed. Kofi Annan personally apologized for the tragedy, because leaders allowed caring, compassion, and social justice to take an extended holiday (Oliner, Gay 1997).

Responsibility for this massacre clearly may be placed on the shoulders of the United Nations and the leaders of the Western democracies—the United States and Britain foremost—because of the abundant warning they had that such a massacre was impending and because of their inaction as it was being conducted (Leitenberg 1997). The current government accuses approximately 120,000 people of genocidal atrocities during this period. Tutsi president Paul Kagame is trying to implement reconciliation but is faced with the difficult reality of being in a political minority in a heavily Hutu nation.

Reconciliation is very difficult under these conditions. Some people feel as though the mass murderers should face trial, and yet there are not enough resources to implement such a legal system. What has been introduced instead is a kind of community court called a *gacaca* court, whereby offenders meet locally to confess and discuss what transpired during those dark days. In this type of system, communities as a whole judge what their families and neighbors did in the terrible months of violence. To represent the offenders, each community elects 19 people who are respected in the community. They sit in a general assembly to hear accusations and confessions. Each assembly is empanelled for a certain amount of time. Their job is to establish who was there during the genocide, who was killed, who lost their property, and who was responsible. Only those accused of killing or rape are tried in conventional court. However, gacaca offers an effective healing tool for society, as the guilty confess their faults and ask the victims to forgive them.

Jande Dieu Cyiza confessed to the gacaca court that he killed five Tutsi children because government soldiers told him to. He argued that he had to commit murder to save his life, so he hacked them with a machete. The perpetrator in this case confessed and apologized for his actions, and he was forgiven by the community and even lives in the same neighborhood as the families of the children he murdered.

Though many acts of apology and forgiveness have been recorded in Rwanda, widespread reconciliation is not discernable. This process takes time and counseling and requires sincere confession and open discussion by perpetrators and leaders. One complication toward resolution in this case is that not only the Hutus committed atrocities. The Hutus claim that Tutsis also committed horrible crimes, including mass murder, torture, and rape. Some say that the situation requires all parties to start by admitting to the killings.

Psychology Professor Erwin Staub, of the University of Massachusetts, and his associate, Dr. Laurie Anne Pearlman, of the Trauma Research Education Institute, are trying to understand the depth of trauma in Rwanda and have enlisted some indigenous and international nongovernmental organizations (NGOs) to conduct research into methods most likely to succeed in reducing resentment and trauma. They have found that many victims with traumatic experiences are less inclined to partake in forgiveness (Staub and Pearlman 2000). Some NGOs are trying reconciliation with the young in the hope of achieving success.

The government supports the gacaca courts to encourage voluntary confession and discussion that may lead to reconciliation at the community level. Truth telling often leads to remorse in the offenders and to forgiveness on the part of the victims (see Tutu 2004; Helmick and Peterson 2001; Enright, Freedman, and Rique 1998, among others). In villages where people experienced the terror, the killers often express deep sorrow and guilt.

Although even critics admit that the gacaca system does offer some opportunities for apology and forgiveness, many claim that the system cannot bring precise justice. For true justice, perpetrators of these atrocities must go through a more traditional justice process involving prosecution and a trial. But some supporters of the gacaca system refer to retributive-style justice as "white man's standards." There is concern with finding a balance "between justice and reconciliation, or between retribution and forgiveness" (Zorbas 2004). Critics of a retributive justice fear it may stimulate violence. One NGO estimates that at least 200 Rwandan genocide survivors have been murdered to prevent their damning testimony in criminal trials (Madre 2005). A Tutsi genocide survivor is afraid that she will be called to testify against her neighbors. The only one of six siblings to survive a slaughter of 40,000 local Tutsis, she says, "They know I could testify against them. That is why I'm scared they will kill me or poison my daughter" (Silverman 2004). This not only prevents any sort of reconciliation from the trials and their verdicts but starts the cycle of violence anew.

Recently there has been interesting new research that sheds light on this tragedy. Administering questionnaires 45 days before the gacaca trial and 45 days after, Patrick Kanyangara, Bernard Rime, Pierre Philippot, and Vincent Yzerbyt (2007) found that the gacaca tribunals have positive potential for future reconciliation. Their data indicate that gacaca ritual has a profound impact on both social psychological and emotional levels. "Our results open up the possibility that when contained within social rituals of gacaca, expression and reactivation of the intense negative emotions linked to the genocide provided an opportunity to (re)process these traumatic emotions and to transform them in such a way that they can participate in a reconstructive process both at the individual and collective levels, rather than being strictly problematic"(401). At the social psychological level, gacaca fosters an increase in social cohesion and a decrease in social prejudicial attitudes. Further research with a larger sample, the authors suggest, would help to understand the consequences of the emotional reaction of both the killers and victims. In the future the authors would like to see if the emotional reactivation of gacaca leads to positive consequences for the social and emotional processing of genocide trauma.

Although it may be too early to judge the efficacy of the gacaca system, it seems to offer a local, more reconciliatory approach that may prove to be a hopeful model for the future.

SUMMARY

Having briefly examined the impact of apologies in several countries, we conclude that apologies do not necessarily lead to forgiveness or reconciliation but have often helped to improve relations and initiate a process that *may* lead to forgiveness and reconciliation.

German apologies for the Holocaust appear to be genuine and have been followed by restitution and remediation that are the basis for reconciliation. Many victims accept German apologies and believe they are sincere. Most victims of Japanese atrocities in China and other areas of Asia have not found official apologies to be genuine and complete. Japanese apologies for these events have not laid the basis for any reconciliation because they have not met the requirements for an effective apology. Japanese leaders have been reluctant to take full responsibility, possibly because of fear of litigation.

In ethnic conflicts in Ireland and past conflicts in Poland, interaction between groups through an apology-and-forgiveness process seems to be crucial. In Ireland, where the hatred and resentment goes back generations, the recent attempts at reconciliation between Catholics and Protestants, based on developing trust between small groups, have shown that true reconciliation is difficult without individuals being able to empathize with eachother. The success of apologies given and accepted can be seen in the increased cultural and business ties between Ukraine and Poland.

Sometimes, an apology itself is all the victims need to "close the book" on a painful incident. President Clinton's apology to those who suffered in the Tuskegee experiment took responsibility for that terrible event and allowed its victims to feel respected. Official apologies on behalf of the American people to African Americans for slavery, lynchings, and civil rights abuses have been problematic because of a lack of unanimity of the Congress, and because the government may fear inviting litigation. The U.S. government did, however, take the "risky" step of apologizing to Hawaiian natives for overthrowing their kingdom and installing an American colonial government. Hawaiians genuinely appreciated this apology and assumption of responsibility on the part of the government, but there already has sprung up a movement for Hawaiian independence based partially on the admitted illegality of American actions in the last century.

Many governments have tried to deal with past inequities suffered by indigenous peoples in their colonial pasts. Canada, the United States, and Australia all have apologized to some or all of their indigenous peoples and have tried to make amends in different ways and with varying degrees of success. The indigenous peoples, who often disagree with the specifics of official attempts to resolve these historical hurts, generally seem to appreciate the efforts, especially when the facts are publicized.

The colonial problems in Africa have generated severe grievances among peoples and groups, and different countries have tried different means to find a way for internal groups to reconcile. South Africa has focused primarily on truth and reconciliation commissions, and these seem to have allowed victims to be satisfied through a public hearing of their grievances, while perpetrators have had the opportunity to take responsibility for their actions and to apologize and be reintegrated into their communities. Other countries, such as Rwanda, are faced with massive genocidal atrocities that are difficult to simply forgive. Rwanda's gacaca courts have had some successes and may prove beneficial in the long run, although some observers see them as a means for the government to enforce mostly Hutu culpability. In Chapter 6 we will learn that Sierra Leone has found a third way, incorporating South African-style truth and reconciliation commissions for the victims, leaving perpetrators of specific acts to be heard by international court through the United Nations, and providing further processes for those who bear the most responsibility for serious violations.

Most studies find that apologies from group to group share similarities with interpersonal apologies, and the success of those intergroup apologies relies on many of the same criteria. The benefits also are similar. We find hope in the fact that many leaders and groups are finding ways to incorporate apology and forgiveness into their public acts. There has been progress, sometimes even remarkable progress, in some cases where inter-group hatred and resentment have festered for decades or even centuries. Taking into consideration the serious nature of many of the grievances, and that violence has often been the main recourse, we note that it may take several generations for many of these conflicts to be resolved and for the pain and suffering to heal.

When we asked respondents the question, "How important is apol-ogy in human relations?" 95 percent of them reported that "apology and forgiveness [are] necessary for the survival of our society and civilization." Apology is more than just saying, "I am sorry." It is more a reflection of an inner ability on the part of the apologizer to take responsibility for his or her actions. When we apologize, we demonstrate our concern for others. Saying "I'm sorry" has become a social lubricant in our hustle-and-bustle society, as we blurt out a quick "Sorry" when we jostle someone on the sidewalk. But an apology for inflicting serious hurt must be heartfelt, or it may end up being worse than not apologizing at all. It seems, in our age of image over substance, and our need to "spin" every possible event in our favor, that we have developed new and improved ways of apologizing badly or ineffectively. Modern Americans have become adept at "apologizing" but not taking blame, or even subtly blaming others. In order to be effective, apologies must be sincere; apologizers must take responsibility for their actions and recognize the harm they have done, and the groundwork must be laid for some sort of making amends. Amends may consist of a heartfelt apology alone, or may take the form of a large cash payment.

Interpersonal apology has been part of human behavior for as long as humans have interacted with one another. Now we are starting to see the ability of groups to admit the harms they have committed against others and to apologize. Intergroup apologies can sometimes be the foundation for a reconciliation process that has a chance to succeed where "negoti-ated" settlements have failed in the past. And in these days of intractable conflicts, high-tech warfare, and fundamentalists who do not discriminate between "combatants" and "civilians," it is imperative that we find processes for reconciliation.

As we have said, spoken or written apologies are just the beginning. When the late Pope John Paul II apologized to some of the groups the Church had harmed over the centuries, it opened a dialogue between groups that had no relationship at all, or a pained one at best. Now, Jews and Catholics are working together in a variety of ways. Of course some conflicts are so difficult to resolve that the process of reconciliation may take longer than our lifetimes. Some, like the Arab–Israeli conflict, have a future that is difficult to predict. But it seems clear that broken relationships like those in the Middle East are not resolved by the traditional diplomacy of arguing over specific points of self-interest. At some point, groups and nations must be able to take another group or nation's interests to heart, too, and often the first step is to recognize the hurts that have been committed.

5

Forgiveness

The one who pursues revenge should dig two graves.

—*Chinese proverb*

If we practice an eye for an eye and a tooth for a tooth,
soon the whole the world will be blind and toothless.

—*Mahatma Gandhi*

He that cannot forgive others breaks the bridge over which he
must pass himself, for every man has a need to be forgiven.

—*Lord Herbert*

All that I'm saying is that the energy of hate will take you
nowhere, but the energy of pardon, which manifests itself
through love, will manage to change your life in a positive sense.

—*Paulo Coelho*

The importance of forgiveness cannot be underestimated. Indeed, a large body of work has grown up around the concept: The teachings and literature of all world religions are filled with persuasive suggestions that apology and forgiveness lead to both emotional and spiritual growth and healing. Many argue that apology and forgiveness ought to be implemented in our educational systems, because scientific evidence indicates that tey do make a difference in people's lives, helping to reconcile transgressors or evil doers with those who have been victimized or hurt. We should perhaps take encouragement from the wide spectrum of research being conducted into the benefits of the forgiveness process in both interpersonal and intergroup relations. These studies are being conducted in evolutionary biology, philosophy, and within virtually every social science.

Religious scholars have addressed the manifestations of altruism and forgiveness in different religious traditions. What one derives from their discussions is that forgiveness is consistent with most or all world religions, but it is addressed in different ways. Christian and Jewish scholars have indicated that forgiveness is central to their traditions, while forbearance and compassion is central to Buddhism. In Islam, personal forgiveness is valued, but Allah's forgiveness is considered to be of paramount importance. Christianity, Islam, and Buddhism all appear to encourage forgiveness irrespective of whether the offenders apologize or express regret. In Judaism, on the other hand, God is not anxious to forgive a sinner unless the sinner seeks forgiveness from those who have been harmed. Buddhist scholars inform us that within Buddhism, compassion and reconciliation are closely related, although one can be compassionate in the absence of reconciliation. In Christianity, forgiveness must always allow for the possibility of reconciliation, even though reconciliation may not always occur (Rye, Pargament, Amir, Beck, Dorff, Hallisey, Narayanan, and Williams 2000).[25]

Secular scholars also have devoted considerable thought to altruism and forgiveness. Philosopher Joanna North defines forgiveness as "a willingness to abandon one's right to resentment, negative judgment, and indifferent behavior toward one who unjustly injured us, while fostering the undeserved qualities of compassion, generosity, and even love toward him or her" (Enright, Freedman, and Rique 1998: 46–47). According to North, forgiveness "does not remove the fact of the wrongdoing, but rather relies on the recognition of the wrong having been committed in order for the process of forgiveness to be made possible." The act of forgiveness does not annul the crime itself but the "distorted effect that this wrong has upon one's relation with the wrongdoer and perhaps with others" (North 1998: 17–18).

Forgiving is not condoning or excusing wrongdoing, nor does it necessarily have any legal status. Robert Enright, Suzanne Freedman, and Julio Rique state that forgiveness "is not the same as legal pardon.

Some are concerned that when we forgive we will open all jail-cell doors, letting the lawbreakers free to further their destructive aims" (1998: 48). The authors go on to argue that forgiveness must be distinguished from reconciliation:

> The basic philosophical distinction between forgiveness and reconciliation is this: Forgiveness is one person's response to injury. Reconciliation involves two people coming together again. The injurer must realize his or her offense, see the damage done, and take steps to rectify the problem. When both parties are guilty of injustice toward the other, both may need to forgive and realize one's own failures, with intent to change. When already in a strong relationship with someone who offends, a forgiver usually reconciles. (Enright, Freedman, and Rique 1998: 49)

There is a wide spectrum of opinion on the essence of forgiveness. Enright, Freedman, and Rique note that Robin Casarjian's approach equates forgiving with "the offer of moral love and acceptance to include one's 'forgiveness' of arthritic hands or a less-than-healthy body. We understand and appreciate her attempt to help a person to achieve a certain inner peace in regard to a failing body. Yet, equating forgiveness with a generalized acceptance brings construct away from the interpersonal, and thus away from the moral qualities of generosity and/or moral love" (Casarjian, cited in Enright, Freedman, and Rique 1998: 51).

Forgiveness cannot be commanded. However, it can be taught as a way of healing not only the victim, but also the victimizer. In 1991, Enright and the Human Development Study Group developed four phases of psychological variables that may be involved when we forgive. Phase one, termed "uncovering," consists of examining one's anger and confronting it, admitting the shame, being aware of the offense, gaining the insight that the injured parties may be comparing themselves with the injurer, realizing that one may be permanently and adversely changed by the injury, and being open to the possibility that the world is just. The second phase, called the "decision phase," includes a change of heart and a new insight that old resolution strategies are not working, a willingness to consider forgiveness as an option, and being committed to forgiving the offender. The third phase is called the "work phase," which addresses reframing through role taking, identifying and viewing the wrongdoer in context, having empathy toward the offender, being aware of compassion as it arises toward the offender, and accepting and absorbing the pain. The last phase is the "deepening phase," which implies that we must find meaning for the self and others in the suffering and forgiveness process. The self has needed the forgiveness of others in the past, and it is aware that we are not alone in this situation. We need to realize that the self may have a new purpose in life because of the injury, and we need to become aware of the decreasing negative effects and the possible increase in positive effects toward the injurer if this occurs. Finally, we must develop an awareness of our internal emotional release (Enright, Freedman, and Rique 1998: 53).

Scholars agree that there are important bases to the forgiveness process. Lewis Smedes (1996) outlines the stages of forgiveness. First, we forgive when we discover the humanity of the person who hurt us. Then, we surrender our right to vengeance. Finally, we reconcile our feelings toward the person we forgive.

Everett Worthington, a psychologist who has studied apology and forgiveness for many years, concludes that those who find the weight of past wrongs to be oppressive must decide to "REACH." In Worthington's model of forgiveness, each of these letters stands for a specific step in the forgiveness process: "R" involves *recalling* the hurt, "E" stands for practicing *empathy* towards the one who has hurt us, "A" stands for giving the *altruistic* gift of forgiveness to another, "C" stands for publicly *committing* to work for forgiveness, "H" is for working on *holding* oneself to forgiveness. Many people see that empathy is the crucial step in the process of forgiveness. If one is not capable of empathizing with the wrongdoer, understanding why he has done harm, knowing his background and what prompted him to do that, it would be difficult to forgive (Worthington 1997; 2004).

Worthington is his own best example. On New Year's Eve 1995, two men broke into Worthington's mother's house and murdered her. At first, Worthington was full of rage. He felt that he could not forgive the people who took his mother's life. It took a great deal of empathy and compassion to try to understand why this tragedy occurred. Being a spiritual person, he thought of the words Jesus spoke on the cross, "Forgive them for they know not what they do." In an effort to be empathetic, Worthington decided that the socioeconomic background of the people who broke in must have seriously impacted their inner world. After soul searching, he decided to forgive the murderers.

Forgiveness helps relieve the pain we felt due to the offense (Hartwell 1999). When we forgive, we take an important step toward mending and rebuilding our relationship with the wrongdoer. We remove the burden that weighs us down. Forgiveness helps us go on with our lives, instead of holding on to the past. It makes us into better people and improves our overall mental and emotional health (McCullough, Rachal, Chris, Sandage, Worthington, Brown, Hight 1998: 1595).

Forgiveness refers to the process people go through when they no longer find it necessary to carry hurt or harm on their shoulders or in their hearts. Donald W. Shriver Jr. (1995) relates the story of a contemporary Native American, a Lakota:

> After my five-year vision quest, I was tempted to go out and shoot every white man…I thought about Sand Creek and Wounded Knee, and I got angrier and angrier…I wanted to grab a gun and start shooting. Then, I thought, my ancestors might honor me…but then I saw the beauty of the moon and the morning star, and I knew that the only way I could live was to forgive…I work on that now every day. If one doesn't work on forgiveness, one will die on the road some day (Shriver 1995: 151).

True forgiveness often requires an emotional or spiritual transformation. It is an exercise in compassion and is both a process and an attitude. "Lack of forgiveness is giving others power over you" (Parachin, 2006: 3). Through the process of forgiveness, we transform suffering into psychological and spiritual growth. Through the attitude of forgiveness, we attain serenity by letting go of the ego's incessant need to judge others and ourselves. To make amends, we must apologize, acknowledge the harm we have done, make appropriate restitution, and change our behavior toward the other person. Amends must be appropriate and should benefit all.

These themes are also present when considering intergroup forgiveness. Archbishop Desmond Tutu (1999), referring to the South African Truth and Reconciliation Commission, says that there is "no future without forgiveness" and that forgiveness is one of the key ideas in this world. Apology and forgiveness are not just nebulous concepts; they contain the realization of wrongdoing on the side of apologizers and empathic understanding on the part of forgivers that has the practical effect of allowing people to unite or reunite. Psychiatrist Richard Fitzgibbons maintains that forgiveness has remarkable healing power for those who are able to use it (1998). Whether it is for small wrongs or for great crimes and injustices, most people struggle to find a way to forgive. The failure of our society to teach young people the skills of dealing effectively with conflicts echoes loudly today in school violence, our high rate of divorce and domestic battering, drug and alcohol abuse, and as criminal acts of ethnic warfare and terrorism. The rediscovered power of forgiveness has great potential for healing society at a number of levels.

What are some of the psychological problems that the injured person, group, or nation faces? On the individual level, psychologists have been able to substantiate that the injured person suffers from anxiety, depression, and the general feeling that the world is unfriendly. The injured person feels a real battering to his or her self-esteem. Members of a group that have been attacked or injured generally feel that they were unjustly treated, that the injuring nation or group is evil, and that vengeance should be sought. This attitude can pose a serious problem, because there appears to be no alternative to injury other than retaliation and vengeance. What is needed is an empathic understanding.

Research was conducted with students to test under what conditions young individuals will forgive parents who deprived them of love and nurturing. Radhi H. Al-Mabuk and Robert D. Enright maintain that "Parental love deprivation is a condition where a child does not receive needed affection and nurturing, is not given assurance of value, respect, and acceptance by the parents" (Al-Mabuk and Enright 1995: 430). The authors designed an experiment in which a group of students who were deprived of parental love were given training that focused on such things as justice and forgiveness. As a result of such training, the students reported that they were able to forgive their parents.

Colin Tipping (2002) has criticized traditional forgiveness. He writes, "With traditional forgiveness the willingness to forgive is present, but so is the residual need to condemn. Therefore victim consciousness is maintained and nothing changes" (Tipping 2002: 45). With "radical forgiveness, the willingness to forgive is present but not the need to condemn. Therefore the *victim consciousness* is dropped and everything changes" (Tipping 2002: 45). Tipping defines "victim consciousness" as "a conviction that someone else has done something bad to you, and as a direct result, they are responsible for the lack of peace and happiness in your life." He claims that radical forgiveness has a divine basis that comes directly from God and is a kind of *divine truth*. By the phrase "divine truth" he means it has no physical form and already carries the energy pattern of eternal life, mutability, infinite abundance, love, and oneness with God. Even though we cannot perceive this world with our senses, and we scarcely possess the mental capacities to comprehend its existence, we can get enough of a sense of it to know that it is real. Such activities as prayer, meditation, and radical forgiveness all raise our awareness of the world of divine truth and allow us earthly access to that world (Tipping 2002: 45).

Radical forgiveness is a purely spiritual path, and traditional forgiveness is more a means of living in this world. Radical forgiveness takes the view that there is no right or wrong or bad or good; only your thinking about it makes it so. Traditional forgiveness always begins with the assumption that something wrong took place, and that someone did something to someone else. In other words, the victim archetype remains operative. But radical forgiveness begins with the belief that nothing wrong happened, and there is no victim in *any* situation. Traditional forgiveness, Tipping says, is effective to the extent that it calls upon the highest human virtues —such as compassion, tolerance, kindness, mercy, and humility—the same virtues always present in radical forgiveness (Tipping 2002: 53).

Others also differentiate among levels or types of forgiveness. Richard Fitzgibbons (1998), coming from a clinical angle, defines forgiveness as the process of relinquishing one's feelings of resentment and thoughts of vengeance. A secondary part of the process is that of fostering compassion, generosity, and even love toward those who have inflicted pain. But abandoning one's angry feelings and thoughts is not an easy task. Fitzgibbons maintains that 40 percent of young Americans do not have biological fathers in their lives. Most of these young individuals have a hard time understanding this and therefore find it difficult to forgive their fathers for the pain of betrayal they struggle with daily. But Fitzgibbons argues that it is understanding that is necessary for true forgiveness to occur.

Fitzgibbons feels that the process of forgiveness can proceed on one of three levels: cognitive, emotional, or spiritual. The cognitive process of forgiveness implies the discussion, the evaluation, and the attempt to understand the victim's anger. By reasoning and reflection one may attempt to forgive, but Fitzgibbons feels that most forgiveness begins at the cognitive level. This is the level at which forgiveness seems like a good idea, when people *decide* to forgive. However, some individuals may feel that cognitive forgiveness is not really forgiveness at all, because they do not truly "feel like" forgiving.

The emotional level of forgiveness is when one comes to deeply understand the offender and his life struggles and is eventually able to develop empathy for the wounded boy or girl within the adult. As a result of this understanding, the offended party truly feels like forgiving. To the victim, being able to offer forgiveness is really a process of catharsis that yields emotional understanding and, ultimately, compassion for the offender. While such forgiveness does not imply an annulment of the wrongdoing itself, it does signify an attempt at an empathic understanding of *why* it happened. Healing may begin for both the injured party and the injurer.

The third level is the spiritual approach accessed when someone suffers from severe pain. Embracing a similar process to that of the Alcoholics Anonymous' 12-step program, victims come to the conclusion that forgiveness is not within their own power and instead look to a higher power to help them forgive. Statements such as "I am powerless over my anger and want to turn it over to God," or "Revenge or justice belongs to God," or "God forgive him, I cannot," or "God free me from my anger" are examples of this spiritual approach (Fitzgibbons 1998: 66).

Fitzgibbons sees the limitations of forgiveness. In his experience as a psychiatrist, he has seen forgiveness diminish the degree of sadness and lessen the severe pain of human betrayal. But he argues that forgiveness does not directly address the person's anger when it results from

> ...character weakness, such as narcissism, grandiosity, and patience, [or] the absence of moral values. While it is a very powerful tool, [forgiveness] alone cannot bring about a complete resolution of the excessive resentment, hostility, and hatred in our culture (Fitzgibbons 1998: 67).

Everett Worthington (1997) proposes five steps for actualizing forgiveness: 1) Do not wait for an apology. Take the initiative to establish relations by giving the offending party the occasion to talk to you. 2) Allow yourself to empathize with the offender. He or she may well have acted out of ignorance and is the person who can heal your pain. 3) Perform a symbolic act. Make it public in some way to show you are willing to forgive. 4) Remember that forgiving is not forgetting. Hurt feelings can linger even after one has forgiven the offender. 5) Offended parties should include themselves in the forgiveness list.

Robert Enright, Elizabeth Gassin, and Ching-Ru Wu (1992) have constructed a similar list from their multiyear study of adults in the United States. They prescribe 18 "psychological variables engaged in a process intervention on forgiveness." Their expanded list shows a thorough appreciation of the steps involved in applying empathic understanding to forgiveness and benefits to the forgiver. All the major theories of forgiveness include processes aimed at reconciliation and restoration of a relationship emphasizing an applied empathic understanding.

Walter J. Dickey (1998) addresses the role of forgiveness in relationships that have been strained by a criminal offense. He considers the harm inflicted on the victim to the victim–offender relationship and to the community. Dickey raises the question of how this kind of harm can be repaired and views forgiveness as an integral part of the repair. In a criminal offense, the restoration of strained relationships must rest on two foundations; community, group, and individual healing must be the goal of any system that purports to administer justice. Apology, forgiveness, and restitution are important components of any restoration or healing. This process needs "undeserved qualities of compassion, generosity, and even love," to which North attaches importance.

Joseph W. Elder (1998) delineates the characteristics and consequences of forgiveness and gives the example of Marietta Jaeger, who forgave the man who killed her daughter. Using the Hebrew and Christian scriptures, she reasoned that, "God is a God of mercy and compassion, who works unceasingly to help and heal." She concluded that her daughter's kidnapper and murderer "was a son of God, and, as such…he had dignity and worth." When the killer tracked down Jaeger in the middle of the night to taunt her, she showed mercy and compassion, asking him what she could do to help him. The killer was unable to reply and simply wept. He eventually confessed to the murder and went to prison. Drawing on the agony of her daughter's murder, as well as the closure brought by this experience, Jaeger concludes, "The only way we can be whole, healthy, happy persons is to learn to forgive" (Elder 1998: 150).

How can offenders ask for forgiveness, and how can victims forgive? Elder notes that the teachings of Judeo-Christian and Muslim faiths include divine forgiveness, and Buddhist/Hindu cosmology maintains that every virtuous act is rewarded, and every sinful act is punished in a manner similar to the law of physics.

> The punishments and rewards might happen in this life or in subsequent lives, but they *will* happen. There is no process of repentance or forgiveness that can affect the inevitability of the punishments and rewards. It would be both wrong and unnecessary to seek revenge. Punishment will happen on its own. Justice will be done through the dynamics of the law of karma…In the center of the Tibetan Buddhist 'Wheel of Life' are pictured a pig, a rooster, and a snake. These are identified, respectively, as the 'three poisons': ignorance, attachment, and hatred. Within the Buddhist cosmology, ignorance, attachment, and hatred are the central cause

of suffering. They infect all sentient preachers everywhere and generate countless lives of misery. To overcome them, one must acquire wisdom and compassion (Elder 1998: 158).

Elder addresses the difficulties that arise when the injured party and the wrongdoer do not share the same moral community. Is forgiveness possible when one does not have moral values in common with the other? How does one deal with this? One answer to this question is to acknowledge that we do share fundamental moral values that are the same in virtually every religious tradition. No religious tradition condones murder, kidnapping, rape, or other violent crimes. Although this answer may not be completely satisfactory, we should realize that some things are universally considered wrong and unjust and simply cannot be tolerated. One example of transcending this problem of lacking a common moral community is the historic handshake between Israeli Prime Minister Yitzhak Rabin and PLO Chairman Yasir Arafat on September 13, 1993. After decades of hatred and violence, both men realized that their groups shared basic human values and had many common interests. Their handshake showed that even though each group considers itself to be the wronged party, forgiveness is still possible as a part of the reconciliation process. But the continuing violence and unrest in that area, and the ongoing hatred between the groups, shows forgiveness is no easy task; in some cases, it may take generations of work.

Charles Klein (1995) maintains that forgiveness is difficult because of a fear of being hurt again. It is only through love that this fear is conquered, and a crucial component of forgiveness is what he calls the "glory of love." Without love it is difficult to see that other human beings deserve a chance. Besides finding the love within us, we must reframe our interpretations and images of wrongdoers, and we must be willing to take a risk for reconciliation that involves reaching out and listening carefully to the person who was hurt or harmed. The person who was harmed must try to understand the reasons for the wrongdoer's hurtful actions. There are no endless tomorrows, and we should seriously consider the notion of reconciling with those we have harmed or who have harmed us. Forgiving another person may reestablish harmony, which is especially important when one of the people involved is dying. To neglect reconciliation with a dying person is to ask for long-term pain for the survivor. From the Jewish perspective, it is vitally important to apologize and to forgive, especially during the high holy days. Klein cites a Jewish theologian, who said, "One who has begged for forgiveness should not be so cruel as not to forgive."

African-American psychologist James M. Jones (2006) speaks about racial inequality and how to overcome it. He focuses on the Truth and Reconciliation Commission (TRC) in South Africa and the concept of *ubuntu*, which is a cultural concept of forgiveness. Ubuntu is the spirit of humanity characterized by the expression, "My humanity is inextricably bound to yours. I am human because I belong, [and] participate in humanity." Forgiveness is illustrated by African psychologist Dr. Pumla Gobodo-Nadkizel, who interviewed a killer named DeKock, hired by the apartheid South African government as a professional murderer. Gobodo-Nadkizel was able to extract a sense of DeKock's humanity from him and was able to forgive. This example illustrates the universal concept of forgiveness as a healing and reconciliation process.

Italian psychologist Pierro Ferrucci's *Survival of the Kindest* (2005) presents an interesting contrast to the concept of survival of the fittest. Ferrucci argues that humanity has survived to a large extent because of its capacity for kindness, and that kindness reflects our true nature. He adds, "You can only be kind if your past no longer controls you" (Touber 2005: 44). Forgiveness is also important; someone who cannot forgive is like a city in which traffic has come to a standstill. To forgive, one must first recognize the suffering that one is experiencing. It is not good to hastily forgive just for the sake of forgiveness. Ferrucci discusses the virtue of attention and says that people who are suffering do not need advice, diagnosis, interpretation, or intervention so much as they need sincere empathy and attention. Once they have the feeling that other people are putting themselves in their shoes, they are able to let go of their suffering and begin healing. Ferrucci stresses this kind of attention as a vital factor in human relations and emphasizes that kindness is a very simple quality that may be able to save humanity.

> It *is* saving humanity. Have you ever wondered why the world still has not fallen apart, despite all its complex structures? Mail carriers, train conductors, newspaper vendors, cleaners…of course they earn their livelihood with what they do, but it all happens largely thanks to their good will, to their kindness (Touber 2005: 47).

"The most sensible way to look after our own self-interest, to find freedom and be happy, is not to directly pursue these things but to give priority to the interests of others. Help others to become free of their fear and pain. It's all really simple. You don't have to choose between being kind to yourself and others. It is one and the same" (Touber 2005: 47).

There are levels and aspects of the forgiveness process that elude easy categorization. Forgiveness presents a large and complex picture, somewhat like the blind men feeling the elephant. At the same time, we can discern some aspects that are universal.

RELIGION AND FORGIVENESS

Muslim scholar M. Fethullah Gulen maintains that Islam, Christianity, Judaism, Buddhism, and Hinduism teach love, compassion, tolerance, and forgiveness as fundamental and universal religious values. These constructive social processes are vitally important, and without them society would simply fall apart. Theologians, thinkers, and social scientists—the Dalai Lama, Everett Worthington, Lewis B. Smedes, Bishop Tutu, Mother Teresa, Nelson Mandela, and others—agree with empirical data that show that altruism, empathy, spirituality, and forgiveness are very important in healing a violent world (Gulen 2003).

The idea of loving one's neighbor is vitally important in religion—and loving not only your neighbor, but loving even strangers unconditionally. The Jewish tradition prescribes loving the stranger because the Jews were strangers and slaves in Egypt. Jews must remember that and practice this great deed, known as *mitzvah*. In Buddhism, there is an important process called *bodhicitta*, referring to a selfless altruism that seeks to relieve the suffering of all. One example might be an effort to make a friend out of an enemy. In Christianity, the idea of love means *unconditional* love, the kind that entails a complete acceptance of the other, forgiveness, openness, being at one with all, and treating others as one would desire to be treated. The Jewish tradition also includes this concept of unconditional love. In the words of Rabbi Robert Kushner, "If you are hurting someone, and you are carrying around this unforgiveness longer than two days, you have failed to do your duty to humanity" (Lama Surya Das 1997).

Religious belief can play a powerful role in our actions. Flying combat in Vietnam in 1968, Richard Cunnare came across a number of bodies of American soldiers executed by the Vietcong. He experienced an overwhelming rage in his soul, as did his crewmembers. As he spotted Vietnamese farmers working in their rice paddies, he felt a tremendous pressure for revenge, but recalls, "I did not kill in rage when every part of my soul was telling me [it] was right. If I had shot the rice farmers, would I have ever been asked why? I do not think anyone would have even questioned the act" (Cunnare 2005). Cunnare felt that "Forgiveness is a powerful grace that the Lord offers us. I chose to take God's will for me and fought to

live. I am sure the VC commander from February 1968 did not lose much sleep over executing American troops, or did he?" (Cunnare 2005).

While responsible for innumerable acts of kindness, caring, and rescuing those in trouble, organized religion also plays a divisive role in human affairs. This is because organized religious groups, by their very nature, are groups that have clear "us" and "them" lines of demarcation. Religion almost always creates "saved" and "unsaved," "righteous" and "unclean," "godly" and "heretical," and so on. To a great extent it teaches us who *we* are and neglects or deemphasizes the histories and cultures, even the very essence, of others. In their edited collection titled *Visions of Compassion* (2002), Richard J. Davidson and Anne Harrington delve into the subject of who taught us to think this way,

> Certainly our religious traditions, the Jewish and Christian traditions, must take part in their responsibility for shaping our thinking here. The Christian tradition, for example, believes profoundly in compassion, but it also teaches that human beings are fundamentally flawed and can only be saved through the intervention of Christ, who alone possesses the compassion for our plight great enough to lift us out of our sinfulness. We have been granted eternal life as a gift we could never deserve on our own (2002: 12).

Of course, there is no mention here of Mohammed or of Buddha, leaving adherents to those traditions out in the cold when it comes to salvation. It is virtually impossible to have equal and empathetic relations when those kinds of distinctions underlie our relationships. At the same time, one can safely say that many religions are based upon similar themes and stress similar beliefs and behaviors.

All religions stress the importance of a foundation of love. The Dalai Lama, referring to love, writes:

> We express our quest for happiness through the language of love. Love not only allows us to access our compassionate nature; it enables others to relate to us at the most human level. In contrast, suffering is closely linked to hostility and anger, for the full realization of hostility's goal is the destruction of the object of your wrath. By instinctually shunning suffering, we also express our dislike for destructive traits such as hostility, anger, and hatred. This is clearly a manifestation in our natural mind state: When we see death, destruction, or decay we feel uncomfortable; whereas

> we feel pleasant and assured when we see life, color, and growth.
> (Dalai Lama 2002: 69)

This most "human" kind of love has been exemplified by a group of Jewish, Christian, and Muslim women who live in Jerusalem and recently participated in a conference. Their statement, which follows, has particular relevance:

> Unless we understand that one life is lived in the other, our attachment to our identities, national and religious, is superficial, presumptuous, and meaningless" (Prince-Gibson 2004).

Precisely because of the potentially divisive nature of organized religion, ecumenism is a desirable attribute and may be strongly associated with forgiveness. Michael W. Foley (1999) reports on an ecumenical approach in his "Memory, Forgiveness, and Reconciliation: Confronting the Violence of History" from a conference on violence held in Northern Ireland. A number of participants in the conference had focused their discussion on ecumenical society. The participants—especially Adam Michnik, editor-in-chief of *Gazeta Wyborcza,* a major Polish newspaper—spoke of religious leaders having a great responsibility for fostering tolerance and acceptance of the traditions of others. Michnik pointed out that in the past, religious leaders had contributed greatly to war, violence, and hatred, but argued that now these leaders have a special responsibility to promote ecumenism and peace. Others addressed the notion of memory and noted that our grievance of historical hurt frequently comes to the forefront, which helps to ignite current conflict between groups. The interesting part of Foley's article deals with the question of forgiveness. Some discussants were somewhat skeptical about the role of forgiveness. Some argued that before forgiveness is possible, one must first overcome feelings of victimization, which may be the most important step toward healing—not only on a personal level, but also on a societal level.

Though there was skepticism among the presenters about the nuts and bolts of forgiveness, they concluded that forgiveness, which requires both acknowledgement and apology, may be a first step toward true reconciliation among groups. Some raised the question considered before by Simon Wiesenthal, of whether only victims can give forgiveness. A similar idea was expressed by Schimmel (2002). Auschwitz escapee Rudolf Vrba (1964) maintains that he cannot forgive for the crimes he has experienced. Others addressed the issue of the importance of understanding cultural backgrounds in considering how forgiveness and reconciliation can be

accomplished. Forgiveness cannot be dictated, however. Hannah Arendt has stated that some crimes are simply not forgivable. However, it *is* possible to have reconciliation *without* forgiveness; for example, in relations between Germany and Israel, Israel does not forgive the Nazi crimes of mass murder, but the two states and peoples are reconciled and have relations on all levels.

Spirituality

Ministers and priests, rabbis and imams, and religious workers are aware of divine forgiveness because we find the concept in virtually all religions. Pastoral counselors try to help heal the pain of individuals by advocating forgiveness, in the image of the divine. Not only does God forgive those who trespass, but so must we as individuals. Forgiveness relieves the offender of shame and humiliation, and, according to John Patton (1985: 16), this is very much related to God's teaching:

> Human forgiveness is not doing something but discovering that I am more like those who have hurt me than different from them. I am able to forgive them when I discover that I am in no position not to forgive. Although the experience of God's forgiveness may involve confession of, and the sense of being forgiven for, specific sins, it is hard to recognize my reception to the community of sinners—those affirmed as God's children (Patton 1985: 16).

Sheffield (2003) sees a strong relationship between forgiveness and religion that helps people cope psychologically in their lives. When we forgive others, we start to establish harmony in our personal lives; God forgives sinners because He is compassionate and wants to see love and harmony in the world.

Rabbi Harold M. Schulweis (2000), a religious scholar, looks at the Jewish Bible to see how religious teaching encourages people to be compassionate and forgiving towards each other and to avoid vengeance or holding grudges. He quotes from Leviticus 18:18 in decrying interpersonal unforgiveness: "You shall not take vengeance or bear a grudge against your fellow man." And similarly, against racism or other exclusionary practices he adds: "You shall not abhor an Edomite for he is thy brother, nor an Egyptian because you were a stranger in his land" (Deuteronomy 23:8).

There still seems to be a consensus among forgiveness scholars that there are methodological barriers to completely understanding the roles played by religion, culture, and the social-psychological facets of everyday life interaction. This must be addressed, or we will remain unable to build comprehensive theories of apology and forgiveness. We must include the situational factors of culture, religion, personality, and socialization to shed proper light on the role of forgiveness in human relations.

There are many nuanced definitions of spirituality[26] today. Facets of spirituality generally include some or all of the following overarching themes: a belief in a power operating in the universe that is greater than ourselves, a sense of interconnectedness with all living creatures, an awareness of the purpose and meaning of life, and the development of personal absolute values. Although spirituality is often associated with religious life, many believe that personal spirituality can be developed outside of religion. Acts of compassion, selflessness, altruism, and an experience of inner peace are all characteristics of spirituality. According to a 1997 survey of spiritual trends in America, "96 percent of Americans believe in God or in a universal spirit." Today, Americans look to their spirituality for practical applications—for example, "to promote healing, especially in cases where medications and other treatment cannot provide a cure." In a 1994 survey of people hospitalized in North Carolina and Pennsylvania, 77 percent felt that their doctors should consider their spiritual needs (*USA Today* 2004). This suggests that Americans appreciate the real benefits that can come through spirituality.

The National Institute for Healthcare Research has initiated a study looking into this important aspect of spirituality. It is believed that a person's most deeply held beliefs strongly influence health, and that a positive attitude towards a serious illness will help with recovery. Forgiveness, interestingly, is also vitally important. A 1997 Stanford study found that college students trained to forgive someone who had hurt them were significantly less angry, more hopeful, and better able to deal with strong emotions than those who were not trained to forgive. These studies found that love and social and emotional support were as important to people's spiritual health as prayer (*USA Today* 2004).

Others speak of spiritual wellness, a sense that life is meaningful, has purpose, and brings humanity together. Many people have spiritual needs, and as social beings, we feel a need to be connected to others. These feelings encourage actions such as prayer and meditation, seeking contentment (to seek the brighter side of life), forgiveness as an effort to reestablish relationships, religious attendance (sharing one's spirituality with a community), and altruistic behavior. So it is faith as well as hope that power most of us on this spiritual journey toward well-being (Hoeger, Turner, and Hafen 2003).

Theologian Dr. Charles Stanley (1996) presents a Christian perspective on forgiveness. Using the letters of the various disciples of the New Testament—including John, Paul, and Matthew—he shows that if you forgive another person, it is the same as if God were forgiving them. Furthermore, God will look at the forgiver with great favor. Stanley passes along some lessons on how to forgive, as well as commenting on the consequences of forgiveness. He gives practical suggestions about how to face the individual who hurt you and how to go about forgiving him or her. He also speaks about self-forgiveness, because in doing so healing is possible. He says that it is psychological and spiritually unhealthy to continue being the victim and suffer as a result.

Addressing the issue of unforgiveness, Stanley has this to say:

> Unforgiveness is actually a form of hatred. 'Oh,' you may say, 'I don't hate anybody.' By such a statement, you probably mean that you wouldn't murder anybody or do anything intentionally to harm another person. But ask yourself these questions: Do I avoid encountering a certain person? Do I find it difficult to speak well of a certain person? Does the very thought of a particular person make me cringe or clench my fist? If your answer is yes, you are harboring hatred in the form of unforgiveness (Stanley 1996: 62).

Stanley maintains that hatred exists in various degrees and that an unforgiving spirit is marked by hatred. We know that when we have such a feeling we cannot shake the pain or memory of the hurt done to us. We cannot honestly wish the offending person well—on the contrary, we often want them to feel pain, to suffer and hurt to the degree we have hurt and suffered.

There are other consequences of unforgiving, according to Dr. Stanley. First, we may experience emotional bondage, and these memories may be tormenting, causing us to relive the pain we experienced. Secondly, we may experience damaged relationships, because we are likely to have relations marked by anger, quarreling, and other emotional eruptions. Thirdly, we will suffer spiritually because we feel that we cannot face certain human beings. Lastly, unforgiveness harbors anger, puts a heavy burden on our nervous systems, and causes us stress and a feeling of betrayal.

Bill Fields (2005) uses the Christian principle of reconciliation. He offers eight steps: confession by the offender; identifying the Biblical principles violated; determining how the offended person was actually offended; recalling similar offenses; having the offenders restate their sins and express Godly sorrow; having offenders express sorrow by restating the offense in their own words; having offenders ask what they might do differently so as to not harm again; and, lastly, offering restitution.

Engaged Spirituality

By *engaged spirituality* we mean sustained moral action on behalf of others that is motivated by selfless love and kindness, rather than by selfish motives on the part of those helping. Jack Berry and colleagues (2005) state:

> Warmth-based virtues (e.g., love, compassion, and generosity) contribute to cooperation and warm emotional bonds. Conscientiousness-based virtues (e.g., self-control, forbearance, and justice) inhibit selfish and antisocial behavior. We suggest that there are individual differences in the degree to which people value and practice the virtues in these two classes. Furthermore, differential preferences for the two classes of virtues should predict differential responses to transgressions (Berry et al 2005: 144).

Dr. Berry proceeds to present data concerning individual differences in preferences for the practice of moral virtues (Berry 2004).

Recent research shows that there is a positive correlation between faith or religion and healing. For many prayer, not only for loved ones but for those one does not know, helps in the healing process. Eighty-four percent of Americans think that praying for the sick improves their chance of recovery, and 28 percent think that religion and medicine should be separate. People who regularly attend church tend to live longer than people who are not churchgoers. Using brain scans, scholars found that meditation can change brain activity and improve immune response; other studies show it can lower heart rate and blood pressure, both of which reduce the body's stress responses. Forgiveness also has been found to have an impact on health and wellness. University of Michigan School of Public Health researcher Neil Kraus found that people who forgive easily tend to enjoy greater psychological well-being and suffer less depression than those who hold grudges (Kalb 2003).

While there are critics of this connection, two thirds of the studies find significant associations between religious belief and well-being: life satisfaction, hope, purpose, meaning, and lower rates of depression, anxiety, and suicide. Seventy of the 120 medical schools in the United States—from

Harvard to Stanford—offer specific courses on spirituality or incorporate spiritual themes into their curricula (Kalb 2003).

Sir John Templeton donates millions annually to study the intersections of prayer, physical healing, love, forgiveness, reconciliation, and related studies. The National Institute of Health spent $3.5 million on "mind/body studies" (Kalb 2003). Many in the medical field, such as Duke University's Harold Koening, Harvard's Herbert Benson, and Stanford's Robert Sapolsky, are finding that this kind of research is valuable.

Stanczak and Miller think of spirituality as "an integral part of everyday life among people who are dedicating themselves to social service. As an integral aspect of everyday life, spirituality is a feeling, an experience, a relationship, a connection of intimate practices that, much like other feelings or relationships in our lives, takes on the texture and color of what is going on around us. For some people, this means that spirituality must address the injustices that they perceive at work, the poverty that they see in their communities, or the global disparities that are so apparent in health services in developing nations" (Stanczak and Miller 2004: 5–6).

Inherited engagement is the connection between social and spiritual commitment that can be derived from family practice or long-term involvement within religious institutions. For example, Rabbi Leonard Beerman's lifelong commitment to justice was founded on his family's experience during the Great Depression. To individuals like Beerman, the combination of social commitment and spirituality is the only way to express faith that is deeply fused with one's sense of identity. The idea of *learned engagement* suggests that the pluralism and diversity of collegiate independence can open up many religious options, such as new ways of practice, discussions on histories of social engagement, or new philosophies about spiritual commitments to social change. Emile Durkheim describes the power of the social encounter as one of the universally fundamental building blocks of religious sentiment and meaning.

A *spiritual epiphany* in the form of visions, dreams, voices, or an overwhelming sense of clarity and direction constitutes the most transcendent and experiential connection between social action and spirituality. The basis of these transformations is perceived as undeniably otherworldly.

Serving as a *community volunteer* is a structured embodiment of the Good Neighbor. The volunteer works within his or her community, providing direct services or aid as part of an organized form of social service and, although spiritually motivated, may or may not publicly express this spiritual motivation. The conventional modern American image is the soup kitchen volunteer, which for many is their first introduction to social service work. Similarly, the *moral advocate* focuses his spiritual motivations on public education of particular issues or attempts to initiate changes in social policy or community development. Advocates are the instigators, the educators, and the mouthpieces for particular platforms or social causes, and they can work either within or outside of institutional channels.

A *visionary prophet* sees the world not only as it is but also as it could be. Often the visionary acts in ways that disregard seemingly insurmountable odds. Spiritual practices are regimented parts of everyday life and often occur at scheduled times or in patterned ways. The five daily calls to prayer at the core of Islamic religious life or the resurgence of the Daily Office among Christians are notable examples of collective daily practice. These strictly scheduled practices connect each day with an otherworldly source.

Other individuals feel *empowerment* directly and literally as an embodied manifestation of a palpable physical force. This force might be articulated through a feeling of courage, strength, or energy but is typically experienced first physically. There is a common thread of *transcendence* or otherworldliness that infuses individuals with power. These individuals continually and solemnly refer to moments that could not be rationally explained.

Many people feel their spirituality in a sense of community, both real—in terms of one's friends, family, or religious congregation—and within imagined communities (for example, historical lineage of others who have engaged in similar endeavors for millennia), or in the greater communal body of the faithful around the globe. These individuals create connections to a tradition that provides cultural roots, affirmation, and validity for socially enacting one's spirituality. In doing so, they generate feelings of solidarity, love, trust, respect, unity, and belonging (Stanczak and Miller 2004).

We are seeing an increase in spirituality in our young people. Alexander Astin (2003) conducted a large survey—112,232 students, from 236 colleges and universities across the United States—that focused on the spiritual development of college students and their involvement with society. One of the questions asked was, "How would you describe your current views on spirituality/religious matters?" Eighty percent of these college students responded that they are interested and tolerant in exploring their spirituality. Even though Elizabeth Svoboda (2005) documents that universities are often reluctant to offer courses that encourage the pursuit of such spiritual investigation, students can find their spirituality through many paths—for example, as community volunteers or moral advocates.

Epiphany

What epiphany promotes some scholars to look at the topic of engaged spirituality? How do scholars become interested in engagement? Recently I reviewed *Flourishing: Positive Psychology From a Life Well Lived* (2003), a collection of essays edited by Cory Keyes and Jonathan Heidt. Martin Seligman, a contributor to that volume, relays the following story: One day, Seligman was in the garden doing some weeding. His five-year-old daughter Nikki was present, but instead of helping with the weeding, she was throwing weeds in the air and dancing around. Seligman became irritated with her, because he had a goal in mind: to finish the weeding. He proceeded to yell at her and caused her to leave. After a while she returned and said to him, "Daddy I want to talk to you. You may not have noticed, but do you remember how I was before my fifth birthday? From the time I was three until I was five, I was a whiner, I whined every day, but when I turned five, I decided not to whine anymore. And that was the hardest thing I have ever done—but I did it, so if I can stop whining, Daddy, can you stop being grumpy?" This real-life episode had a profound effect on Seligman, who realized that he indeed was always grumpy and grouchy and that his daughter Nikki was correct. For 50 years he had walked around acting grumpy despite being surrounded by a wife and children who were all "rays of sunshine." In some sense, this single event made Seligman the father of "Positive Psychology," a field that has recently come into its own.

One dramatic example, previously mentioned, is the story of psychologist Everett Worthington and the murder of his mother. Stanford psychologist Frederic Luskin (2002) was motivated by an unpleasant and dramatic fall-out with a friend he valued greatly. Psychiatrist Aaron Lazare (2004) relates a similar experience, in which two friends betrayed his trust, causing anger and a need for understanding. Sociologist Nicholas Tavuchis (1991) had a similar experience of hurt. He says, "I trace my interest in apology to a bitter argument I had many years ago with someone close and dear to me. The precise details have faded from memory, but I can still recall feeling hurt, wronged, and angered by the accusation of misconduct and insensitivity" (1991: 1).

We can see that there are a variety of reasons why people get passionately involved with a subject. But is it possible, in the absence of dramatic epiphanies, to move more people from simply being bystanders to getting involved with others? How can we begin to inculcate and disseminate the behaviors of helping, getting spiritually engaged, and acting as moral exemplars so that more people will benefit their neighbors, their communities, and the world?

LOVE, EMPATHY, AND FORGIVENESS

One word frees us of all the weight and pain of life. That word is love.

—*Sophocles*

Closely connected with forgiveness is the power of love. "Without love what have we got? A world without a heart." This quote, from one of the more than 500 rescuers of Jews in Nazi-occupied Europe that we interviewed, had an important impact on our thinking. In considering the ways that we interact when we apologize and forgive, love must take a central role.

"Love is the language that can be heard by the deaf, seen by the blind, and felt by the loneliest of hearts. [It] is being happy for another person when they are happy, being sad for the other person when they are sad, being together in good times, and being together in bad times. Love is the source of strength…Love is the source of life," according to an Ohio-based Christian church (Agape Love Ministries 2004).

Stephen Post, in *Unlimited Love: Altruism, Compassion, and Service* (2002), and with others in *Research on Altruism and Love* (2003), outlines an important process he calls *unlimited love*. Citing Vladimir Solovyov (1853–1900), he says, "The meaning and worth of love, as a feeling, is that it really forces us, with all of our being, to acknowledge for another the same absolute central significance, which because of the power of our egoism, we are conscious of only in our own selves. Love is important not as one of our feelings but as the transfer of all our interest in life from ourselves to another, as the shifting of the very center of our personal lives." Post believes that those who have the virtue of meaningful spirituality shape our love, and any spiritual transformation that is not a migration toward love is suspect" (Post 2003: 42).[27]

David Augsburger (1981) informs us that love helps us care enough to forgive. The following steps are part of this process: 1) See the other as having worth and value; 2) See the other as equally precious; 3) Recognize that changing the past is impossible; 4) Work through anger and pain in order to risk trusting again; 5) Drop demands for a perfect, risk-free future. 6)

Celebrate the forgiveness with love and compassion. Augsberger reports that letting go allows feelings, views, and emotions to be fluid, and that accepting our humanity and our powerlessness to force others into perfection relaxes our grip on pain and allows ourselves to flow forward with time and be present with us, our companions, and the universe. He argues that this is only possible when love is part of one's cognitive and emotional being, which is strongly coupled with empathy and altruistic predisposition.

Menachem Eckstein (2001) argues that "Love, compassion, caring, [and] empathy are contagious and spread from those who are fortunate to have these positive processes to others who do not have [them]." It comes about as a matter of kindness and expression of caring. It is beautiful and "endless," and we would like to see more of it diffused. These ideas are "not just for the hassidically inclined, nor even just for Jews." Rabbi Eckstein focuses on a "release from self-centered consciousness, living the compassionate life, and the experience of oneness with the universe. These ideals are common to all traditions." (Eckstein 2001: 15)

My experience tells me that love is of the utmost importance, especially during childhood. At the age of 12, I found myself trying to survive in a dangerous world without parents, family, friends, or loved ones. The Holocaust had deprived me of all love and compassion. Until I was rescued, I felt lost, terrified, and alone. Then compassionate people took an interest in me and saved my life. After the war ended, other people showed me not only that they loved me, but also that they cared about me and respected me. It is easy for me to understand the ways in which love-deprived children suffer. The research on the topic of love shows that children who do not experience love early in their lives suffer the consequences for the rest of their lives.

At the "Works of Love" conference, held at Villanova University in 2003, attending scholars produced the following statement:

> Unselfish love for all humanity is the most important point of convergence shared by the world's great spiritual traditions. We marvel at the…power of love, and find in it the best hope for a far better human future. People from all walks of life, often those disadvantaged themselves, excel in love and kindness, not just for the nearest and dearest, but also as volunteers and advocates on behalf of all the strangers (Works of Love: 2003).

Great numbers of scholars have dealt with this positive social process we call love. Psychologists, theologians, philosophers, social activists, marriage counselors, psychiatrists, and healing professionals of all stripes have made a convincing case that without love human beings cannot flourish. Harry Harlow's famous experiments with baby monkeys are instructive as to the importance and value of love to our successful development. Harlow separated infant monkeys from their mothers and raised them in separate cages with two substitute "mothers," one of cloth and one of metal wire. The wire "mother" had a bottle for the infant; the cloth "mother" did not. Although the infant monkeys were quick to determine that the wire mother had the bottle, and quickly learned to feed there, afterward they went to the cloth "mother" for comfort. Harvard Medical School professor Mary Carlson was influenced by the Harlow study and its relevance to human deprivation and lack of loving contact between mothers and their infants.[28] When the infant monkeys were raised in a cage from which they could see, smell, and hear the mother monkeys but not touch them, the baby monkeys developed what Carlson called an "autisticlike syndrome" with grooming, self-clasping, social withdrawal, and rocking.

Reporting on a study she did on orphanages in Romania, where conditions were shocking, the children were devoid of caring human contact, and their institutionalized care was not sufficient to maintain the social capacity for the human baby. The dictator Nicolae Ceausescu was a strong believer in technological progress and was highly skeptical of all things "touchy-feely." He clamped down on psychology and social work, preferring engineering and science. He greatly favored policies to raise the birth rate and established institutions for orphans and children whose parents could not care for them. Carlson's observations have many implications for our society, where she sees a consistent relationship between poor care and increases in cortisol levels, which are associated with stress. Her research raises questions about what happens to American children in poor day care centers.

Thomas Lewis, Fari Amin, and Richard Lannon address the importance of love in their major work, *A General Theory of Love* (2000). They seek to answer questions about the definition and meaning of love, why people are unable to find it, and about loneliness and why it hurts. The authors raise the question of the importance of attractors, which are patterns that are more or less imprinted in the limbic system from infant and childhood limbic connections. Lynn E. O'Connor notes that "Less than optimal limbic connecting, in whatever manner it fails to do the job, tends to get repeated throughout life in terms of choice of love partners and other close relationships" (O'Connor 2002). She agrees that people who have experienced dysfunctional and unloving parents tend to select and continue to select partners who essentially match the parents in some limbic way and that in the end are not good for them. Psychotherapy, when it works, helps to change the limbic patterns just enough to allow the person to begin to select more comfort-inducing partners and friends" (O'Connor 2002).

Faith-induced love is emphasized and embraced by every major religious tradition. For Christianity the notion of love is unconditional and emphasizes acceptance, forgiveness, openness, oneness with all, and treating others as you would wish to be treated. In Buddhism, especially Tibetan Buddhism, we have seen that the concept of *bodhicitta* means selfless or unselfish altruism, aspiration to relieve the sufferings of all, compassion, and service—also meaning love and forgiveness. There are a number of examples from real life in which unlimited love and loving kindness are exhibited, including in the hospice system and in L'Arche communities of people who have developmental disabilities.

There are different kinds of love, according to Anders Nygren in his book, *Agape and Eros* (1953). Nygren distinguishes romantic love (*eros*) from altruistic love (*agape*). Agape love is spontaneous and unmotivated, indifferent to values, creative, and initiates fellowship with God. Divine love is spontaneous, in that it does not look for reward. Divine love seeks those who do not deserve it and can lay no claim to it. Agape love is God's creative activity, and it initiates fellowship with God. It is deep, intimate, and selfless love, as portrayed in Christianity, Judaism, Islam, Buddhism, Hinduism, Taoism, and Confucianism. Judaism carries the message of agape in the passage from Leviticus that states, "You shall not hate your brother in your heart…you shall love your neighbor as yourself" (Leviticus 19:17). There is a similar statement in the New Testament: "You shall love your neighbor as yourself" (Mathew 22:39).

Stephen Post says, "In essence, unlimited love is abiding, regarding perspective and emotional attunement that affirms and serves all of humanity unselfishly and unconditionally, without any exception whatsoever" (Post 2002: 5). Others, such as John Templeton (1999), maintain that unlimited love is a form of love that arises from every conceivable limit to embrace all of humanity in joy, creativity, compassion, care, and generativity; it lies at the heart at of all valid and worthwhile spiritual, religious, and derivative philosophical traditions. It is often associated with a divine presence that underlies the cosmos and makes life a meaningful gift. Indeed the life of unlimited love probably begins with the sense that every life is a gift. These explanations are the heart of agape.

In his book, *The Model of Love: A Study of Philosophical Theology* (1993), Vincent Brümmer maintains that *agape*, what he calls "gift-love," is the attitude of giving oneself in service to the other. He notes that two of the most important classical examples of the view that love is to be understood in terms of *eros* or "need-love," were Plato and St. Augustine. Brümmer discusses gift-love in some depth. "There is thus no way for man to come to God, but only a way for God to come to man: the way of divine forgiveness, divine love. *Agape* is God's way to man" (Brümmer 1993: 128). Brümmer continues "that all love that has any right to be called *agape* is nothing else but an outflow from the divine love. It has its source in God—God is *agape*" (Brümmer 1993: 131). Brümmer argues that the way in which God loves us is the perfect example upon which we should try to pattern our love for each other. Thus, God's love of human beings can be understood as a supreme appreciation of the individuality of each person. Discussing gift-love, Brümmer says that *agape* love is a kind of devotion for individuals to serve the good of others. A residual, though latent, effect of so doing is that we actually end up serving ourselves. In this sense, love is indeed unconditional love or gift-love, rather than a desire for fulfilling our own needs or interests.

In the Jewish tradition, it is stated that when we help others lovingly and unconditionally, we at the same time help ourselves in the eyes of God and humanity. Similarly, David J. Hassel (1985) states that love is other-centered and necessarily includes a discovery of God within this love. Understandably, Karol Wojtyla, the late Pope, said that "The desire for unlimited good for another person is really the desire that God has for that person" (Brümmer 1993: 139).

Rolf M. Johnson (2001) speaks about care-love and union-love. Care-love means concern for the good or welfare of someone or something. To love he says, in this case, is to care for or care about objects. The lover is concerned with the beloved and is supposed to act on its behalf. If the object of our care-love is endangered, our impulse is to protect it. Care-love is a form of agape love. Also he cautions that it should be clearly understood that care-love has a universally moral purpose only because one could also lovingly care for someone who is evil and destructive. Johnson cites Russian philosopher Solovyov in arguing that "we must join with others in order to join with God: we have no access to the divine as separate egos" (Johnson 2001: 95). Ilham Dilman speaks of "gift-love, which is always directed to objects [that] the lover finds in some way intrinsically lovable. . .divine gift-love in the man enables him to love what is naturally unlovable: lepers, criminals, enemies, morons, the sulky, superior, sneering" (Dilman 1998: 162).

I became acquainted with the philosophy of Pitirim Sorokin in the late 1950s, when I was an undergraduate at Brooklyn College. One of my sociology professors told me that Sorokin might have lost his sociological direction and might instead have become a "philosopher of love." This implied that Sorokin was not worth reading, because he was not sociological or scientific—despite the fact that he had written 40 important books in sociology and had 400 articles published in professional journals. Sorokin's major works have been translated into at least 19 different languages and are read and discussed around the world. That single, somewhat offhand comment by my professor made me curious about this philosopher of love. In 1976, I became even more interested in his philosophy because of his creation of the Center of Creative Altruism at Harvard University. I wanted to know what he meant by "creative altruism," so I started investigating his writings. Besides reading his works, and the thoughts of those who critiqued him, I also wrote to some of his famous students who were by then full professors—scholars such as Neil Smeltzer, Robert Merton, and Edward Tiryakian—because I wanted to find out what kind of a scholar Sorokin was. Each of them had something profoundly positive to say about Sorokin and his work. Some also commented on his conflict with the new upstart, Talcott Parsons, who later succeeded him as chair of the Department at Harvard.

Sorokin's monumental work, *Social and Cultural Dynamics,* and numerous other works, including the *Ways and Power of Love* (1954), have examined major social processes and how change occurs. Sorokin looked at 2,500 years of civilization to determine what causes social change. One of the positive social processes was love, which he felt was not well examined by social scientists. Sorokin felt love to be less well understood because social scientists tried to emulate the methods of physical scientists, involving themselves deeply in measuring and testing hypotheses. He was not very impressed with this direction. As a matter of fact, he accused social scientists, especially sociologists, of being involved in "quantomania" and "quantophenia"; testing little theories, subjecting them to rigorous statistical analysis, and coming up with results that are not earthshaking. Sorokin proposed another way of knowing: He introduced the notion of *integralism,* which is a system of thought that has the potential to fundamentally alter and redirect the social scientist in a positive and creative direction. The fundamental ideas of integralism are found in the writings of St. Thomas Acquinas, Pope John Paul II, and Sorokin himself. Integralism, which Sorokin formulated in the 1940s, offers a unique perspective in the social sciences, because it rests on the fundamental assumption that reality contains physical/empirical, rational/meaningful, and supersensory/superrational components. Therefore, the development of social scientists should include components that affect each part of this reality, and the epistemology should include methods of cognition that can be adapted to each of these aspects.

Sorokin's approach was a blending of Eastern and Western philosophical focus, fusing the truth found in human experience—truth of the mind, the senses, and the spirit. Sorokin maintained that integralism would free us from the pitfalls of one-dimensional thought and instrumental knowledge. He found it to be a necessary corrective to past domination by an instrumental but shortsighted and often destructive form of knowledge. Sorokin argued that sociologists spend too much time studying destructive social behavior, crime, violence, and war. If we wish to improve the human condition we should start emphasizing and understanding the positive aspects of humanity. With the help of a Lilly endowment, Sorokin established the Harvard Center of Creative Altruism, which sponsored many studies. Sorokin's research now positively impacts psychology and the topics of altruism, apology and forgiveness.

BIOLOGY AND FORGIVENESS

There is little emotional activity that goes on in our brains that does not have a corresponding physical (bodily) reaction. For more than two decades, scientists have used various types of devices to scan brain activity while subjects are conducting certain tasks or thinking certain types of thoughts. Functional Magnetic Resonance Imaging (fMRI) scanners are now used by researchers. Human activity "lights up" one or more parts of the brain on the fMRI screen. A luminous spot represents intense electrical firing of nerve circuits or an unusually intense blood flow and oxygen consumption at a certain locale in the brain.

Science writer Keay Davidson (2004) reports that scientists have used fMRI evidence to find a link between empathy and physical pain: "When someone says, 'I feel your pain,' it isn't just an expression of empathy—it may literally be true." The pain-sensing part of our brains switches on when we're aware that someone else is in pain. And the more we feel empathy for someone else's pain, the greater the activity in the pain-sensing regions of our brain. Empathy, the ability to grasp the feelings of others, is one of humanity's most cherished traits. It is associated with great humanitarians, social activists, philanthropists, insightful novelists, and artists.

Recent research by Dr. Tania Singer of University College London points toward a neurological basis for empathy: "our brains' ability to mimic the 'internal bodily states' of others inside the neural jungle of our own noggins" (Davidson 2004: A2). The subjects were 16 male–female couples who were placed inside an fMRI scanner. The scientists applied painful stimulation—electric shocks or heat—to the women's right hands." Each woman faced a computer screen, and before each stimulation, she was informed by the computer when she was about to be hurt and by what intensity of pain. Later, the women's brains were scanned while they observed similar pains inflicted on their husbands. The fMRI scans showed that when women observed the suffering of their mates, the same parts of the women's brains illuminated as when they expected, thanks to the computer alert, to be hurt themselves.

Our ability to empathize may have evolved from a system for representing our own internal bodily states. Our capacity to tune into others when exposed to their feelings may explain why we do not always behave selfishly in human interactions but instead engage in altruistic, helping behavior. The journal *Neuron* reported fMRI evidence of how our brains distinguish between people who "play fair" and those who cheat (Davidson 2004: A2). The result of brain imaging experiments shows that human beings activate something within their brains when they see another person performing an action. That concept is currently understood as "mirror neurons," which implies that when people see joy or stress, they reflect the emotion they witness in sympathy. Singer and her colleagues had volunteers play the game "Prisoner's Dilemma," which tests how well two "prisoners" cooperate with each other. In the game, under certain circumstances, cooperation pays dividends; in other instances, cheating pays off. By fMRI-scanning the volunteers, Singer and her team discovered that the volunteers' brains illuminated in certain ways to players perceived as fair and differently to those regarded as cheaters. Such fMRI research is a new, high-tech contribution to long-standing debates over the possible biological roots of moral behavior.

For decades evolutionary biologists have argued over why humans and other animals risk their lives to help others. According to the "selfish gene" hypothesis, altruism make little sense—at first glance anyway—because it is only our own lives and genes that matter. But scientists have offered interesting arguments for why, under certain circumstances, altruism makes more sense. For example, it makes genetic sense for an elderly male to rescue a healthy young female relative who is genetically close to him, because her fertile years are still ahead of her.

Neuropsychological analysis of forgiveness may help us to understand mechanisms by which forgiveness contributes to improved psychological functioning. By utilizing autonomic and neurophysiological measures, in addition to more traditional psychological ones, some of the direct effects of forgiveness may be measured. Decrease in heart rate, respiratory rate, anxiety, depression, feelings of hostility and anger, and improved self-esteem have been associated with practices such as meditation designed to augment parasympathetic activity. Changes may therefore occur in patients going through the forgiveness process. One might utilize brain-imaging techniques to measure aspects of cerebral functioning related to forgiveness. Forgiveness may improve a person's standing within the social group and enhance interpersonal relationships, and the forgiveness process may strengthen interpersonal bonds. Thus, encouraging forgiveness might be a powerful therapeutic intervention with transforming consequences.

Neuropsychological models suggest that forgiveness may ultimately have beneficial effects on the body, such as decreased levels of stress hormones and improvements in sleep patterns. Forgiveness and healing may go hand in hand. It is difficult to accomplish one without the other, and neuropsychological analysis of forgiveness may help to delineate why forgiveness is such an important phenomenon psychologically, physically, and spiritually.

INTERPERSONAL AND INTERGROUP FORGIVENESS

There are different types of forgiveness, from interpersonal to intergroup, and the factors and influences involved range from spirituality to love and empathy. Researchers have found neuropsychological correlations to forgiveness, and scholars see forgiveness as a critical distinction between restorative and retributive justice (see Chapter 6).

Apology can be an effective tool in reconciliation, but not if it is perceived as insincere. Similarly, false forgiveness also obstructs reconciliation. Just as there are conditional false apologies, such as "I am sorry for what you made me do," there is false forgiveness, which does not really resolve the issue for the offender or for the offended. Some who are skeptical of forgiveness as a part of reconciliation are quick to point to these kinds of ineffectual instances of apology and forgiveness as the norm. But, as we know from our own experience, though some apologies and forgiveness exchanges may be attempts at a "quick fix," there are also many examples of sincere apology and forgiveness that form the basis of understanding and reconciliation.

There is evidence that people who are hurt and in pain are looking and longing for forgiveness. Recently, when conducting research on the Internet, we found numerous messages of apology asking for forgiveness. One example was found at the "Home Reading Room Message Board":

> Please forgive me for I know not what I do. All I wanted to do was make you happy. All I wanted to do was show you how nice and tender I can be. Please forgive me. I know sometimes I might have made mistakes. But I come to you, asking you, please forgive me. I just want you to know how I feel about you. So, I come to you asking, please forgive (Forgivenessweb.com 2001).

We don't know how effective such public notices are, but there are many of them, which seems to indicate that many people feel they have done wrong and are seeking reconciliation and hoping to reestablish harmony in their relationships.

Interpersonal Forgiveness

Mark Umbreit relates the following story as an example of a victim with a need to forgive in order to restore her own well being:

> Sarah contacted me shortly after the parole hearing and expressed her strong inner sense of needing to meet the very man who killed her father so many years ago. Other than her husband, the rest of her family had no interest in following this path. From the very beginning it was clear that she was yearning to find peace within herself and her immediate family. Many months of separate preparation followed with both Sarah and Jeff. During our in-person separate meetings, I was able to understand the life context and needs of Sarah and her husband Rick, as well as Jeff, the offender. In addition to much deep compassionate listening to their stories, I explained how the process works and the fact that there are both benefits and risks in such a dialogue, particularly if people enter the process with unrealistic expectations. I also pointed out that even though many who have chosen a similar path of restorative dialogue have reported the encounter to be very therapeutic; the actual dialogue is not a form of psychotherapy. Jeff felt tremendous

remorse for what he had done and was willing, though scared, to meet with Sarah. For all, this must be an entirely voluntary process. It became increasingly clear in Sarah's own words that she was on an intense spiritual journey to reclaim her soul, her sense of meaning, balance, and wholeness in life.

The mediated dialogue was held in a maximum-security prison. Sarah's husband was present, as well as a support person that Jeff chose. Mediated dialogue refers to a humanistic approach that is very nondirective, honoring the healing power of silence and one's presence. My comediator and I practiced mindfulness through centering and breath work both during the preparation and in the dialogue so that our egos and voices stayed out of the way, to allow Sarah and Jeff's strength and wisdom to emerge and flow as it needed to. After very brief opening comments by the mediators, we entered an extended period of silence as Sarah sobbed and tried to find her voice to tell her story. As mediators, we did not intervene to move the process along. Instead, we remained silent. We knew she had the strength, and our mindfulness practice allowed us to stay out of the way. Sarah and Jeff told us later that the energy of our presence, the nonverbal language of our spirit, was vital to the process being safe and respectful of their needs and abilities. After nearly four minutes, Sarah found her voice and her story of trauma, loss, and yearning for healing flowed out with strength and clarity. Jeff then offered his story of what happened, how it has affected his life, and the enormous shame he felt.

They continued to share deeper layers of their stories, interspersed with lingering questions both had. After five hours, and shortly before the session ended, following another moment of extended silence, perhaps a minute, Sarah looked directly at Jeff and told him she forgave him for killing her father. She made it clear that this forgiveness was about freeing herself from the pain she had carried with her for more than twenty years. She hoped this forgiveness might help him as well, but Sarah said she could not set her spirit free without forgiving him. Sarah had never indicated in our many months of preparation that forgiveness was an issue she was struggling with, nor did we raise the issue. When she and her husband came to the prison for the dialogue with Jeff, she had no plan whatsoever to offer forgiveness. Yet in the powerful moment of confronting her greatest fear, Sarah [spoke] of how she felt within her soul that "this is the moment to free myself." In post-dialogue interviews with Sarah and Jeff, they both indicated the enormous effect this encounter had on their lives. Sarah spoke of how meeting Jeff was like going through a fire that burned away her pain and allowed the seeds of healing to take root in her life. She spoke of how before meeting Jeff she carried the pain of her father's death like an ever-present large backpack. After meeting Jeff, the pain [became] more like a small fanny-pack, still present but very manageable and in no way claiming her life energy and spirit, as before. Jeff reported a sense of release and cleansing, as if his spirit was set free as well (Umbreit 2005 with permission from the author).

There are many definitions of interpersonal forgiveness (Enright and North 1998). Interpersonal forgiveness, as distinguished from divine forgiveness, has as its major purpose to reduce the possibility of vengeance, revenge, or retaliation against those who have harmed us, thereby increasing reconciliation. This is pragmatic. Michael McCullough, Everett Worthington, and Kenneth Rachal (1997) define forgiveness as "a summary term representing efforts to reduce the motivation to avoid and to seek revenge and increase the motivation to reconcile or seek conciliation" (McCullough et al 1997: 229).

There are many situations that may call for forgiveness from people, including victims of crime; unethical work practices, workplace aggression, or discrimination; people who are unemployed; targets for racial, ethnic, gender, age, or religious discrimination; and members of ethnic groups that have a history of conflict and harm. Other groups that also may be included are separated or divorcing parents and their children, victims of child abuse, people involved in interfamily and intergenerational conflict, people dealing with unfaithful partners, and those who have been harmed or rejected by deceased parents. The list truly is endless. Forgiveness would help heal these wounds by decreasing the likelihood of vengeance and increasing reconciliation.

How can we sensitize, inform, and "prove" to people around the world that it is possible for mankind to live without hate, harm, war, and degradation of the environment (Dozier 2002)? There are two powerful human forces ultimately capable of reversing the trend of alienation and separation: The first is teaching, inculcating, and disseminating the positive consequences of altruistic behavior. We have seen that genuine altruistic behavior is helpful and regenerative, that it is strongly associated with enhanced general health, and that it leads to more harmonious relations. The second powerful force is apology and forgiveness. We know that hurt and alienation have been proven to have negative effects on mental and physical health, causing stress and physical and psychological pain. Professional healers are aware of this pain and the positive consequences of interpersonal forgiveness. They advocate apology, forgiveness, and reconciliation as a process of restoring loving and caring relations between individuals. A small percentage of people avail themselves of these healers. However, we do not see the results of the vast amount of research being done in these areas by schools and universities around the country.

It will take a focused vision on the part of educators to implement these ideas. In addition to the very important subjects of reading, writing, math, science, and computers, should we not also spend time learning about the consequences of harming? There is evidence that not only the victim is harmed, but the offender suffers for hurting or shaming another person, often feeling guilty for these actions but not knowing how to resolve them. Those who have been offended tend to carry anger and resentment, feeling that somehow they deserved the treatment. Their resentment often leads to a desire for vengeance. But positive, powerful social forces of altruism and apology/forgiveness can serve as an antidote to the spiraling need for vengeance. There are more than 80 million students in classrooms from elementary to college levels. Surely some way ought to be found, with our present state of knowledge, to impress upon them how hurting or shaming others in their immediate environment has painful consequences and should be avoided.

The classic sociologist W. I. Thomas (1923) made a profound observation about how we treat each other as human beings. He is well known for his explanation that when a person defines a situation as real—whether it *is* real or not—it then becomes real in its consequences. This explains much about human behavior. For example, if an employer defines African-Americans as "lazy," an unfair stereotype, that employer will be less likely to hire them. The employer has defined reality and makes real-life choices based on that interpretation. We tend to define people as good or bad, as one of "us" or one of "them," and then treat them accordingly.

There also is a psychological basis for forgiveness that consists of the need to overcome guilt, rage, and the desire for revenge, as well as a strong desire for reconciliation. There are several theories on the relationship between apology, forgiveness, reparations, and the restoration of harmony or reconciliation. Psychologist Seiji Takaku (2001) tested victims' abilities to take the perspective of the transgressor to facilitate the process of forgiveness as a result of dissonance/reduction motivation. He also investigates forgiveness as a model of dissonance reduction. Takuku challenges some of the explanations offered by authors such as Enright (1995, 1998) and others. He agrees with the notion that sympathy, compassion, and love increase the likelihood of positive behavior toward the offender. However, he feels that unless the offender takes the perspective of the other, and is thereby able to generate positive attributes toward the offender, forgiveness is less likely to be successful.

Takaku discusses other authors on perspective-taking. According to the correspondent inference theory (Jones and Davis 1965), if a transgressor apologizes for a transgression, the victim is less likely to infer a negative judgment of the transgressor's personality. The offense and the intention that produced it are less likely to be perceived as corresponding to some underlying trait of the offender. By breaking the link between the negative act and negative dispositional attributes, apology facilitates the process of interpersonal forgiveness. Forgiveness is more likely when others perceive the offender as having had good reasons for committing the offense, as in self-defense.

Holley Hodgins and Elizabeth Liebeskind (1999) analyzed two studies in which participants imagined themselves in "face-threatening" predicaments, examining the reproach and evaluation phases of predicament management. In the first study, participants gave accounts of their behavior after receiving hypothetical reproaches that were mild, moderate, or severe. Results showed that the severity of the reproach influenced the so-called perpetrators' accounts in opposite ways for females and males. Male perpetrators became more defensive under severe reproach, whereas females became less defensive. Expectations for a future relationship were more negative under severe reproach, and this was greater when the victim was an acquaintance rather than a friend. Individuals scoring high in self-determination were less defensive under mild-to-moderate reproach but not under severe reproach. In the second study, participants gave evaluations after receiving hypothetical accounts that varied in responsibility-taking. Results showed that greater responsibility-taking led to more positive victim evaluations and more positive expectations for future relationships. The advantage of responsibility-taking was especially pronounced when the perpetrator was a friend, suggesting that friends are more likely to be forgiven than acquaintances when they do take responsibility and apologize, but not if they fail to do so. Although claiming the results as useful in analyzing apology and forgiveness, the authors do offer the caveat that the experiment scenarios may not fully and accurately reflect real life.

Another quandary occurs when someone does not ask for forgiveness, such as Ali Agca, who attempted to assassinate the late Pope, John Paul II. The Pope personally forgave his potential murderer when he went to see him. Ali did not appear to be repentant. Major religious teachings maintain that a person has to repent first in order to be forgiven. We also must forgive ourselves and not blame ourselves for being the victim.

Lewis B. Smedes reminds us that forgiving a person does not require us to reunite with the person who broke our trust (1984). We do not forgive because we are supposed to, but rather when we are ready to be healed. Waiting for someone to repent before we forgive is to surrender our future to the person who wronged us. Forgiving is not a way to *avoid* pain but to *heal* pain. Forgiving is done best when it is done tolerantly.

Smedes maintains that forgiving is the only way to be fair to ourselves. Forgivers are not doormats; to forgive a person is not a signal that we are willing to put up with his behavior. We do not excuse the person we forgive, we blame the person we forgive. Forgiving is essential; talking about it is optional. When we forgive, we walk in stride with the forgiving God. When we forgive, we set a prisoner free and discover that the prisoner we set free is us.

Forgiving is a remedy for our pain but not for everybody else's pain. It is not our pain until we own it. An odd notion: How does one "own" pain? We appropriate and acknowledge that we have it and take responsibility for it. Smedes advises us of five steps in forgiveness: 1) Think; come to as much clarity as you can on what actually happened. 2) Evaluate; what is an accident? A misunderstanding? Lying? 3) Talk; consult with friends or counselors, and get the counsel that is needed after having been damaged. 4) Feel; take time to be alone with yourself to contemplate and clarify your feelings. 5) Pray; forgiving is a tough act to perform when bad things have been done to us. Give yourself a chance to be alone with yourself and your spirituality.

Smedes maintains that forgiveness should not be done in haste. It has to take time. He suggests ten stages: 1) take your time; 2) size up the risks; 3) wait for a signal; 4) do it sideways—talk about other things first; 5) begin at the end–forgiving hits its stride when the victim wishes good things for the victimizer; 6) don't claim holy motives; 7) improvise;

8) make it short; 9) keep it light–don't be too dramatic; and 10) give the other person time to respond.

The power of forgiveness is formidable, Smedes says. The most creative power given to the human spirit is the power to heal the wounds of a past it cannot change. We do our forgiving alone inside our hearts and minds; what happens to the people we forgive depends on them. The first person to benefit from forgiving is the one who does it. Forgiving happens in three stages: We rediscover the humanity of the person who wronged us, we surrender our right to get even, and we wish that person well. We forgive people only for what they do, never for what they are. We forgive people only for wounding and wronging us; we do not forgive people for things we do not blame them for. We cannot forgive a wrong unless we first blame the person who wronged us. Forgiving is a journey; the deeper the wound, the longer the journey.

In her recent book, Kathleen Griffin (2004) discusses steps for individual forgiveness. She maintains that forgiveness is liberating, and those who are unforgiving carry a burden with them that diminishes their joy in life. She realizes that for forgiveness to take place, one must forgive oneself for being a victim. Griffin gives us various examples of the positive effects of forgiveness, including Michael Lapsley, an Anglican priest in Africa involved in the antiapartheid struggle. In 1990, South African authorities sent him a letter bomb, causing him to lose both hands and one eye. He did not want to be stuck in his state of anger for the rest of his life. Despite his suffering, he used the power of forgiveness to transform himself from a victim into a victor. Griffin concludes that those who have already been hurt and have forgiven their offender, or who have experienced forgiveness themselves for hurts they have caused others, are more able to forgive. Our study shows that these people understand forgiveness better and are thus better able to forgive further hurts as they go on in life.

Kathleen Griffin had been sexually molested, as had Suzanne Simon, who also found release in writing about her own molestation. Those who have been hurt, like these two women, may be motivated to study and write about it in order to liberate themselves. Simon and her husband and coauthor clearly take this approach. Their book (1990) offers explanations of forgiveness and discussions about its difficulties. Forgiveness can be a long process. There is self-blame involved; the victim may feel that they themselves actually caused the pain. Forgiveness consists of an internal process to seek liberation (Simon and Simon 1990). The Simons view it as a sign of healthy self-esteem to let go of intense emotions attached to past pain. They say that forgiveness involves accepting that nothing done to punish others will heal us. In order to heal, one must get rid of self-blame, victimhood, and indignation. Forgiving frees up all the energy consumed in holding the grudge and nursing wounds. An important first step in the forgiveness process is to refuse to deny the hurt or to downplay its impact. The victims will find themselves integrated when they are able to acknowledge that the people who have hurt them may have been doing the best they could, and they may come to the realization that if we are more than our wounds, then the ones who did harm must be more than their infliction of those wounds. It is possible that healing our wounds can result in being an acceptance of more loving relationships with people around us; it is possible to become closer, feel safer, experience more affection, experience more attention, as well as to feel more encouragement and validation of our self-respect. Suzanne Simon described her own victimhood:

> I reached the point where I no longer believed that being pretty or anything else about me drew my painful past experiences to me. Nothing I did made my father molest me. He did not have to do what he did—and because of him, my life was a mess. I was as powerless to change my life as I had been to prevent the abuse, I now thought. The situation was hopeless, I believed. I was not responsible for what he had done—or anything else. I had been victimized, and that was reason enough not to do anything more than just getting by (1990: 122).

This victimhood stage has many negative effects, from low self-esteem to the perceived need to victimize others. These effects occur until victims, as Simon said, "take off their blinders" and make room for a positive outlook, visualizing a different, brighter future. Smedes mentions the story of the German seeking forgiveness from Simon Wiesenthal, a holocaust survivor, for having committed atrocities in the village of Dnepropetrovsk. The German had murdered many Jews by trapping them in a framed house, dowsing the house with gasoline, and setting fire to it. When people jumped out of the windows, he and other soldiers shot them. Wiesenthal could not forgive him, because he felt that only the victims could forgive.

Patterson and Roth (2004) address the important question, is forgiveness possible after Auschwitz? And if so, how can the victims who are dead forgive those perpetrators who are still alive? Thus, it raises a quandary: perhaps forgiveness is not possible. Haas (2004) addresses forgiveness from the Jewish perspective, citing the famous Jewish philosopher Maimonides, who maintained, "For one who sins against his fellow and his fellow dies before he asks forgiveness of him, he is to bring ten people and stand at the grave of the victim, and say in front of them, 'I have sinned against the LORD, God of Israel, and against so-and-so by doing such-and-such,' [such as mass murder]. And if he owes him recompense, he returns it to his heirs, and if he does not know who the heirs are, he gives the recompense to the court and makes confession" (9). There are some victims of the Holocaust who have forgiven the Nazis their atrocities. For instance, Sidney Finkel, a Holocaust survivor who went through hell in various concentration camps, has since forgiven the Nazis for the trauma he experienced. "I began the unthinkable process of forgiving the German people, and it has released me."[29] Another example of forgiveness is the recent Virginia Tech massacre. Christine Hauser—in her article published in 2007, titled "Virginia Tech Sets Out to Preserve Objects of Grief, Love, and Forgiveness"[30]—describes several students' reactions to the shooter, Seung Hui Cho, who murdered 32 people, including students and faculty at Virginia Tech in April of 2007—and then turned the gun on himself. The students are quoted in the article as saying, "Dear Cho, you are not excluded from our sorrow in death, although you thought you were excluded from our love in life." Another student wrote three words, "I forgive you" (A17).

Smedes believes if we concentrate on getting even, we will never see an end to cruelty and violence. There is no chance that Muslims will get even with the Serbs, or that the Bloods will get even with the Crips. The more likely scenario is that in following the lure of vengeance and retribution, they will kill each other until all are dead, which does not resolve anything. We have to break the chain of retribution and start thinking about forgiveness.

Likewise, philosophers such as Emmanuel Levinas and Paul Ricoeur imply that forgiving does not mean forgetting; but if we refuse to forgive, we may block a brighter future and any relation between the offspring of the harmed and the harm-doer. As I have maintained, some acts are unforgivable, but perhaps we need to look at the offspring of victims and victimizer, who may have an obligation or moral authority to have an honest conversation about the tragedy affecting their families and subsequently themselves. This notion that only the victims can forgive gets us nowhere when the victims are dead. Pollefeyt (2004) speaks about *substitute forgiveness*, meaning that the descendants of the victims may have to get involved in forgiveness. He says, "I believe, however, that it is as illogical to refuse forgiveness in the name of the victims as it is to grant forgiveness in their name. Refusing to grant forgiveness is also a way of speaking in the name of the victims. Such acts are inappropriate attempts to 'manage' history"(65). Pollefeyt suggests that an intergenerational bond may be formed between victims and victimizers. One should not blanket the entire German population as those who were perpetrators and murderers of Jews. One reason offered is that offspring of both the perpetrators and the victims were born after the Holocaust; neither were involved in the event. Goodstein (2000) suggests that the document, *Dabru Emet: A Jewish Statement on Christians and Christianity*, which was signed in 2000 by Jewish leaders of all ranks, may be a hopeful step in the direction of reconciliation.[31]

To further emphasize the importance of offspring leading the way to forgiveness, authors Ervin Staub and Laurie Anne Pearlman (2001) believe the incorporation of offspring in education is a step in the right direction. If the offspring of Jewish Holocaust survivors share the same schoolrooms as German descendants, through mutual learning and understanding they may be able to begin the process of reconciliation. The authors' emphasis upon this incorporation of offspring into mixed groups stems from their research in Rwanda, where they observed that the truth telling of victims of the Rwandan genocide seemed to aid the forgiveness and reconciliation process after decades of political unrest between the Hutu and Tutsi.

Truth telling as a path leading to forgiveness can be eminently practical, as in Nelson Mandela's implementation of the Truth and Reconciliation Commission in postapartheid South Africa. There, the first step in forgiving is speaking honestly about what has happened and taking responsibility for doing wrong. Forgiveness is the price of reunion; it requires honesty about the person who wounded us and weighs future possibilities if one forgives or remains angry. Smedes says:

> The heart of my answer to the complaint against forgiving is that forgiving is the only way to get ourselves free from the trap of persistent and unfair pain. Far from being unfair, it is the only way for a victim to be fair to himself or herself. Far from being a dishonest denial of reality, forgiving is not even possible unless we own the painful truth of what has happened to us. Far from being alien to our human nature, forgiving dances to the melody of our own true humanity (Smedes 1996: 62-63).

Forgiving serves the forgiver and forgiven as a kind of reciprocal act. Forgiving must heal our pain before it helps the person we forgive. The act of forgiving is a wish for our perpetrator to heal as well. For those who are not repentant, forgiveness is a waste of time. It is important to understand that those who caused the pain and hurt are responsible. In this regard, Smedes mentions "the blame-share fallacy," which consists of blaming ourselves for having caused the victimizer to victimize us; for example, blaming the Allies for the Versailles Treaty of World War I, which crashed Germany's economy and sparked World War II.

Arie Nadler and Tamar Saguy (2004) discuss what it would take to end conflict between nations. They maintain that apology alone may not be enough. As in interpersonal forgiveness, it is necessary to first build trust between the groups, followed by social and emotional reconciliation. In some cases a simple apology alone may not work. An example might be in the conflict between Israelis and Palestinians, in which much hatred and mistrust has developed over the years. What is required is slowly and surely building trust, beginning with face-to-face contacts between leaders, followed by other trust-building activities between people, organizations, and associations of both groups. Nadler and Saguy conclude that trust is a necessary condition to lead to the resolution of conflict.

Intergroup Forgiveness

In August 1995, the Prime Minister of Japan, Tomiichi Murayama, gave a "heartfelt apology" for the brutal crimes his country committed during World War II. The question naturally arises: Can a national leader ask for forgiveness for an entire nation? We conclude it is possible, because leaders represent groups that were perpetrators of the harm, even though not every member of the group agrees. Even if all the individuals who perpetrated the wrongs are dead, and none of the current group members are in any way responsible for these past wrongs, the leader can still take the moral high ground on behalf of the group. This can lead to the elimination of hatred and ultimately to reconciliation. Hatred is one of the most basic human emotions and is frequently justified, but it also proves to be a very persistent obstacle to forgiveness and reconciliation.

Forgiveness is not about reunion, nor does forgiving obligate us to go back to previous situations. Forgiveness does not necessarily mean restoring relationships. Smedes maintains that we must have an inner push to forgive, and that with some people or in some situations, it is not possible. He cites a story from Fyodor Dostoevski's book *The Brothers Karamazov*, about a young boy, the son of a poor peasant woman, who throws pebbles at a cruel landowner's dogs. The landowner, wanting to teach the boy a lesson, sets his vicious dogs on the child, and they tear him to pieces. How can a mother forgive someone for this?

Christina Montiel (2002) maintains that much of the discourse on public forgiveness actually addresses private forgiveness and calls for the development of ideas and practices for public forgiveness in the social arena. Social political forgiveness occurs when all members of the group of offended people engage in the forgiveness process in relation to another group that is perceived to have caused a social hurt or offense. Montiel writes that "Public forgiveness requires sensitivity to the historical, cultural, and political contexts of both conflicting groups" and "Collective forgiveness arises along with cultural transformations" (Montiel 2002: 271). When Germany apologized for the Holocaust, for example, it transformed its society as it introduced democratic institutions and changed its curriculum from dictatorial to democratic.

Intergroup forgiveness does not take place rapidly. It takes time, especially between unequal groups; the weaker group must not be pressured into a quick accommodation. Healing has to take place slowly. This is especially true when harm has been done to the weaker group. Asking for forgiveness, in this social/political sense, must be performed by some prestigious authority, such as a president or another important leader. While the consequences of private and interpersonal apology are much better known, social/political forgiveness, or *collective forgiveness,* is understudied.

Social thinkers, such as Vaclav Havel and Albert Einstein, maintain that we need to rid ourselves of the destructive and straight-jacketed views of human relations that guide us to confrontation rather than forgiveness and reconciliation. A global revolution in the sphere of human consciousness and forgiveness is needed to improve human relations. A number of solutions have been suggested to bring about a more caring world. The Buddhist monk Thich Nhat Hanh (1993) tells us that what is needed is revitalization of established religions, enabling them to be more relevant to the changes in our time. Religions seem to have become stagnated in practices and rituals and have become hostile toward other religions.

We are concerned with how nations or groups can forgive those who have committed unspeakable mass murders or genocide. How can Jews forgive those who participated in the Holocaust? How do Armenians overlook the genocide committed by the Turks? It is much easier to forgive lesser crimes and hurts; it is not so easy to forgive major crimes such as genocide. Leaders can make a profound difference. Chancellor Willi Brandt of West Germany knelt in silent atonement at the site of the

Warsaw Ghetto. It may not have been therapeutic for the chancellor, but it raised global consciousness of a hurt perpetrated by the German nation. Forgiveness has the power of breaking the cycle of victimization and opens up space for political exploration that would otherwise be closed. Forgiveness is important toward reestablishing peace. The emergence of new sociopolitical institutions, nongovernmental organizations (NGOs), and citizen diplomats are opportunities for people to take part in improving international relations by facilitating helping, healing, and reconciliation. Also encouraging is the important push by some NGOs for economic, political, and restorative justice for all people on a global scale.

Henri Tajfels (1982; Tajfels and Turner 1986) developed a theory of group identity, which suggests that human beings divide the world into manageable categories to simplify matters. One of the ways in which we do this is to define and join groups. Our sense of identity depends upon our group memberships. This greatly eases the complexity of our daily interactions with others, because we are not constantly redefining ourselves. Instead, the underlying assumptions that go with our group memberships give us a ready-made and fairly solid framework for action. At the same time, unfortunately, discrimination, ethnocentrism, and hostility toward outgroups can be explained by this tendency to engage in categorization and identification. The notion of ingroup virtues and outgroup vices is implied.

There is a universal human tendency to form ingroups and outgroups: members of the "family" and strangers. The ingroups have positive attributes—they are civilized, they are cultured, they are friendly, and they are "us." Negative characteristics are attributed to the outgroup. Statements such as "They are really evil," "They get what they deserve," and "They are not my people" are common; such beliefs make it more difficult to forgive those who are in the outgroup.

For thousands of years, philosophers, theologians, psychologists, and others have attempted to explain the nature of evil. In the recent past, sociologists, social psychologists, and therapists have tried to give evil a social or cultural explanation, such as being the absence of love, compassion, or caring and the presence of neglect or abuse. Those suffering would manifest destructive ideological beliefs—such as Nazism, racism, or homophobia—by relegating the other to a status of being less than human and not deserving to live among us.

In their article on the willingness to forgive among adolescents, Genevieve Vinsonneau and Etienne Mullet (2001) report on their cross-cultural research on forgiveness between two young groups in France. They assessed willingness to forgive in a sample of 203 ages 15 and 16, adolescents from different cultures: French, Western Europeans, and a group from Maghreb of Islamic origin, residing in France. The aim of the study was to measure willingness to forgive under varying circumstances, and it noted the scarcity of cross-cultural studies on forgiveness. Some studies suggest stages of forgiveness, including revengeful forgiveness, restitutional forgiveness, expectational forgiveness, lawful expectational forgiveness, forgiveness as social harmony, and forgiveness as love (Al-Mabuk, Radhi, Enright 1995; Enright, Santos, and Al-Mabuk 1989).

Vinsonneau and Mullet (2001) included samples of Druze, Shiite, and Sunni Islamic communities and Catholics, Maronites, and Orthodox Christians. These studies consider the effects of a number of circumstances on the willingness to forgive, such as intent to harm, cancellation of consequences, religious and social similarity to the offender, apologies from the offender, as well as variations of these effects as a function of age, gender, and educational level. The sample living in France was mainly Christian and Maghrebi. France, though a very multicultural society, experiences quarrels and unrest between the two groups on a frequent basis. One of the main findings of Vinsonneau and Mullet is that willingness to forgive is not substantially different between the groups. Forgiveness is far from being conditional, the authors say. The apology factor appears to be extremely important; when remorse and apology are present, it is much easier to forgive. Willingness to forgive extends to the members of "the other" group. "The overall level of willingness to forgive was clearly different from zero, but not very high: among other lessons, forgiveness is far from being unconditional. The apology factor seems to be extremely important: when remorse and apologies are present, it is much easier to forgive. Willingness to forgive extends to the members of the 'other' group. All these results hold true, irrespective of the respondent's origin" (Vinsonneau and Mullet 2001: 267).

This ingroup/outgroup mentality, which is one ingredient of enemy-making, regards the outgroup as having negative attributes; this is represented by the old adage, "We are the Greeks, they are the barbarians." Theoretician Fritz Heider's (1958) theory aims to explain how individuals attribute causes to events and how these cognitive perceptions affect their motivation. In a nutshell, this theory divides the way people attribute causes to events into two types: One common way people explain causality of events is through external attribution, which assigns causality to an outside factor, such as the weather, or simply to the idea that "they" did it. Internal attribution, on the other hand, assigns causality to factors within individuals, such as their level of intelligence or other variables that make the individual responsible for an event. Generally, people are more likely to make external attributions that are negative. Thus, those people who are "bad" are not only bad, but they "bring it upon themselves." Ulrike Niens and Ed Cairns (2002), who conducted research on intergroup forgiveness in Northern Ireland, have used Henri Tajfels's theory to demonstrate that much of human social behavior is determined by social group memberships. Human beings are more likely to forgive acts of violence perpetrated by ingroup members than to forgive similar acts by outgroup members. Understanding the insights gained from this type of research is important, because they explain basic aspects of human behavior. If we understand these behaviors better, we might be able to reconcile with the enemies that we make or perceive.

On an intergroup level, it is not easy to initiate the process of apology and forgiveness. If a leader apologizes, it will not be very productive if there has been no change in the perception of those who have been degraded and offended. Skillful and compassionate mediators may find a way for both sides to understand each other. From this foundation a relationship may be established, leading to apology, reconciliation, and ultimately to peace and cooperation. We know that humans are enemy-making animals with infinite ways to hurt one another. Hurts are frequently unintentional and are caused by unforeseen circumstances, misunderstandings, or misinterpretations. People are capable of carrying grudges for many years, making forgiveness a difficult process to initiate. How, then, do we motivate people to reconcile and release their heavy loads of resentment and revenge?

Researchers at the Conflict Research Consortium at the University of Colorado (2005) conclude that there are important steps in the process of easing pain between harmdoers and victims. The first step is to establish or reestablish a relationship between the victim and the victimizer. A personal relationship offers the opportunity to progress beyond the problems that come with group memberships. This is usually not a simple task, and frequently a third party is necessary to get two conflicting groups together. Another goal of reaching out is to help deescalate the animosity felt by the harmed person. Some German chancellors apologized to other nations and groups that they hurt during the Nazi years. Reaching out at a grassroots level occurred when Jews and Arabs in the United States sought to create dialogue as a first step in fostering reconciliation.

In attempting to reestablish contact between harmdoers and the harmed, the first step is to build trust and respect between the groups. Once the parties sit at the same table, they can consider the problem. Harm must be acknowledged, anger admitted, and the offending side must genuinely promise to change its ways. At this point group members may perceive each other in a different light.

SUMMARY

Benjamin Franklin once said, "Doing an injury puts you below your enemy; revenging one makes you but even with him; forgiving it sets you above him." While agreeing with the idea that forgiveness shows that one is a "big person," we feel that the whole point of forgiveness is to attempt to restore balance in relationships, and that using the imagery of someone being "above" or "below" another is not helpful.

Frederic Luskin of the Stanford Forgiveness Project shows that forgiveness is teachable and can reduce stress, blood pressure, and anger; it can also help lessen depression and hurt and increase optimism, hope, compassion, and physical vitality (Luskin 2003). Yehudith Auerbach (2004; 2005) maintains that an apology made by a nation's leader to a nation that was harmed is one of the major ingredients in conflict resolution and reconciliation. For Auerbach, forgiveness means the forswearing of resentment and the resolute overcoming of anger and hatred that are naturally directed toward a person who has done an unjustified and unexcused moral injury.

Beverly Engel (1990; 2001), Enright and Fitzgibbons (2000), and Kathleen Griffin (2004) document the benefits of forgiving those who have harmed us. Luskin, Ginzburg and Thoresen (2005) and Luskin (2004) have shown a positive relationship between forgiveness and physical health. The rage that a victimized person carries is debilitating, and it is in need of being released from the burden this individual carries. Not so long ago, the discussion of forgiveness and apology had been assigned as a weakness or deemed the domain of religious functionaries, whereas now the culture of apology is much more prevalent. When the world between the harmdoer and forgiver is "right again," it may foster self-confidence and a sense of efficacy. In the medical arena, it may actually reduce disease, preventing pathologies that result in hostile feelings, depression, and hopelessness. Forgiveness also may provide a higher level of perceived social and emotional support, which may also include a greater sense of community. Lastly, forgiveness also may encourage self-healing, as well as help to refocus on the goodness and altruism that exists in the world. The forgiveness process helps us think in terms of higher values beyond the pain of the individual's ego.

There are literally hundreds of studies that show the power of forgiveness (Enright, Freedman, and Rique 1998). This proliferation of studies focusing on the positive effects of apology and forgiveness has begun to diminish some of the pessimistic views that have long held sway, such as with those who see only the "disuniting America," or the "fraying of America." Popular literature has taken notice of this trend. Jane Jacobs authored *The Death and Life of Great American Cities* in 1961. She said that the cities were being devastated by automobiles and showed a photograph of Manhattan, where thousands of cars occupied six lanes, bumper to bumper, hardly moving. Jacobs maintained, "This sort of culture and life will ultimately destroy us." Another pessimist is Samuel P. Huntington, who wrote *Who Are We: The Challenges to America's National Identity* (2004). He points out that massive Latino immigration threatens the fabric of American culture, and says, "this will be disuniting America." Huntington is known for his earlier book, *Clash of Civilizations and the Remaking of World Order* (1996), in which he predicts the cultural battle for supremacy between Christendom and Islam. These writers predict that our proud American, or Western, culture and democracy will cease to exist. We will suffer from debilitations of bilingualism and multiculturalism. America will be negatively transformed, according to Huntington. Other pessimists, including evangelical Christians—such as Tim LaHaye and Jerry B. Jenkins, in their *Left Behind* novels (1995 and others)—warn us that we are on this earth for the last days, and that Armageddon is inevitably coming.

While some social critics offer valuable insights into our rampant individualism, acquisitiveness, waste, degradation of the environment, and perpetual engagement in wars, many promote their personal causes. But a profound question, one we are not sure is answerable, is this: What is the answer to the gloomy pictures that we regularly see? We are bombarded by media reports of how we harm and hurt, and yet we are still murdering each other on a mass scale. In the twentieth century, we killed approximately 100,000,000 people: innocent men, women, and children, as well as soldiers. What causes this massive universal separation, and what can we do about it? We are not so naïve as to think there is an immediate solution. For thousands of years, since the dawn of civilization, we have been murdering each other and making enemies of the "other." But perhaps we are now evolving as our world shrinks. Are we willing to listen to new evidence that we do not need to murder and harm each other, that there is enough space and food if we are simply willing to become true neighbors on both local and universal levels? Is this an impossible dream? Perhaps, perhaps not; however many social scientists, philosophers, theologians, physical scientists, and others believe in this possibility. Perhaps not today or tomorrow, but there is an opportunity to change the minds, attitudes, perceptions, and hearts of humankind to see the "other" as a member of the human family. There is overwhelming evidence that almost all human beings are capable of feeling empathy, social responsibility, love, and compassion.

6

RECONCILIATION AND RESTORATIVE JUSTICE

Reconciliation has many meanings. Although most authors agree that it is a process intended to end animosity between parties in conflict, essentially it is the cessation of violence and polarization. Reconciliation implies a restoration of conditions prior to the rupture in a relationship.

When a rupture occurs on an interpersonal level, the consequences generally entail material or psychological loss and a feeling of betrayal, victimization, and loss of trust. The needs of the victim and offender often can be resolved in a process with positive consequences for both.

Walter J. Dickey (1998) relates the case of a youthful burglar who stole from a local church. A face-to-face meeting between the offender and the minister of the church helped the youth see his actions from a new perspective. The minister explained that churchgoers were now fearful of experiencing violence in the church, and the offender realized that his actions had more consequences than he had considered. His apology that day was genuine, the minister's forgiveness was sincere, and the pair worked out a community service sentence that involved the youth working for 100 hours at the church. Through this process, the participants met as sincere individuals and restored balance.

Dickey acknowledges that it is easier to seek vengeance and punishment than to do the extra work that a truly moral approach to restoring balance requires. He laments that in the American criminal justice system, vengeance competes directly with the possibilities for compassion, empathy, and forgiveness, and that "the latter are losing the competition" (1998: 116).

On an intergroup level, the ideas and concepts are similar. In broken personal relationships, and in contentious historical relationships between groups, the ultimate goal of the apology and forgiveness process is reconciliation. If a person or group apologizes, and the victim or offended group does not forgive, the process is one-sided and ineffective. No successful reconciliation can take place on that basis.

Reconciliation scholar Luc Huyse argues that reconciliation is both a goal and a process with three stages: achievement of peaceful coexistence, building of confidence and trust, and generation of empathy. "Empathy comes with the victim's willingness to listen to the reason for the hatred of those who cause their pain, and with the offender's understanding of the anger and bitterness of those who suffer," but it does not necessarily lead to a fully harmonious society. "Moreover, empathy does not exclude the continuation of feelings of anger. Nor does it require that the victim be ready to forgive and forget" (Bloomfield et al 2003: 21).

Reconciliation is a slow process and cannot be dictated, although some governments, and lately even international NGOs, feel they can induce the process of reconciliation. The Rwandan government has designated, in response to popular movements, more than 200,000 local officials to judge the guilt of those involved in genocidal atrocities. The Truth and Reconciliation Commission (TRC) process in South Africa was instituted by the government. The people came before the commissions and told the truth about their suffering, allowing aggrieved people to start the process of understanding and forgiveness and allowing perpetrators to take responsibility for their actions. However, sometimes reconciliation introduced from the top down may be resented by the victims as a smoke screen that prevents real healing.

Bloomfield, Barnes, and Huyse claim that there are certain main ingredients to the reconciliation process. Healing the wounds of survivors is a central need of the victimized group, as is justice, either restorative or retributive. Although retributive justice often plays a part in the reconciliation process, restorative justice embodies the concepts necessary to repair a broken relationship. Another key ingredient is the historical truth-telling and airing of grievances of reconciliation commissions. Finally, compensation for physical and psychological damages inflicted upon the victims must be made. "There are close links between these four mechanisms," (Bloomfield et al 2003: 23); these are shown in *Figure 1*.

Figure 1. Reconciliation: The Instruments

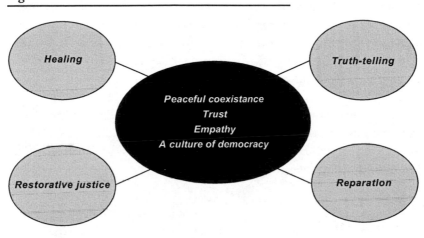

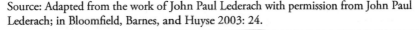

Source: Adapted from the work of John Paul Lederach with permission from John Paul Lederach; in Bloomfield, Barnes, and Huyse 2003: 24.

Empathy is the necessary precondition to repairing a relationship. Only through an empathic understanding of those who were or are our enemies may we begin the process of apology and forgiveness. Apology and forgiveness can be the foundation of a real reconciliation between parties on an individual or intergroup basis.

But there are still many potential pitfalls in the process. Those in power who do not want to make substantive changes to an existing system have sometimes used a reconciliation process as a smokescreen. A victim of apartheid testified to a South African Truth and Reconciliation Commission, "Reconciliation is only in the vocabulary of those who can afford it. It is nonexistent to a person whose self-respect has been stripped away and poverty is a festering wound that consumes his soul" (Bloomfield et al 2003: 22).

Trying to hurry the process is usually counterproductive. If the parties to a conflict are recovering from recent violence, they are generally too preoccupied with their individual troubles to pay enough attention to societal issues in a positive manner. "Coming to terms with human injustice is a deeply personal process, [touching] the cognitive and the emotional, the rational and the nonrational in human beings" (Bloomfield et al 2003: 32). Reconciliation must be homegrown. Although international bodies, such as the United Nations and other national and international NGOs, see violence prevention and reconciliation activities as their province, the people in the country experiencing the violence must come to embrace the process. "The credibility of the UN and of NGOs is often damaged because of an explicit disregard for this central rule that a post-conflict society must 'own' its reconciliation process,"although such agencies can be helpful by "supporting and monitoring local reconciliation programs, giving advice and training, and providing material resources" (Bloomfield et al 2003: 23).

Some scholars see reconciliation as a process that lies outside of the need for apology, forgiveness, and empathic understanding. Philosopher Susan Dwyer (1999) states that reconciliation may be possible where forgiveness is not. She writes:

> This understanding of reconciliation applies at the micro and macro levels. It makes the application of the concept appropriate, even in circumstances where there is no prior positive relationship to be restored. In this sense, reconciliation does not pretentiously masquerade as *wiedergutmachung*—making things good again. Coherent incorporation of an unpleasant fact or a new belief about an enemy into the story of one's life might involve the issuance of an apology and an offer of forgiveness. But it need not. Reconciliation, as I have presented it, is conceptually independent of forgiveness. This is a good thing. For it means that reconciliation might be psychologically possible where forgiveness is not (Dwyer 1999).

Dwyer's insistence on a "core notion" of "bringing apparently incompatible descriptions of events into narrative equilibrium" seems little more than a rewriting of history and a refashioning of narratives, personal or national, although she denies it. Reconciliation must confront the real causes of the rupture in the relationship, and though memory and perception of course play pivotal roles, the necessary end must be genuine repair rather than a simple restatement of the problem.

INTERPERSONAL RECONCILIATION

The objective of forgiveness is to help healing occur, which often leads to an immediate improvement in the emotional and physical well-being of the forgiver. Holding on to resentment serves only to disrupt one's life. Frederic Luskin conducted workshops on forgiveness, teaching people how they hurt themselves by holding on to resentment and disappoint-ment, developing a grievance story that ends up dominating their lives and preventing them from moving forward (Luskin 2002).

The opposite happened in the case of Amy Biehl, who was a Fulbright Scholar working on the transition to democracy in South Africa in 1993, when she was killed by a mob of angry young blacks outside of Capetown. Amy's parents, Peter and Linda Biehl, decided that instead of seeking vengeance for their innocent daughter's death, they would establish the Amy Biehl Foundation to help with reconciliation in South Africa (Amy Biehl Foundation 2006).

The purpose of apology is to restore dignity and social harmony in a society and among individuals. Susan Alter (1999) examines why apologies are necessary to reconciliation and what kind of apologies should be made and when. Forgiveness and apology can restore one's moral compass, she says. Alter maintains that forgiveness has to come willingly and cannot be forced. Forgiving indicates a basis for reconciliation and the restoration of trust. But even court-ordered apology and forgiveness processes may be helpful in restoring trust; if the parties recognize and affirm the importance of restoring their relationship and promise to work together, they can produce some meaningful results.

There are definite cultural imperatives in the reconciliation process. In American society, unlike in Japan, apology is not advised by the legal system, because it may be perceived as admitting legal guilt. Our legal system redresses wrongs and attempts to return the situation to its pre-injury status, which is exactly what the reconciliation process of apology and forgiveness can accomplish. But lawyers generally discourage official apologies, becasue they may end up being interpreted as an unlimited legal assumption of liability. Thane Rosenbaum, in his book *The Myth of Moral Justice: Why Our Legal System Fails to Do What's Right,* says, "One of the dirty little secrets of the legal system is that if people could simply learn how to apologize, lawyers and judges would be out of work" (Liptak 2004: 19). Rosenbaum concludes that treating people with respect and dignity, and acknowledging responsibility for harms one has committed, is not only the decent thing to do; it is practical and often actually prevents the filing of lawsuits.

There is a new movement in the United States and elsewhere to pass legislation amending the use of an apology as an admission of guilt. But apologizing and making a good faith effort to repair broken relations should be taught in kindergarten.

One doctor involved in the movement said:

> For decades, lawyers and risk managers have claimed that admitting responsibility and apologizing will increase the likelihood of a

patient filing a malpractice suit and be used against a doctor in court if they sue. However, this assertion, which seems reasonable, has no basis in fact. There is to my knowledge not a shred of evidence to support it. It is a myth (SorryWorks.net 2006).

California has already passed legislation protecting apologies, and several other states and nations are considering similar measures. The key to this movement is the idea that there is more to litigation than mere economic damages; there is often a greater need for acknowledgement of the hurt and acceptance of responsibility (Cohen 2001).

Formal apologies tend to be less individualized, meaningful, and effective, because the attempt is to address the harm done to a number of people who feel differently about it. Apologies from church or political leaders may be well intended but will be perceived differently by individuals. Some will feel that the apology is meant for them, and will feel that it is insufficient or not applicable to them; but some will be touched by an apology, and they will perceive it as a step in the right direction. For an apology to be meaningful and reconciliatory, especially when it already may suffer from coming from and being directed to a group, it must acknowledge and accept total responsibility for the wrong done. It is an expression of sincere regret and profound remorse, an assurance or promise that the wrong will not occur again, and a remediation and reparation that will have the best chance of obtaining concrete results. Timing of the apology is important; one should not wait to apologize because the injured person or group has been unrecognized and neglected for a long time. Apology must be done in an appropriate manner with an appropriate message and by appropriate individuals. Cultural sensitivity is also vitally important as to when one apologizes and how one apologizes.

From a mediation point of view, apology involves an exchange of shame and power. Carl D. Schneider (2000) argues that apology is involved with role reversal: the person apologizing relinquishes power and puts himself at the mercy of the offended party, who may or may not credit the apology. Restitution and reparation should follow. Apology in mediation is particularly important, because it means acknowledgement. Another important observation made by Schneider is that apology is a form of power balancing; the power is no longer in one person's hands.

Other scholars stress that reconciliation through apology and forgiveness should be broadly studied in positive psychology. Malver Lumsden (1997) maintains that breaking the cycle of violence requires that individuals, groups, and nations negotiate shared meanings, including coherent and compatible identities in patterns of social relations. "It is in a transitional zone between society and individuals that shared meanings can be 'informally' constructed and negotiated, and it is shared meanings that form the core of group identity and culture, as well as peaceful interpersonal and intergroup relations" (Lumsden 1997: 15).

Listening is a core skill in reconciling, and it can be taught and strengthened. Dr. Rachel Naomi Remen of the Compassionate Listening Project (2006) has found that there are five practices of "compassionate listening" involved in reconciliation. These are:

1. Cultivating compassion and a willingness to connect even when not in agreement;

2. Developing the "fair witness" by remaining neutral in conflicting situations;

3. Respecting self and others by developing boundaries that protect yet include;

4. Listening with the heart to create a spaciousness that allows divergence and finds a deeper point of connection;

5. Speaking from the heart with language that reflects a healing intention (Compassionate Listening Project 2006).

The apology and forgiveness paradigm has become clearly associated with conflict resolution and healing among both individuals and groups. A number of scholars have vehemently rejected Nietzsche's notion that those who forgive are merely weak and unable to assert their right to a "just" solution. On the contrary, we discern a very real strength in the processes of apology and forgiveness, not a weakness.

Truth is one of the most important ingredients of reconciliation—not the kind of truth that consists of simply retelling what has happened chronologically, but rather an open acknowledgement of the hurts sustained and a claiming of the moral responsibility for them. The foundation of reconciliation lies in moving beyond competing narratives to a truer understanding of the facts and putting those facts into a context aimed at reconciliation.

INTERGROUP RECONCILIATION

The reconciliation efforts we are exploring include explicit apologies on the part of the offending group to the group that has been offended—as Nicolas Tavuchis describes it, an apology of the many to the many (1991). Collective apologies function both politically and symbolically. Leaders apologize on behalf of the state or church, and their authority and position suggest that the apology has the support of the people they represent.

Research in the field of alternative dispute resolution indicates that apologies alone often do not bring about reconciliation; instead, there must be ongoing changes in behavior on the part of the offending group, and in many cases, reparations. We have explored the origins of the apology and how it is linked to additional steps towards reconciliation.

To understand reconciliation, remember that it is "a process rather than a state" (Bretherton and Mellor 2006: 95). Individuals or groups may have different reasons for taking part in a reconciliation process. We distinguish between peace-building approaches that manage conflict and improve relationships, and social justice movements that aim for a more equitable distribution of resources. While these can be complementary processes, there are times when these approaches conflict (Bretherton and Mellor 2006: 93). Peace founded on reconciliation is more stable than peace based on less complex processes or on short-term self-interest (Bretherton and Mellor 2006: 95).

Di Bretherton and David Mellor underscore the importance of making sure the goals of all parties are aligned. "In Australia, the process officially described as reconciliation has been adopted as the means to redress the past [but] the term is used variously to describe the need for, the strategy to achieve, and the goal of achieving better relationships between Indigenous and other Australians." They assert:

> For many people, the term [reconciliation] denotes the need to address a lack of positive and empathetic attitudes towards Aborigines and Aboriginal culture. For others, it refers to relationship building to promote harmony, in contradistinction to more adversarial means to restore justice, such as advocating for a treaty. The current Federal government sanctions the process of reconciliation, but the choice of the word "reconciliation" is a diplomatic one that can mean different things to different people. For those at the more conservative end of the political spectrum, it can mean the need to settle disputes and resolve uncertainty (e.g., about the

ownership of land), even at the cost of diminishing Aboriginal rights. The use of a word like *reconciliation* allows discussions to skate over depths of division in the community and to contain disagreements beneath a veneer of apparent progress and accord (Bretherton and Mellor 2006:94).

Japan has offered apologies to China through the years. The Japanese prime minister expressed "deep remorse" for Japanese conduct during the period before and during World War II. The Chinese wanted a formal, written apology and Japan consistently refused. It would be difficult and painful to write a nationally self-incriminating document about the horrible abuses the Japanese committed in China, including the rape of Nanking, where 300,000 people were massacred by Japanese troops. Japan refused to offer a formal apology, though it had offered apologies for its conduct during its occupation of the Korean Peninsula (Kristof 1998).

Sociologist Anthony Giddens, in *Modernity, Self, and Society in the Late Modern Age* (1991), notes that political life should imply direct emancipation of politics. He asks how we can remoralize social life without falling prey to prejudice. The more we return to substantial issues, the more we find moral disagreements; how can these be reconciled? If there are no trans-historical moral principles, how can humanity cope with the clashes of "true believers" without violence?

Joseph Montville, at the Center for Strategic and International Studies, and others have made forgiveness central to "two-track" diplomacy; that is diplomacy occurring outside of government by private citizens. Forgiveness has been visible in several countries, including South Africa, where the Truth and Reconciliation Commission was established on June 26, 1995 in Chile, the Middle East, Rwanda, the Balkans, and Chechnya. Reconciliation, a restoration or even a transformation toward an intended wholeness that comes with transcendent or human grace, expresses the result of a restored relation in behavior (Montville 2001). Forgiveness expresses the acknowledgement and practices of this result. In this sense, *forgiveness* is not so much a middle term as one that includes both justification and reconciliation (Marty 1997: 13). Our research shows that reconciliation is possible when there is a desire by both harmdoers and victims to repair the relationship.

FACTORS IN RECONCILIATION

Steps and stages have been proposed in the reconciliation process, and they are similar in both interpersonal and intergroup reconciliation efforts. The starting point is usually grief and loss for one party and guilt and anger for the other. Author Olga Botcharova, working at the Center for Strategic and International Studies (CSIS), a Washington-based independent research institute focusing on international affairs, deals with conflict resolution training. Botcharova has worked in Bosnia, Herzegovina, Croatia, Serbia, and Montenegro to resolve some of the issues in the Balkan States. Botcharova (2001) addresses the problem of official diplomacy and notes it has had less than 50 percent success in international negotiations. She relates its failures to three major factors:

1.   Failure to attend to the deep need for healing from victimization of parties in violent conflict;

2.   Strategies that impose foreign recipes for peace; and

3.   Strategies that appeal to the political hierarchy as the exclusive decision-makers.

Botcharova also notes that after experiencing the effects of aggressive action on the part of "the other," the victim can either stay in the cycle of violence by seeking vengeance or pursue reconciliation through empathizing with the other, what she calls "rehumanizing the enemy." The victim who chooses to stay in the cycle follows th "Seven Steps Toward Revenge" shown in *Figure 2*. These steps consist of 1) giving way to anger; 2) desiring justice or revenge; 3) creating myths and heroes and the "right" conflict history; 4) committing an act of "justified" aggression; 5) feeling injury, pain, shock, and denial; 6) realizing loss; and 7) suppressing grief and fears.

When the victims choose to take the risk of forgiving the offender, they can start on the path to reconciliation, through a justice process incorporating apology and forgiveness. She adds seven additional steps, "The Seven Steps Toward Reconciliation." These seven steps, are: 1) mourning and expressing grief; 2) accepting the loss and confronting fears; 3) rehumanizing the enemy; 4) making a choice to forgive and a commitment to take risks; 5) taking the first step in establishing justice through the admission of guilt; and 6) taking the second step in establishing justice by reviewing the history of the offense and jointly negotiating solutions.

Botcharova argues that there is a "critical role of two-track diplomacy in dealing with contemporary conflicts, filling the void left by the often rationalized, politicized, and militarized approaches of official (track one) diplomatic initiatives" (Botcharova 2001: 303). Forgiveness must be con-

Figure 2. "Seven Steps Toward Forgiveness"

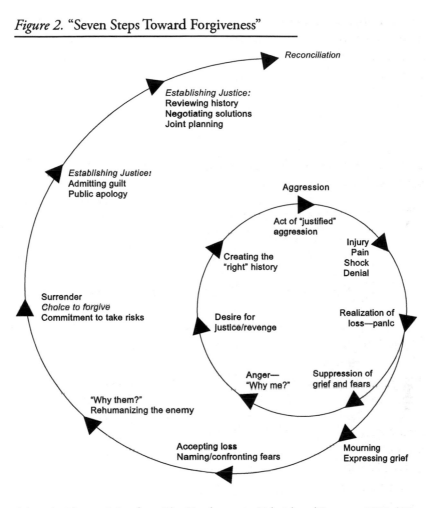

Reconciliation

Establishing Justice:
Reviewing history
Negotiating solutions
Joint planning

Establishing Justice:
Admitting guilt
Public apology

Aggression

Act of "justified"
aggression

Injury
Pain
Shock
Denial

Creating the
"right" history

Surrender
Choice to forgive
Commitment to take risks

Realization of
loss—panic

Desire for
Justice/revenge

Anger—
"Why me?"

Suppression of
grief and fears

"Why them?"
Rehumanizing the enemy

Accepting loss
Naming/confronting fears

Mourning
Expressing grief

Adapted with permission from Olga Botcharova in Helmick and Patterson 2001: 298.

sidered the practical strategic process in the diplomacy of peace building, she says. "Within this framework, 'outsiders' must be willing to go beyond 'fixing the problem' and to reach beyond the traditional political hierarchies, to create an environment that allows those hurt by conflict to find and nurture their capacity for forgiveness" (Botcharova 2001: 303–4).

RELIGION AND RECONCILIATION

We live in a world profoundly distressed and torn by a multitude of conflicts, many of which are deeply rooted in past acts of oppression.

Reconciliation efforts have been organized by national, state, and local governments and promoted by faith-based organizations. Until recently, forgiveness was dismissed as a "merely" religious activity, rather than a helpful personal and intergroup tool for reconciliation. The concept caught the attention of the secular world after serious conflict, when it was reasoned that it might persuade former enemies to find a way to live together once again.

We know that religious traditions have encouraged forgiveness. In Judaism, humans imitate divine forgiveness and consider it to be a moral obligation. But forgiveness can take place only when the harmdoer has apologized and genuinely promised a change in behavior toward the victim.

We often find religion central to both fueling and healing conflict. Suchocki, in *The Fall to Violence* (1995), views violence as "original sin" and places forgiveness in the context of a relational process theology that has both a social and a personal dimension. Sin, the violence of rebellion against creation and therefore, God and forgiveness, "willing the well-being of victim(s) and violator(s) in the context of the fullest possible knowledge of the nature of the violation," are social in nature (253).

According to da Silva, "Forgiveness is most associated with religion, which in turn tends to cast it in the realm of individual sinners making their peace with God. However, in the present-day discourse, forgiveness is also viewed as a societal event, whereby whole peoples or nations forgive others or receive forgiveness from others. Hence forgiveness has presently moved from the private to the public domain" (da Silva 2001: 303).

From a religious perspective, sacraments such as repentance, forgiveness, healing, reconciliation, restoration, penance, and holy confession serve as a model. The first core value is that we all live in God's world. Muslims, Christians, and Jews answer to the same God. The world is His, not ours, and His authority is not there to affirm our sectarian biases, but for us to become attuned to the presence of God in all of life. The second core value is the recognition that human beings are created in the image of God. "Human beings have been given sacred worth as their birthright and are therefore deserving of dignity and respect in all relationships," writes Islam scholar Abdulaziz Sachedina (Sachedina 2001: 109).

Narratives and Reconciliation

When people who have been harmed have the opportunity to tell their story, they can find peace for themselves. At the same time, they are strengthening or adding to a consensus of narrative. It is this consensus that eventually dictates how a group feels about events in its past. According to Julia Chaitan,

> Telling one's story, through oral or written means, has been shown to be a key experience in people's lives, especially those who have undergone severe social trauma. This has been the case for many of the thousands of Holocaust survivors who have given their testimonies in institutions around the world, such as Yale University, [13] the Survivors of the Holocaust Visual History Foundation project, and Yad Vashem, the national Holocaust museum and memorial in Israel (Chaitan 2003).

Storytelling and narratives have been used since the 1990s to help parties in conflict work toward reconciliation. These conflicts include some of the most contentious and long lasting; for example, between Catholics and Protestants in Northern Ireland, blacks and whites in South Africa, Palestinians and Israelis, and descendants of Holocaust survivors and Nazi perpetrators.

One international NGO has initiated a project aimed at reducing tensions in the Middle East by formulating a study group of Israeli Jews and Palestinians. The project takes a unique approach:

> Each side's narratives are being translated into the other's language, with blank pages left for the students to write down their thoughts, feelings, and understandings of the texts. The textbooks will be used in conjunction with class discussions and activities that will aim toward a reduction in animosity and hatred of the other (Chaitan 2003).

Mark A. Steele studied conflict resolution in the Balkan countries where narratives compete. He proposes four stages of relational expressions that need to be worked through before common problems might be faced across racial or ethnic lines. These four stages are "an expression and acknowledgement of a grievance, a clear understanding of the identity of the other, the acceptance of basic needs and concerns of others, and critical honesty and how we view our history and that of others" (Steele 1998: 11).

In South Africa, narratives were at the heart of the difficulties faced by the TRC:

> The hearing thus incorporated a number of different communities, each with quite different conflict dynamics and types of victimization. There was no obvious underlying cohesion to the various

stories told. Trying to construct such a unifying narrative or to engage victims about the meaning of their experience would be complicated. If one included the hundreds of other victims who made statements but did not appear at the hearing, the task would be even more daunting (Van Der Merwe 2003).

Van der Merwe goes on to explain how narratives of victims may differ based on their relation to the larger political situation:

> A third layer refers to national political struggles. Victims draw a connection between their experience of victimization and key national events or dynamics. They often demonstrate a deep political awareness, which allows them to describe their own suffering in relation to a particular phase or campaign in the broader liberation struggle, or in relation to particular political organizations and repressive state strategies. Some victims, especially those who were activists or leaders, place their stories mainly in this national context. They see their opponents not as independent actors but as agents of the apartheid system (Van Der Merwe 2003).

Narratives have driven conflict in the Middle East because they provide competing explanations for events. One observer distinguishes between the narratives of victimhood and those of reconciliation. She describes the hopelessness of the current struggle between Hezbollah and Israeli Jews, because Hizbollah is stuck in victimhood:

> Hezbollah presents…a Narrative of Suffering but without any complementary Narrative of Reconciliation. And I believe that the way Hezbollah presents this is largely representative of the way the vast majority of Lebanese people—not just Shiites—feel about the way Israel has treated their country for the past 35-plus years (Cobban 2004).

Many historians and political analysts point to narratives involved with nationalism or hypernationalism that reinforce the conflict between nations or groups. Narratives clarify the boundaries between groups. They contribute to serious conflict when the nation or group being attacked is put under some kind of strain, perhaps economic, or must ask more of its citizens or members. Past events have been woven into the narratives of the groups. The greater the responsibility attributed to one group, and the less that group accepts it, the higher the likelihood of continued conflict. The more clearly a victimized group remembers unresolved hurts, the greater the chance of continued conflict. How groups incorporate events into a shared narrative dictates the possibilities for peace (van Evera 1994). This helps explain the importance of truth commissions in creating a narrative that all may embrace, in which old hurts have been aired, grief expressed and understood, and responsibility taken. The complexity of these simultaneous goals explains the often tortuous path that reconciliation efforts must take. As in interpersonal reconciliation, adjusting our views of events from the past in light of new facts and subsequent apologies and explanations is painful.

Contact Hypothesis and Reconciliation

The idea of bringing together two sides to a conflict in an effort to help them better understand each other hardly seems radical on its face. Gordon W. Allport's (1954) hypothesis proposing contact as a necessary part of reconciliation has been accepted as fundamental to conflict resolution. If individuals from groups in conflict are brought together with equal power and status, having a common goal and under conditions conducive to building trust, they will start to reform their images and feelings about each other.[32]

Frederic Luskin (2002) partially bases his groundbreaking work on forgiveness on the idea of contact. A small group of Protestant and Catholic women came to Stanford and participated in six-week sessions. The indicators from the forgiveness session showed the participants felt better when they went back to their communities and were able to reduce the distorted images of the other.

Habitat for Humanity is one active NGO directly involved in building contact among parties in conflict. The head of Habitat in Ireland, Peter Farquharson, says, "We are at the front lines of working with organizations to define more clearly what effective peace building means." The founder, Nobel Prize winner Jimmy Carter, has had a profound influence in peace building through building homes for poor people throughout the world. Operating in Northern Ireland—where violent conflict has existed for the last 30 years, and where 3600 people, both Catholic and Protestant, have been killed—has allowed individuals from both sides to work together and even to build friendships. Commonly heard comments from participants relate a surprising discovery of each other's humanity. Habitat for Humanity is concerned primarily with the need for decent housing in places like Belfast, but in this case, notes one observer, "the more fundamental need in this battle-weary country is reconciliation" (Reeves 2006: 8). If the Peace Wall constructed by authorities to separate the warring factions was one approach to building peace in Northern Ireland, the concept of putting the people together to work on common problems like building affordable housing is another.

Another example that facilitates mutual understanding and friendship building is the Seeds of Peace, a camp in Maine, which now has satellite offices around the globe, where youths from groups in conflict can come together in peace. A main focus has been to bring together Israeli and Palestinian youths with the hope that living and playing together will enable them to develop trust and friendship. The heart of the program is the idea of "dialogue groups" that facilitate opportunities of learning about the other, with many other features based on the contact premise.

> Using acting, puppetry, storytelling, and music, a group of Israeli and Palestinian Seeds of Peace participants are creating a performance which is imbedded with messages they see as important... The show will be created throughout this year and performed starting next summer for family... [in] Arab and Jewish communities. Before or after watching the show, the children will participate in a "hands-on workshop" in puppetry or acting, led by Seeds participants, where they can express their own creativity (Seedsofpeace. org 2006).

Building on the links between participants, advanced efforts include language training, cultural education, and even the production of a common calendar showing the important holidays, festivals, religious traditions, and schedules for both Israeli Jews and Palestinians. These youths bring their experience back to their communities. The success of this kind of grass roots effort is often difficult to see, but if, as the name implies, the youths who are attending now become tomorrow's leaders, perhaps at a later date, the greatest changes will be noticed.

The film *Hotel Rwanda* helped many people around the world learn about the Rwandan genocide. Recently, Prosper Ndubishuriye—recognized by the Giraffe Heroes Project for "sticking his neck out" to work for peace and reconciliation in that war-torn area—was able to assemble over 100 Hutu and Tutsi youths to build simple homes for poor families from both tribes. Simply meeting each other was a major accomplishment for some, but working together to help solve the housing problem resulted in members of both groups recognizing the humanity of the other (Giraffe Project 2006).

People, especially children, are able to learn to interact with "the other" easily, and the result of that interaction is a new ability to frame the narratives by which they live. It is hard for a Hutu boy to think of Tutsis as "cockroaches" if they have helped each other build a home, or for a Palestinian youth to call for the extermination of Jews when they have acted in a puppet show together. Contact is certainly not the goal, but it is an important step in the reconciliation process.

Obstacles to Reconciliation

We have learned what factors lead to a successful reconciliation: A legitimate and widespread description of the facts of a grievance must be arrived at and accepted. Everyone must realize that damage was done and losses were suffered. According to Walter Wink (1998), "Truth is medicine. Without it, a society remains infected with past evils that will inevitably break out in the future" (Wink 1998: 53). Included in the need for truth is the idea of the acknowledgement of guilt or responsibility on the part of the harmdoer. The sense of moral responsibility on the part of the perpetrator is key to empathy between the parties and underlies the possibility of a sincere apology. Of equal importance, the victim must relinquish his "right" to vengeance or pure retribution. Empathy for the perpetrator is the first step toward reconciliation for the victim.

But there are many potential barriers to reconciliation. Parties to the conflict may not perceive the efforts at justice to be fair and impartial. A truth commission may become, or be perceived as becoming, a witch hunt; therefore both sides must sincerely wish to heal the rupture. All immediate causes for violence and dissension may not have been ameliorated in the apology-and-forgiveness process. A reconciliation based on economic need or immediate political necessity is bound to fail and may cause a backlash in relations. Parties to the conflict must look to the future as the basis upon which policy is made and steps are taken, not immediate self-interest. True empathic understanding of the other, and a balancing and equalization of competing interests for the future, are essential.

Although we may not find Susan Dwyer's discussion of narrative in the reconciliation process as proof of the insignificance of the apology-and-forgiveness process, her work is helpful in terms of discovering some of the obstacles to reconciliation. She makes a crucial distinction between what seems *right* and what is *possible* on the personal level:

Consider the black youth whose entire self-understanding has been built around resisting apartheid; or the white businesswoman who, although not an active oppressor, never objected to apartheid and comforted herself with the thought that the system couldn't really be that unjust. In such cases, the scope and depth of narrative revision required may be too great for some individuals (Dwyer 1999).

RESTORATIVE JUSTICE AND RECONCILIATION

There is no separating the concept of justice from reconciliation. There are many gradations of justice, some oriented toward reconciliation and others toward retribution. According to Audrey R. Chapman (2001), "Criminal justice involves the investigation, prosecution, and punishment of the leading architects and executors of serious abuses, but...it is frequently not a feasible goal in a transitional society." Restorative justice, on the other hand, seeks to heal a breach in a relationship. It seeks to "repair an injustice, to compensate for it, and to effect corrective changes in relationships and in future behavior" (2001: 266–67). Restorative justice is concerned with a healthy foundation for the future, although retributive justice can sometimes leave the victim in the trap of cyclical violence.

Recent studies show that Americans are still more likely to seek retributive rather than restorative justice, although this is starting to change. John Braithwaite (2006) relates an example of the new trend towards restorative justice. In North Minneapolis, they use the concept of "circles" for each defender. First, there is the interview circle, in which the program is described in detail, so that the young offender can decide whether to participate, and the crime is discussed. The second circle discusses the harms caused by the crime and what may need to be done to put things right. And finally, there is a celebration circle, in which a kind of agreement is reached about when the steps have been completed and justice has been restored; both victim and victimizer participate.

According to Braithwaite, New Zealand is the leader in restorative justice. They have recently tended to embrace a Maori custom that goes against the whole Western notion of exacting a punishment for every crime, employing it especially in cases where retributive punishment does nothing to either restore the victim or rehabilitate the offender. A one-to-one innovation is implemented, in which the victim and the offender, in the presence of a mediator, discuss the crime. An important attribute of restorative justice is *shame*. It is helpful for the accused to be confronted by the victim in the presence of his or her loved ones.

Studies have shown that restorative justice processes are perceived by offenders and victims as more procedurally fair than courtroom-style justice. "It may be that restorative justice is perceived as more procedurally fair because stakeholders are given a direct voice rather than having to channel their communication through the mouthpiece of a lawyer" (Braithwaite 2006: 397).

Braithwaite examines the Xhosa concept of *ubuntu*, which incorporates restorative, procedural justice; distributive justice—people with ubuntu "share what they have"; and relational justice ("We belong in the bundle of life"). Bishop Tutu says ubuntu is a holistic kind of justice, which may ultimately lead to a restoration of peace.

Restorative justice can be seen in a number of settings, including Australian enforcement of laws against corporate crime. Braithwaite says that restorative justice "can foster a public discussion that transforms the regulation of an industry or create a tax system that is more structurally just in the burdens it imposes on super-rich individuals and corporations in comparison to the poor." According to Bishop Tutu, restorative justice is more likely to result in "the restoration of broken relationships" (Braithwaite 2006: 401), as opposed to retributive systems where the victimizer simply goes to jail.

Building on the view of Thomas Scheff (1994), Braithwaite discusses "vulnerable emotions such as shame, fear, and grief, as opposed to aggressive emotions such as anger, rage, and self-righteous indignation" (Braithwaite 2006: 403). The result of vulnerable emotions is more likely to follow from "vicious circles of hurt begetting hurt into virtuous circles of healing begetting healing" (Braithwaite 2006: 403). The role of forgiveness is also important in restorative justice.

Apology also plays a role. Braithwaite observes that research has lagged behind theory, and theory has lagged behind practice. He cites Morrison as having developed a "new paradigm of emotionally intelligent justice" (Braithwaite 2006: 407). This idea is that justice should involve "opportunities to empower people to learn how to learn in civil society" (Braithwaite 2006: 407).

Just as we are beginning to see a culture of apology and intergroup forgiveness in the United States and around the world, we may discern movement toward acceptance of the idea of restorative justice. There are now more than 45 centers of restorative justice in the United States and also in other parts of the world, including the European Union, Australia, New Zealand, South Africa, and Canada. Increased interest in studying and applying restorative justice has followed the appearance of satisfied victims and offenders. The process seems to result in a greater likelihood of a genuine resolution of conflict, reduced fear on the part of victims, and reduced frequency and severity of criminal behavior on the part of the offender. Mark S. Umbreit and William Bradshaw (2001) focus on the harm caused by wrongdoing, as opposed to the fact that rules have been broken, showing equal concern to both victims and offenders. Their goal is to involve both parties in the process of justice. This process can empower victims while responding to their perceived needs.

There is support for offenders who are encouraged to understand, accept, and carry out their obligation to the victim. Molly Ryan Strehorn (2004) shows that countries around the world are using restorative justice to heal relationships damaged by crime. The philosophy is based upon four key values: *encounter, amends, reintegration,* and *inclusion.* This holistic process brings justice back into the community and offers remediation for the victim and offender. Traditional theories of retributive justice and treatment offer the simplistic option of punishing offenders in an "eye for an eye" sense and generally fail to adequately address the needs of victims. The victims' active participation in defining the harm of the crime, and shaping the obligation placed on the offender, is necessary but often ignored when there is a focus on retribution. The restorative justice process helps to redefine the traditional and meaningful role of the community, which is responsible for supporting and assisting victims, holding offenders accountable, and ensuring opportunities for offenders to make amends. The offender actively participates in competency development. The major intended function of restorative justice is to enable and develop rehabilitation for the offender and to generate reconciliation between the offender and the victim.

Through reconciliation, community may be restored. For restorative justice to work, all the parties must learn to take the perspective of the other. Marilyn McNamara and Mandeep Dhami (2003) offer an interesting conceptualization of restorative justice. They see crime as a conflict between individuals that results in harm to both individuals *and* communities. Victims, offenders, and community members come together in a restorative justice process to repair the harm and restore peace. An offender's offer of apology and a victim's acceptance of the apology can promote this restorative process. An apology can take various forms, such as a polite expression of regret. The process involves the victim's receipt of a sincere admission of guilt; empathy then develops in the victim and victimizer. Besides admitting wrongdoing and offering restitution, the victim often seeks reassurance that the offender will not offend again. The authors present an interesting model of apology and restorative justice (McNamara and Dhami 2003: 8), which states that when the offender offers responsibility, he or she is remorseful and gets involved in restitution and forbearance. The effects on the victim might be fear reduction, anger reduction, vengeance reduction, increased self-confidence, increased self-esteem, increased feelings of safety, and a more positive perception of the offender. This leads to the acceptance of the apology and restoration and reintegration of the offender.

McNamara and Dhami maintain that "apology has to be commensurate with a particular hurt or offense and should be an expression of responsibility, remorse, reparation, and forbearance" (2003: 9), and it must emphasize the important role of empathy in the apology/forgiveness process. They conclude that the restorative justice process offers offenders the opportunity to accept responsibility, feel remorse, make amends, recover their self-esteem, and refrain from such antisocial action in the future. The offender also may reintegrate into society with a restored social identity.

Julie J. Exline, Everett L. Worthington, Jr., Peter Hill, and Michael E. McCullough (2003) address aspects of the relationship between forgiveness and justice. Why are individuals motivated to choose restorative justice? Some find in forgiveness and restorative justice "warmth-based" virtues like compassion, empathy, and altruism. Others assign higher values to the "conscientiousness-based" virtues, such as responsibility, honesty, accountability, and duty. In many situations, the authors say, warmth-based virtues and conscientiousness-based virtues should complement each other. Individuals who are more altruistic and empathic are likely to perceive restorative justice as important to reconciliation and will value reconciliation. The authors conclude that psychologists and social scientists should understand the interface between forgiveness and justice.

If a goal of our justice system is to restore community and heal the relationships broken or bent by crime, the concept of restorative justice must be considered. The main distinction between retributive and restorative justice is that retributive justice is assessed by the extent to which the retributive act measures up to the past wrongs, and restorative justice orients toward the future. The contributions of restorative justice are evaluated through the process of individual and community healing. Restorative justice also serves the dual purpose of restoring a sense of fairness between the victimized individuals and their offenders, while establishing fairness and social equity between groups. Both of these goals are equally important as elements of healing. A process of restorative justice, encompassing both true apology and genuine forgiveness, seems to be necessary for successful reconciliation.

Gordon Bazemore has emphasized the importance of restorative justice. In his article "Restorative Justice and Earned Redemption: Communities, Victims, and Offenders Reintegration" (1998), he discusses how different cultures deal with crime and restorative justice, focusing on crime and justice in New Zealand and Japan. Like Christina Montiel (2002), Bazemore accentuates the need to pay attention to the personal level and the sociopolitical level. He argues that active participation in defining the harm of the crime helps to shape the obligations placed on the offender. The community is responsible for supporting and assisting victims, holding offenders accountable, and ensuring opportunities for offenders to make amends. Many juvenile justice professionals argue that our goal must be to restore community. Restorative justice programs can encourage this by providing ways for offenders to earn funds for restitution, developing creative and restorative community service options, engaging community members in the processes, and educating communities on their roles. This develops new roles for young offenders to develop and practice competency, assesses and builds on youth and community strengths, and develops partnerships and relationships. Public safety is enhanced through the process of developing a range of incentives and consequences to ensure offenders' compliance with supervision objectives, assisting schools and families in their efforts to control and maintain offenders in the community, and increasing the prevention capacities of local organizations.

COMMISSIONS AND TRIBUNALS

Truth commissions are becoming increasingly common in states and areas emerging from sectarian violence (Chapman 2001: 257)[33] and are generally composed of leading citizens carefully selected and vetted. They must meet political needs both inside the state and in the world community to have credibility and legitimacy. Archbishop Desmond Tutu observed that truth commissions must be a "third way, or compromise between the Nuremburg trials at the end of World War II or the prospective International Criminal Court and blanket amnesty or national amnesia." The effectiveness of truth commissions comes from the accountability and acknowledgement they can offer and the ability to frame an event so that it can be incorporated into a new, impartial narrative acceptable to all sides emerging from a conflict (Chapman 2001: 258). This makes it crucial for the commission to balance truth and reconciliation. If the intent is simply to punish those guilty of crimes, the truth commission will be perceived as a prosecutorial tribunal, which will seriously impair reconciliation efforts. Any commission that too easily grants amnesty to guilty participants in atrocities also suffers from a lack of legitimacy.

The International Criminal Tribunal on the Former Yugoslavia (ICTY) was established to reconcile the country after the brutal atrocities committed during the war. There were serious doubts that the successor states would be able or willing to prosecute guilty parties, and there was a need to channel the widespread grief and anguish of the victims. Michael Humphrey (2003) writes that in Bosnia, reconciliation meant the ability to work through the recent events, putting the past behind and finding a way for all to live together again.

Olga Botcharova (2001) makes the key distinction about those areas emerging from conflict: they can either run through the cycle of vengeance or go through the process of forgiveness aimed toward an overarching reconciliation. When those who perceive themselves as victims of others prefer vengeance, the "justice" produced merely changes the position of the parties to the conflict: the victim stands in the position of aggressor, and the guilty party is in the position of the harmed. This cycle can be repeated endlessly. Reconciliation can occur only in cases in which the hurt people are willing to throw off old baggage, abandon vengeance, and accept the enemy as an equal. Finding empathy for the victimizer is essential to reconciling fractured relations.

The ICTY is an example of the new international strategy of individual nation-states—established international entities like the U.N., and, increasingly, international NGOs—to stop violence and help restore peace and achieve national reconciliation through restorative justice.

THREE AFRICAN APPROACHES TO RECONCILIATION AFTER HUMAN RIGHTS ABUSES

According to Lyn Graybill and Kimberley Lanegran (2004), one of the main problems facing Africans and African nations today is people getting along with former enemies in past interstate and intrastate conflict. The recent focus on attempting reconciliation (restorative justice) instead of mere punishment (retributive justice) among many African nations represents an innovative approach.

Three African nations recently attempted to reconcile internal dissension and violence. South Africa, Rwanda, and Sierra Leone chose different paths to find reconciliation for their people, although all chose to incorporate the idea of restorative justice into their reconciliation methods. South Africa had to deal with 25 years of human rights abuses and violent conflict. Its leaders chose to establish a Truth and Reconciliation Commission as a mechanism to bring the abuses and crimes to the light of day. Rwanda chose to use the United Nations in a more retributive process of bringing leaders of the massacres to justice. Sierra Leone trod both paths by establishing a criminal court for those most directly responsible for abuses and a truth and reconciliation commission for a more general airing of grievances.

South Africa

For 45 years of apartheid, and 30 years of struggle between the African National Congress and the white-dominated government of South Africa, thousands of atrocities were committed. Nelson Mandela was elected president in the elections of 1994, and discussion began about a national truth and reconciliation commission. Leaders of both sides realized that for reconciliation to occur in South Africa, perpetrators needed to repent and victims to forgive. The Truth and Reconciliation Commission (TRC) was established in 1995 to investigate human rights violations occurring between 1960 and 1994. It established committees, the Human Rights Violations Committee and the Amnesty Committee, each with its jurisdiction for pursuing perpetrators, and the Reparations and Rehabilitation committee to design a reparation program. Both justice entities had powers of search and seizure, subpoena, and a witness protection program.

Perpetrators were offered amnesty in exchange for full disclosure of past crimes. The goal was to document, as completely as possible, the atrocities of that period to facilitate the collective healing of the nation and to allow a smooth transition from apartheid to democracy. More than 23,000 people testified in open court, including 2000 victims and witnesses. South African media was saturated with coverage of the testimony, and the TRC held public hearings on a series of topics.

Because full public testimony was required of those seeking amnesty, it was clear that only those who reasonably feared prosecution would come forward. This seemed to spur applications for amnesty, although some trials of major figures that ended in acquittal must have encouraged others to opt out, including most of the top apartheid-era political officials and most of the top army and police commanders. Another issue was improper use of the amnesty system. Of the approximately 7000 people who applied for amnesty, many were common criminals attempting to convince the committee that their crimes were politically motivated. Few applicants were top leaders of the apartheid system: nearly half were from the African National Congress. Contrition was not a requirement for amnesty; many individuals seeking amnesty did not apologize for their actions. Of the 7000 applicants, about 1000 acknowledged their responsibility and were granted amnesty and reintegration back into society.

Most analysts view the South African TRC as an ambitious, even daring, success. The crimes committed over the decades were vicious, and the effects were felt across a wide spectrum of the population. That black and colored South Africans offered a violent resistance to apartheid both complicated and simplified matters. It was harder to simply blame the perpetrators of the crimes, but it was perhaps healthier for both sides to realize that each had its atrocities and criminals. The legitimacy enjoyed by the TRC, and the fact that criminals faced serious prison time if they did not avail themselves of the amnesty offer, gave the true impression that it was an effort to reconcile the sides, rather than a retributive effort to punish one side only. Although many major figures were not prosecuted or were acquitted in controversial trials, hope remains that others will still face justice for their crimes. The TRC, in its 1998 report, included recommendations for concluding the process.[34]

Rwanda

In contrast to the South African model of restorative justice, Rwanda's leadership sought retributive justice for those responsible for and taking action in the genocide. The Rwandan Patriotic Front had politically defeated the interim Hutu government and was under no pressure to compromise with outside influences. The religious-redemptive model of forgiveness and reconciliation was severely undermined by the implication of religious leaders in the genocide. Rather than acquiescing to international calls for truth and reconciliation commissions, Rwanda asked the United Nations to assist in repairing and overhauling the traditional criminal justice system, and more than 100 justice-related projects have been funded by outside donors.[35]

But, by 1999, Rwandan government officials had recognized the importance of restorative justice, and they began to implement a traditional method of conflict resolution known as *gacaca*, although it was not widely used until November 2002.

Gacaca is a traditional form of conflict resolution historically used to settle disagreements and feuds between family members and minor offenses between neighbors. This community-based system administers justice with the intention of restoring harmony between the community and those responsible for discord. Jurisdiction and punishment are hierarchically organized. Tribunals composed of 19 local leaders and others of integrity are elected by members of communities. The next levels become more centralized and less tied to specific localities. The high number of local gacaca tribunals—about 10,000—offers the potential for a widespread dissemination of the events of the massacres, but its "localness" leaves many opportunities for the settling of scores among families or tribes that have little to do with actual events. Another advantage of the high number of local tribunals is that it allows a rapid resolution of cases.

Gacaca encompasses three primary components of justice: it rewards those who confess their crimes with the halving of their prison sentences, it highlights apology, and it emphasizes state-provided reparations to the victims of crime. The frank admission of crimes, and the truthful and detailed accounts by the perpetrators, help to air out grievances and lay the foundation for apology and forgiveness between perpetrators and victims and their families. The gacaca tribunals include a mixed judge/prosecutor function and do not stress competent legal representation, permitting the likelihood that innocents are coerced to confess and therefore fingered through the testimony. Community service may be offered as a substitute for some prison time, but only if the defendant has confessed and publicly asked for forgiveness for his crimes. Reparations for both material and emotional losses are made more immediately payable through the speed of the system and by the frank and full confessions often given in court. These confessions, including names of those killed or harmed and details of material losses, provide a legal basis for victims and their families to receive compensation from the victim fund set up by the government. A quick and efficient reparations system seems to help victims accept the process while blunting emotional responses to the crimes.

The gacaca system has proven to be somewhat successful, though some argue that the process has been politicized by the Tutsi leaders and has become merely a means of assigning collective guilt to the Hutus. Most victims and offenders seem to favor this system as the best way to relatively quickly lay the groundwork for a restoration of civil relations. Analysts and participants in the reconciliation agree that in Rwanda, there are no cheap, easy, or fool-proof solutions.

Sierra Leone

On April 21, 1999, after a long history of civil strife between the Sierra Leone government forces, Ecomog,[36] and the Revolutionary United Front (RUF), a massacre broke out prior to scheduled peace talks in Togo, a West African state near Sierra Leone. The peace talks were intended to close the eight-year civil war between RUF and President Ahmad Tejan Kabbah's Sierra Leone government, but violence ensued instead. After scores of civilians were brutally murdered, Ecomog forces were eventually able to contain the rebel uprising.

Sierra Leone set up a U.N.-funded Special Court, as well as a South African-style Truth and Reconciliation Commission (SLTRC). The entities were a mix of Sierra Leonean law and internationally developed and approved TRC procedures. The Special Court was responsible for those who bore the greatest responsibility for crimes against humanity, war crimes, and other serious violations of humanitarian law; actual perpetrators and their victims were heard in the TRC hearings. But the institutions had very different objectives. The purpose of the Special Court was to emphasize retributive justice, determining punishments for those involved in planning and overseeing the atrocities. The SLTRC was designed to promote reconciliation through a process of truth telling, apology, forgiveness, and pardon.

There were several positive features of the Sierra Leonean approach. SLTRC members were picked through an international consultative process in which all sides of the conflict, including the public at large, nominated judges with the finalists picked by the UN. This created a high degree of trustworthiness and a direct connection to the people, resulting in high legitimacy for it as an entity. As the result of an internationally brokered peace initiative, forces outside the country were able to form a counterweight to national interests that may have skewed the performance of the commission. Follow-up was built into the mandate, allowing for a tying up of "loose ends."

A primary concern was the lack of incentive for persons to testify before the SLTRC. The SLTRC resembled the South Africa model but lacked the power to grant amnesty to the perpetrators of violence. It was feared that prosecutors for the Special Court could use testimony as evidence against persons committing violent criminal offenses. Due to the lack of incentives to testify before the SLTRC, many former combatants hesitated to come forward in the early stages of testimony. As it became apparent that the Special Court was not interested in testimony, those numbers increased. The SLTRC was unable to address the needs of the major stakeholder groups—women and girls, children, amputees, and ex-combatants—it could only make recommendations to the government.

A Failed Attempt at Reconciliation: Mexico

In the southern state of Chiapas, there has been a 20-year human rights struggle between the Zapatistas and the state and federal government on behalf of the poor—in particular, the indigenous citizens. The Zapatista Rebellion, led by the *Ejercito Zapatista de Liberacion Nacional* (EZLN) was spawned by past injustices based on years of government expropriation of indigenous land, directly reducing the life chances of Chiapas citizens.

We have discussed the difficulty of the reconciliation process and some of the potential obstacles. Two African states we examined were partially successful. The recent Truth Commission instituted under former President Vicente Fox in Mexico is perhaps an example of a failed effort at using a truth commission as a reconciliation device. It can be characterized as the use of a truth commission as a political ploy in a situation in which the parties in power are not really interested in the truth.

Proposed during his historic campaign as the first successful challenger to the *Partido Revolucionario Institucional* (PRI) in Mexico for decades, Fox promised accountability, an end to impunity, and the "resolution of horrific crimes committed by the Mexican state against its own citizens" (Ross 2006). Six years later, when President Fox left office, those crimes remained uninvestigated. In fact, there have been dozens more "disappeared" individuals since the commission was created. The truth commission, known as Special Prosecutor for Social Movements and Political Crimes of the Past (FEMOSPP) was disbanded without making a final report. The effort, underfunded and ignored by government bureaucracy, resisted by the army and the police, and often run and staffed by the perpetrators of the crimes, was perhaps doomed from the start. Those in power in Mexico had no interest in airing grievances or reconciling. There was a massive though hidden interest on the part of many to hide the past, deny the crimes, obfuscate the facts, and let sleeping dogs lie. Angeles Magdaleno, director of the historical analysis section of the truth commission said, upon leaving the special prosecutor office for the last time, "The only truth is that no one wants to know the truth" (Ross 2006).

SUMMARY

We find a circular relationship among empathy, altruism, apology, forgiveness, and restorative justice; all are aimed toward reconciliation.

Figure 3

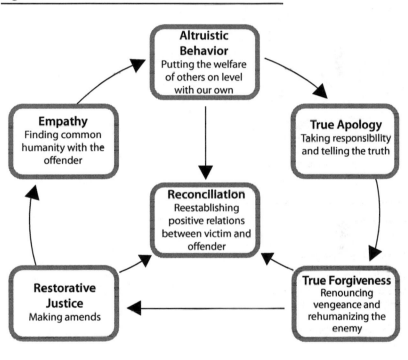

"To be social is to be forgiving," said Robert Frost, and "if we started counting each other out for the least sin, we'd soon have no one left to live with." There are many ways of increasing tolerance and empathy of people, starting with apology and forgiveness and continuing through a meaningful reconciliation. Many of the lessons we have learned through the study of apology and forgiveness between individuals are directly applicable to groups. Genuine interest in the process, airing of grievances, opportunity for contact and dialogue, rebuilding of trust, and the sincere processes of apology and forgiveness are similar in individual and group reconciliation.

Reconciliation is a positive social process and should be used more to help establish a more peaceful world. The alternatives to peace are bleak.

7

Collective Guilt, Apology, and Reconciliation: The Polish Case

The massacre by Poles of almost the entire Jewish community in Jedwabne was described in Chapter 4. The public revelation of the events in the book by Tomasz Gross evoked a heated debate. Thousands of commentaries and publications—not only in Polish media, but also in Western media—followed. Scholars and representatives of the general public shared their opinions on collective guilt and responsibility and on the official apologies made by the Polish Catholic bishops and especially the former president Aleksander Kwaśniewski. The debate was valuable for all who strive to reconcile immoral aspects of past relations between nations or other large groups.

In this chapter we will start by discussing the issue of collective guilt as it is seen by scholars. The second part of the chapter will report on the research we conducted in Poland with a nonrandom sample of 100 respondents. In addition, we interviewed two high-ranking persons, the former president of Poland, Aleksander Kwaśniewski, and the icon of Polish Jewery and the last living leader of the Warsaw ghetto uprising, Dr. Marek Edelman. We felt that these two prominent persons could add valuable information about the Jedwabne tragedy.

In recent years different nations, ethnic groups, and religious groups have started to consider their wrongdoings toward other groups (Barkan 2000; Oliner 2004). Barkan claims that since the Cold War, groups and nations have begun to examine their moral obligations toward each other and the hurt and harm they have done to their neighbors. This has resulted in increased research interest in the phenomenon of collective guilt.

According to Doosje and Branscombe (Doosje et al 1998; Branscombe and Doosje 2004), members of a given group may experience specific emotions in reaction to the actions of that group. Therefore, one may experience guilt on behalf of their group when the behavior of other ingroup members violates norms or values of either the group or the individual. Collective guilt reflects the remorse that is felt when one's group has illegitimately harmed another group and not repaired the damaged. Although collective guilt as a psychological experience does not need to involve actually being guilty, it is often grounded in the context of real misdeeds committed in the past by representatives of the individual's own ingroup. In this chapter we use the terms *collective guilt* and *collective responsibility* interchangeably, although on theoretical and/or ethical grounds, a person may be found guilty but not responsible (Baier 1991). However, as our research shows, ordinary people use both terms as equivalents.

Do Collective Guilt or Responsibility Exist?

There has been much controversy whether collective guilt or responsibility is a legitimate category that can be looked at as some sort of entity identifiable beyond personal experience to be described in legal, moral, or other terms. Let us start with historical instances of such debates. Colt Anderson (2002) thoroughly analyzed the history of the notion of collective guilt in the teaching of the Catholic Church. It is a topic that became particularly vital in the context of Pope John Paul II's apologies to communities harmed by members of the Church throughout its 2000-year history. The biblical book of Exodus proclaimed that God would visit the sins of parents on their children up to the fourth generation. The consequences of original sin were debated, and Christian communities often were found to be tainted with a real, long-lasting guilt inherited from past generations. Sometimes, even children of serious sinners—for example, the offspring of unchaste clergy—were considered to be carrying temporal guilt.

Larry May and Stacey Hoffman (1991) distinguish two basic, opposed approaches to collective responsibility. One argument is that collective responsibility is nothing but the aggregation of individual responsibilities of members of a group. Another is that collective responsibility, if it exists, is nondistributive in nature, meaning that the entire responsibility can be ascribed only to the group itself and not to its members individually. Most of the authors who study the subject seem to take an intermediate position.

H. D. Lewis (1991) represents the critics of the aggregate approach, who argue that no one can be responsible in the properly ethical sense for the conduct of another, and therefore responsibility belongs solely to the individual. "We cannot answer for one another or share each other's guilt (or merit)," Lewis writes, "for that would imply that we could become directly worse (or better) persons morally by what others elect to do—and that seems plainly preposterous" (Lewis 1991: 26–27). Other authors add: "If we all are guilty, then no one is." The latter notion stems from apprehension about the possible diffusion of moral responsibility by major perpetrators who ascribe responsibility to those who were not directly involved or who even actively resisted the wrongdoing.

One advocate of collective guilt, Karl Jaspers (1961), argued that there is a form of guilt which is based on who a person is and not on the person's actions. He called it "metaphysical guilt" and believed it is not necessarily equivalent to moral guilt (blameworthiness), but that it entails some form of moral responsibility.

> Metaphysical guilt is the lack of absolute solidarity with the human being as such.... This solidarity is violated by my presence at a wrong or crime....If it happens and if I was there, and if I survive where the other was killed, I know from the voice within myself: I am guilty of still being alive (Jaspers 1961: 71).

According to Larry May (1991) this sort of guilt arises from the fact that nothing has been done to prevent harm or at least to indicate that one disapproved of it. May postulates that "shame" or "taint" are moral categories more appropriate than "guilt."

There are two relevant issues to consider: The first pertains to the question of which collective may legitimately be called responsible. Democratic societies (Baier 1991), nations (Miller 2004), or even—under some circumstances—random collections of people (Held 1991) may be charged with collective guilt. The other issue is whether one can fully deny or diminish one's collective responsibility by condemning evil practices or by just dissociating oneself from the collective. Jaspers (1961) claimed that by disavowing crimes committed by the collective, people change that part of themselves that depends on personal choices or preferences. He believed such disassociating is enough to diminish a sense of shared responsibility for what other ingroup members have done. Others, like David Miller (2004), believe an individual may actively oppose such practices and still be legitimately considered responsible.

IN SEARCH OF CONTEMPORARY EXAMPLES OF GROUP-BASED GUILT

Collective guilt has become a hot topic worldwide. It seems no national, ethnic, or religious group may find itself free of substantial "moral debts" toward others. As Stephen Baskerville (1996) shows, the concept of collective guilt has existed for centuries and now plays a vital role as a political tool. Discussions on collective guilt or responsibility, especially for past wrongdoings, overtly or covertly pervade many intergroup relationships. We will mention just a few instances currently considered a legitimate basis to experience shared guilt.

- Abuse of colonized countries by imperial nations: relatively recent exploitation of African and Asian nations by Great Britain, France, Spain, and Portugal; earlier extermination of Indians in the West Indies, and semicolonial exploitation of former Soviet bloc countries by the Soviet Union.

- Persecution by religious groups, including the mistreatment of Jews by Christians or among Christian denominations.

- Interethnic atrocities: Hutu with Tutsi, Turks with Armenians, Chinese with Tibetans, apartheid in South Africa, and ethnicity-based extermination of Jews.

- War crimes: abuse of Chinese or Filipino women by Japanese soldiers; detention camps during World War II in the United States for Americans of Japanese descent; massive bombardments of civilian facilities by the Allies and the German Army; massive executions of soldiers by Soviets or the German Army; execution, promotion, or acceptance of extermination of civilians, such as Srebrenica in Yugoslav, Mai Lai massacre in Vietnam, and the atrocities at Shabra and Shatila in Lebanon.

Additional examples will provide some insight into the complexity of acceptance or rejection of collective guilt for the past. For example, for more than 50 years after World War II, Austrians have been trying to determine if their country was the victim of German aggression, or the co-responsible agent of war atrocities as an active partner with the Germans. The long-lasting national and international debates over Kurt Waldheim's and Joerg Heider's roles have revealed the painful relevance of the issue of national guilt in that country (Berg 1997).

World War II continues to be an unhealed wound in the collective memory of Germans, despite the fact that in the 1950s, Germany voluntarily launched a program of compensation for the victims of Nazi terror. (This approach was much different from, say, the Japanese policy of moral detachment from war crimes, like The Rape of Nanking.) On the one hand, organizations in Germany claiming properties lost during the forced displacement of Germans at the end of the war have been proliferating in Germany. On the other, those victimized by the Third Reich unceasingly remind Germans of their past. The debates culminated after Daniel Goldhagen (1996) published *Hitler's Willing Executioners: Ordinary Germans and the Holocaust.* He gathered evidence to argue that not only those in power, but also ordinary Germans, had been to some extent personally responsible for the Holocaust.

Kim Forde-Kazrui (2004) reports that currently in the United States there has been a new wave of debate on the legitimacy of affirmative action. Generally, there is no argument on the moral evaluation of slavery and discrimination of the African-American population. However, there is disagreement on the extent of collective responsibility of American society to improve present conditions for African-Americans. Recently, as polls show, even Western societies have dramatically increased blaming the United States government directly, and the entire American society indirectly, for events surrounding the invasion of Iraq and the "War on Terror." These include occasions of torture—so-called "extraordinary renditions"—a very high death toll among Iraqi civilians, and the unlawful status of the Guantanamo detention camp. It is recurrently said that the moral responsibility of a superpower is particularly large.

In Australian society collective guilt for the treatment of indigenous inhabitants of the country is a prominent issue (Pederson 2003; McGarthy and Bliuc 2004). Strongly varying opinions on the government's apology to those Australians, as well as to perceived non-indigenous responsibility for past mistreatment of indigenous people, have been pronounced.

TOWARD THE ADMISSION OF COLLECTIVE GUILT AND ITS CONSEQUENCES

Debates on the guilt of collectives are initiated either by the group itself, evaluating its past actions or nonperformance, or by external agents. Most often admission of collective guilt or responsibility results from pressures exerted by the persecuted group.

Several factors underlie the reluctance to assume collective guilt. When people are confronted with the ingroup's substantial mistreatment of another group, they may distance themselves from their group by either avoiding categorization or denying collective responsibility; they also can minimize the severity of the harm done. When these justifications fail or become impossible to sustain, people may feel collective guilt to the extent that the ingroup's past actions are perceived as violating the current moral standards of the group (Branscombe and Doosje 2004).

Furthermore, it is difficult to accept shared guilt if the group generally tends to perceive itself as a historical victim, rather than a perpetrator of recent events. This is the case to a large extent in Poland, which was recurrently exploited by neighboring nations for about two centuries. The other potential cause of reluctance to shared guilt is the fear of consequences. Fairly often the acceptance of inherited guilt entails facing demands for reparation made by the members of a victimized group. And a final obstacle is a sort of collective pride in the group, which significantly prevents admission of guilt, because part of a person's identity is based on his or her group membership. The desire to feel positive about the group will frequently result in exonerating explanations of ingroup actions. It is much nicer to maintain in schoolbooks, and in official and personal narratives, that one's country provided the colonized country with technology and legal and social regulations, rather than reporting on human casualties, unlimited greed of the colonizers, exploitation of the workforce and the country's resources, or theft of the art or monuments of the local culture. Confronting the difficult past is a real challenge for the leaders of communities and their members alike.

Self-righteousness of this type stems from the very nature of human identity. According to social identity theory (Tajfel and Turner 1986), a person's self-image consists of an individual and a group component. This implies that people mold part of their self-image in close relation to the characteristics of the social groups they belong to. Similarly, they tend to defend the moral aspects especially of the group's image, just as they protect their own self-image—which, if predominantly negative, hampers effective functioning and diminishes the individual's sense of well-being. There have been other factors identified as relevant for the emergence of a collective guilt experience: These include intensity of identification with a given group, level of interdependence of its members, and political preferences. Some of them will be outlined later in this chapter.

The recognition of past harm done is often accompanied by a willingness to make reparations in terms of some sort of compensation. Brian Lickel, Toni Schmader, and Marchelle Barquissau (2004) found that feelings of *collective guilt* predict the desire to make reparations for the ingroup members' immoral behavior feelings of *collective shame* predict a desire to distance oneself from the blameworthy ingroup event. Barkan (2000) names three possible methods of amending past injustices: 1) *restitution* refers to a return of whatever specific actual belongings that were sized or stolen; 2) *reparations* refer to forms of compensation for what cannot be returned; 3) *apology* refers to admission of wrongdoing, a recognition of the effects, and acceptance of responsibility for those effects.

RESEARCH ON COLLECTIVE GUILT OR RESPONSIBILITY

As we have tried to show, collective guilt, or responsibility, is an issue of vital importance for diverse intergroup relations, attracting some interest in theoretical considerations. Until very recently there has been limited empirical research on collective guilt in the social sciences. Let us present a few studies that demonstrate some lines of the relevant investigation.

Diane Kappen (2001) examined the effectiveness of an ingroup member versus an outgroup member in producing feelings of *collective guilt*. She found that attempts aimed at acknowledgment of *collective guilt* are more successful when made by ingroup members; outgroup members' influences appeared likely to be more harmful than beneficial.

In a study by Chi-yue Chiu and Ying-yi Hong (1992), the collectivistic nature of Chinese culture was identified as an important context for understanding individual and collective responsibility among Chinese Hong Kong businessmen. Based on ratings of scenarios, the authors found that responsibility for a protagonist's misdeed tended to be generalized to members of the protagonist's collective. The target, to whom collective responsibility was attributed, varied with the context in which the act was carried out.

The shootings of high school students in Littleton, Colorado, inspired Brian Likel, Toni Schmader, and David Hamilton (2003) to analyze the perception of collective responsibility for the event. The researchers assessed perceptions across a range of groups, including the shooters' parents and the shooters' peer group. The research showed that perceptions of a target group's identity predicted judgments of collective responsibility. Encouraging or facilitating the event, failing to prevent it, and perceived authority significantly affected judgments of collective responsibility.

Richard Harvey and Debra Oswald (2000) examined whether expos-
ing Caucasian Americans to collective guilt and shame-inducing stimuli
by means of showing them civil rights videos would lead to heightened
support for African-American programs. Findings showed that Caucasians might react antisocially to guilt-and-shame-inducing situations
—here suppressing their support for African-American programs—or
they might react prosocially, depending on whether their personal integrity would be endangered or reaffirmed.

In two crucial studies (Doosje et al 1998), it was proved that people
who have not personally harmed an outgroup, but who belong to a
group that has acted in a harmful way toward the other, may feel guilty.
When subjects have personally harmed an outgroup, they feel relatively
guilty, and their group's behavior does not influence these feelings.
Other research participants were asked to indicate their level of national
identification with being Dutch. It turned out, paradoxically, that low
identifiers—as compared with high identifiers—felt more guilty and
were more willing to compensate the people of a former Dutch colony.
In turn, the level of willingness to compensate was a function of feeling
group-based guilt.

Naturalistic Conception of Collective Guilt

The research described in this next section explores naturalistic conceptions of collective guilt. It is assumed here that the analysis of naturalistic
notions—that is, ones embedded in common understanding and ordinary
language—can yield ideas of collective guilt operating in everyday life but
not necessarily overlapping with current research and ethical theorizing.
Particular interest was focused on the arguments people employ to defend
or reject legitimacy of the notion of collective guilt when they belonged
to either a victimizing or victimized group.

Method

This part of the research was conducted in Poland with a nonrandom
sample; controls were put in place relative to participants' attitudes
toward religion.[37] Out of 100 participating subjects, 51 were Christians
(27 females, 24 males), 17 persons identified themselves with Judaism
(9 females, 8 males), and 21 were non-believers (11 females, 10 males).
Moreover, 11 participants (4 females, 7 males) did not specify their
religious affiliation. Participants' ages varied between 20 and 58 years
(the average age was 31). The educational level was above the national

average (70 percent of participants had some college or a higher degree). Most participants were from large Polish cities.

The questions administered to the subjects were derived from the Apology-Forgiveness Interview Schedule by Oliner (2004). Two of the questions, one explicit and the other implicit, implying collective guilt were taken into consideration: 1) Has there ever been anything like collective guilt of a nation, citizens of a state, or of a religious group? Give reasons for your answer. 2) Have you heard about the Pope John Paul II apology to the Jewish people? How did you react to the apology?

Most participants—93 percent—were contacted by e-mail and returned their responses to the researchers by e-mail. Other participants were interviewed personally. Person-to-person interviews were substantially more lengthy; they reflected both unprompted and prompted responses to the questions. On the other hand, e-mail versions provided more anonymity and therefore are believed likely to yield more sincere responses.

Results and Discussion

The most important issue for us here was whether people who are not professionally dealing with collective guilt/responsibility accept or reject collective guilt and what sort of rationales they use in either case. As many as 44 percent of interviewed subjects denied collective guilt, but 43 percent favored the concept. Gender of the respondents did not matter in this respect, which is congruent with earlier Polish findings (Wolniewicz 2002). As many as 13 percent were not explicit enough or were unsure about the concept of guilt. Of those with a specified attitude toward the concept, roughly two thirds of subjects identifying themselves in religious terms as Jews accepted the notion, but only 48 percent of Christians and 44 percent of nonbelievers accepted the existence of collective guilt.

First, the views of those who rejected the notion of collective guilt are considered in the arguments that follow. Qualitatively different relevant reasons have been shown; sometimes we have provided exemplary statements of the subjects to highlight the content of the given argument.

TYPES OF ARGUMENTS PROVIDED AGAINST COLLECTIVE GUILT/RESPONSIBILITY

- There is no other responsibility than that of the individual (an individual never equals the whole; guilt is by nature individual;

collective responsibility makes all people equally moral or immoral).
Example: *"Everyone is unique."*

- Decisions are not made by all group members.
  Example: *"The worst decisions have never been undertaken by an entire group."*

- The group leaders are guilty. In attributing guilt to all group members, they would absolve their responsibility.
  Example: *"The leaders are guilty, because they direct individuals in the group."*

- All human actions are context specific, and there cannot be any transfer of guilt across time.
  Example: *"Everything has its specific historical context."*

- The notion of collective responsibility has been used to persecute different outgroups.
  Example: *"Nazis persecuted such groups as Gypsies, Jews, homosexuals, and other outgroup members."*

Many of those who rejected the notion of collective guilt based their belief on uniqueness; that is, on the individual quality of human responsibility/ guilt. A second argument they made that in large groups, decisions are not made by all group members. In our research, participants were asked solely about possible large-scale collective guilt by nations, religious groups, and so on. A third argument on the validity of personal dissociation from the misconduct of the group (Jaspers' type of argument) does not exclude the occurrences of other cases in which collective guilt might be at stake.

The affirmative beliefs on collective guilt were more diversified.

TYPES OF ARGUMENTS FAVORING COLLECTIVE GUILT/ RESPONSIBILITY

- Some people oppose the evil being committed by others.
  Example: *"You can try to prevent the minority or the majority from committing acts of evil against an outgroup."*

- Others identify with a given group, and share in its beliefs.
  Example: *"Accepting principles of a group, one must assume responsibility for its harmful actions."*

- One is guilty by belonging to a group of extremists.

- Groups or nations have fixed qualities, including the negative ones.
  Example: *"Authoritarian upbringing and obedience to authority may be malevolent behavior."*

- Accepting responsibility for the past is a precondition for reconciliation between groups and reestablishing a sense of harmony.
  Example: *"There has been responsibility for the sins of our forefathers [...] and this acceptance of harms done by the offspring can reestablish a sense of community."*

- People experience negative emotions after misconduct of other group members; asking for forgiveness for their misdeeds would be healing.
  Example: *"A person or group member who has experienced some sort of harm would welcome genuine apology from the offending individual, group, or nation."*

- To prevent shifting responsibility solely onto group leaders, we must recognize our own role as a bystander.
  Example: *"When an individual witnesses a tragedy, such as what took place in the Jedwabne Massacre, and looks the other way and does not get involved to prevent such horrors, he or she is indirectly responsible for the act."*

- Whenever a nation chooses leaders, it is responsible for the decisions and actions of those leaders.
  Example: *"People who voted for Adolf Hitler as chancellor of Germany are responsible for his actions."*

Those respondents who favored the notion of collective guilt most often reflected the argument by Jaspers (1961), and repeated by other authors, on the blameworthiness of not resisting the misdeeds of the group to which belong. Group members were perceived as trying to hide behind the leaders; when they witnessed evil, they could not justify being innocent bystanders. Goldhagen (1997), addressing the responsibility of ordinary Germans who supported Nazi leadership crimes, is a good example of this sort of thinking. Robert Lifton (1996) has indicted Nazi doctors for performing medical killings.

Finally, there is an argument relating to collective guilt in a democratic society. Members of such societies are deemed to be responsible for the misconduct of their leaders. Kurt Baier (1991) maintains that in democratic societies, people are sovereign although they operate in two roles: on the one hand they are politically low-ranking members of the society; on the other hand, as sovereigns they are of the highest rank and therefore are collectively responsible for their superiors, including the government and elected leaders.

In our research, we also analyzed responses to the implicit collective-guilt question, how did you react to the Pope's apology to the Jewish people? which implied the collective responsibility of Catholic Church members for past wrongdoings. We took into consideration the religious affiliation of the respondents. It turned out that only 29 percent of nonbelievers and 35 percent of Christians reported positive reactions toward the Pope's pronouncement. By contrast, 52 percent of Jews were positive. One person identifying himself/herself as a Jew, said: "I rejoiced that the greatest authority in the Catholic Church apologized on behalf of the Church and nations." None of the Jewish participants in the study had a negative view of the Pope's statement, but some expressed skepticism. "Well, they finally pleaded guilty, but what's the profit for us if so many had died?" asked one. Another said, "I am glad, although it will not help or convince those who are intolerant." As many as 55 percent of nonbelievers and 45 percent of Christians did not mention any personal response to the statement, while less than 20 percent of those identifying themselves with Judaism had no response. For the nonbelievers the apology may have been neither personally relevant nor universally important. In turn, for nonresponding Christians, the collective guilt toward Jews may be a personal issue still to be resolved.[38] A few Christians overtly undermined the statement ("I do not like Jews very much, so I was not particularly interested in the statement"), and some nonbelievers tended to find the Pope's statement "just useless."

In summary, taking into consideration that this study details the potential guilt of large groups, societies, and nations, the majority of our respondents would accept the legitimacy of collective guilt under at least some circumstances. Most of those who unanimously reject the notion are congruent with those theoreticians who highlight the individualistic character of guilt. In turn, for most of the subjects, solely belonging to an ethnic, social, or religious group is not a sufficient reason to attribute collective guilt. A person's involvement or lack of involvement—as in not reacting to some sort of group member's misconduct, or free-will identification with the wrongdoing collective—usually seems a necessary prerequisite of collective guilt or responsibility. Asking for forgiveness for the wrongs of the group a person identifies with can have a positive impact on intergroup reconciliation. The case of the Pope's apology shows the potential importance of intergroup forgiveness. American writer Ann Roiphe (2004) reported that Poland's offered apology was 60 years late.

We felt that two well-known personalities of Poland would have some deep insight into the important topic of collective guilt, and we offer their interviews here.

Interviews with Dr. Marek Edelman and Former President Aleksander Kwaśniewski

Dr. Marek Edelman, born in 1921, was a co-founder of the Jewish Fighting Organization and one of the leaders of the heroic Warsaw ghetto uprising during World War II. After the war he became a cardiologist and a first-line member of both the anticommunist Workers' Defense Committee and later of the Solidarity movement. During the martial law imposed by Polish communists in 1981, he was temporarily imprisoned. Eight years later, Dr. Edelman was instrumental in the so-called Round Table Talks, which enabled a peaceful turnover of power from the communists. Later he served four years as a member of the Polish parliament. He strongly resisted pressure to leave Poland.

Interviewer: Do you believe there has been any form of guilt we could call collective?

Marek Edelman: Of course there has been. If a group of people supports war criminals, it is an example of collective guilt, especially if they were taking profits from those who were murdered by Germans. In the conquered countries, Germans plundered food and other goods. They believed it was their right as Übermenschen. So 'til now every German housewife [bore] collective guilt for the past. This guilt appears not because you personally killed somebody, but due to the fact that, witnessing genocide, you turned your head away, telling yourself, "Well, it was not me and I am okay"

Interviewer: Even relatively young persons in our current research point at indifference and the omission of relevant counter-action as critical examples of collective guilt. But what is the collective guilt 60 years after the war?

M. E.: You know 60 years is not a particularly long time period. It is no more than two generations—two generations that were reared by parents and grandparents who do not tend to change their opinions in a day's time. They also feel much has been taken away from them, and that produces resentment and even more hatred.... The best proof of relevant German attitudes is that of unceasing fighting 'til the very end of the war.... these were German parents who pushed their children into the trenches. Nobody else was forcing them to do it. There was everything but German Resistance.

Interviewer: But what is the relationship between the terrible past and the present? What sort, if any, obligations arise [from] these experiences?

M. E.: First, the person's past requires [mental] change. And that takes a long time, as we see. To change attitude implies ceasing to hold oneself as Übermensch *and starting to be a normal human being...and not treating yourself now as a victim or perpetrator.... Of course the expulsion of Germans from postwar Poland was not nice, especially for those who were doing fairly well here, but it was war here, and people had been massively slain. And we, that is neither Poles nor Jews, did not start the war!*

Interviewer: Four years ago, in Jedwabne, Polish president Aleksander Kwaśniewski asked Jews for forgiveness. How did you react to that? What sense does such a pronouncement have?

M. E.: I reacted very positively. However, first of all, these words had only political character. Any words, except ones eliciting hatred, have no particular causal effect. Whenever you speak about love or goodness, the results are very poor.

Interviewer: And what is necessary for reconciliation among groups tainted with a difficult or painful past?

M. E.: There must be appropriate politics behind it. The issue is establishing interpersonal connections. The politics of mutual trust must prevail. Hatred is to be absolutely excluded and old resentments prohibited. Prohibition here means punishment.

Interviewer: So what about the current Palestinian–Jewish relationships? They are so often mutually loaded with hatred.

M. E.: Israel and the Arabs [are] a completely different story. It is not just Israel against Palestinians, but it is a tiny Israel surrounded by an ocean of 100 million Arabs who are against Jews....Very often economic affairs are embedded. In general, we cannot say their mutual relationships are founded on hatred. If there is no current upsurge of hostile events, then both communities get along relatively well. One party does not live at the expense of the other....

Interviewer: And the last question: Do you believe that contemporary Poles should forgive the other nation for the crimes committed against their forefathers?

M. E.: Such forgiveness is ungrounded! It is only the victim himself or herself who can justifiably forgive. And this the victim can do but does not need to. If the criminal killed my father, mother,...why do I have to forgive? I cannot kill him. If he spent even a year in prison, it would bring some moral satisfaction. If he is 90 years old, he may not go to the prison, but at least he will be socially branded for what he did. What does it mean to forgive? If someone just said he is sorry for his crimes, is it enough to say from now on everything is okay? [39]

Aleksander Kwaśniewski is a Polish politician who served as president of Poland from 1995 through 2005. He is a former leader of the left-wing Democratic Left Alliance. Kwaśniewski defeated the incumbent, Lech Wałęsa, former Solidarity leader, and was reelected to a second five-year term as president in 2000. He strengthened ties to the European Union and NATO and played an instrumental role in improving relationships with Lithuania, Ukraine, and Israel. Aleksander Kwaśniewski signed a law granting special rights to those who saved Jews during World War II.

As the Polish president, Kwaśniewski decided to ask for forgiveness for the crimes committed by Poles against Jews in Jedwabne during the commemoration of the sixtieth anniversary of that atrocity, held on July 10, 2001. The action was met by some furious reactions, including attempts to try him for national treason. In March (2001a) he told the Israeli newspaper *Jedijot Ahronot,* "It was a genocide done by Poles from Jedwabne against their Jewish neighbors. Therefore we need to bow down and ask for forgiveness. Maybe Poles afterwards will become better."

In an interview by the German *Spiegel*, Kwaśniewski (1991b) said, "Arriving at Jedwabne on this very day is the greatest challenge of my presidency." In a nationwide poll carried out after the anniversary, it was found that as much as 44 percent of the population dismissed the value of the apologies by Catholic Church bishops and president Kwaśniewski, and 36 percent claimed the apology would positively affect Polish–Jewish relations (CBOS 2001).

> *Interviewer:* Do you believe collective, transgenerational guilt exists? The guilt of the kind named by Karl Jaspers, when he referred to the crimes Nazi Germans committed before and during World War II?

> *Aleksander Kwaśniewski: I reject, in the case of Poles, direct comparisons with Nazis. It was the Germans who adopted the concept of Final Solution* [Endloesung] *as a basis for the upcoming Holocaust. Polish guilt for this time period was substantially different. It was basically of situational character, resulting from the contemporary drama the Polish nation was experiencing. There is no doubt that our national conscience got tainted with shameful deeds. But, at the same time, the Polish conscience can count extraordinary acts, like rescuing Jews. However, when we look at the scope of suffering of Polish Jews, we must also admit the numbers of the righteous who helped was too small. Still it is they who gave us a pass to the moral world. As we all know, the majority of Polish Jews [were] annihilated. About the Polish guilt of silence, the Polish guilt of omission, the Polish guilt of antisemitism, and the Polish guilt of excluding those others than Poles, calmly but consequently we have to speak.*

> *Interviewer:* How do you perceive now your act of apology in Jedwabne in 2001? Do you find, more generally, that this sort of apology makes any deeper sense?

> *A.K.: The case of the Jedwabne crime was a real shock to me, and it activated very unusual processes. When I read the book* Neighbors *by Jan Gross, I already knew that it had special significance. But first of all, what I could not believe was that, until the late nineties, we as a society did not know the facts. It was in disguise, it was a secret. Second, there was my personal reaction that we must go further with*

all this knowledge, that we have to honestly face the truth about everything that occurred then. The third critical moment was that of the enormously extensive social debate. Fourth, I felt we must keep responsibility in this debate. Polish accountability for the crime was accurately grasped by the title of the book.... The discussion of whether there were 600, 800, or only 400 people in the barn is of minor importance, because each and every crime considered individually was terrifying and horrible. I find Jedwabne was a great lesson, a sort of mental transformation for the Polish society. However, it was a very difficult lesson. I shall never forget that during the anniversary in Jedwabne, there was no one there from this locality. I shall never forget: someone across the field produced [a] disco music session while the cantor Joseph Malovany was singing. And all with this process of breaking the stereotypes, our habits, and at last ourselves. Everything in order to be able to finally admit, "It was we who did it." At the same time, it was obvious to me that Polish accountability for the Holocaust is very limited. It was a Nazi concept perfectly realized. Some Poles showed exceptional moral strength while helping persecuted Jews.... On the other hand, there was antisemitism in different parts of the country. There were blackmailers, betrayals, taking over of Jewish houses.

Interviewer: So I understand that despite heavy criticism, you seem not to regret your apology of 2001, considering it necessary and significant; am I right?

A.K.: Currently, I am a person speaking in a very personal way, solely in my own name. For 10 years of my presidency, I spoke foremost in the name of Poland. But what I did then in the name of Poland for the sake of Polish–Jewish relations I still consider valid, accurate, and effective.

Interviewer: Now I would like you to compare ongoing changes in Polish–Ukrainian and Polish–Jewish relations, both of which you were much involved in. While Polish–Ukrainian relations clearly improved in recent years, Polish–Jewish relations tended rather to deteriorate. What is your opinion about that?

A.K.: First, in Polish–Ukrainian relationships we made enormous progress, with the substantial involvement of Ukrainian president Leonid Kuchma, who showed much rationality in this respect. You know he was from the eastern part of Ukraine, which was less historically troubled by conflicts with Poland. With his successor Victor Jushchenko it was much more difficult, as he comes from the western part of Ukraine, and his close family was linked with nationalists during the war. One must keep in mind that Western Ukraine fought for her independence in tough battles against the Soviet Union and Poland. Those from the East show a much more relaxed approach.

Year after year we strove to further the reconciliation, to remove all the difficulties we faced. I myself had a difficult situation at home, because the father of my wife comes from the current Ukraine, and he, because of Ukrainian nationalists, ran for his life into the forests carrying his ill mother. When I was explaining to him that reconciliation has to come, he asked me only to do everything in truth. When during my presidency I had a crucial reconciliatory meeting with Kuchma, I invited my father-in-law and many other people linked to those events. I knew even among my members of parliament there were people against the reconciliation process. In Volyn 200,000 to 300,000 Poles perished, and 100,000 to 200,000 Ukrainians in retaliation. The ceremony proceeded in great dignity. We told the entire truth. I remember one Pole telling the story of villagers driven to the wooden church and burned. He himself managed to escape the ordeal. But the fact he was given an opportunity to speak in front of Polish and Ukrainian presidents was very cathartic. After the ceremony one senator approached me. I got shivers as I knew she was against this process. But she said: "You were right, not me. It was absolutely great." She started to cry, and I cried as well. This happened among all those people who suffered, like my father-in-law, who during the Soviet time unveiled an illegal memorial in this region. But in general, among most of the Polish and Ukrainian groups involved in this process, there was no mutual aggression. I had many encounters with emotional difficulties, because always there were perished family members behind us.

As regards Jews and Israel, we also strove to foster reconciliation. However, it is much more complicated now to react on. Although, on the one hand, there is still marginal homemade, traditional antisemitism: you know, sometimes someone writes something on the walls, or the like. But the real trouble is somewhere else. Now, we have little to say in global affairs in [the] Middle East or especially in Israeli–Iranian relations. Right now, by ourselves we can do nothing to support a balance of power in that region. America, Germany, and even smaller states like Poland must realize that antisemitism will not disappear unless a modus vivendi between Israel and the Arab states is worked out. Conversely, anti-Islamic tendencies will not evaporate, as long as we arrive at this modus vivendi. That is a challenge for the entire international community, including the U.N., U.S., or even countries like Poland. In the traditional work against antisemitism at home, politics is of lesser importance now because many positive events have occurred. The key question remains how we can help the Israeli state to safely continue its existence in the place where it is now, and how we shall foster Arab–Israeli reconciliation....

Pretty often I am asked, in particular by Americans, if I am a Jew or if I have Jewish roots. I always answer: I am not. I am not because of the genetics, because of the specific history of my family. But I warn all in Poland who seem 100 percent sure they do not have Jewish blood. It is just risky, because most probably have! It might have been a grandmother, uncle, or a lover in a former generation. And therefore, we have a special prerogative to fight for preservation of the Jewish heritage. We of course have behind us the terrible events of the year 1968 and the undeserved tragedy of Nazism. But now we are in NATO and the European Union, and it is Israel [that] currently has more troubles than we have. That gives us the capacity to be a gentle friend to Israel. One thing we cannot do, as it will completely ruin our international reputation, is to allow any antisemitism. It must be at absolute zero because of history, because of culture, because of our international position. We may have odd concepts on some things, but in Jewish–Polish relations, we must be ultimately coherent. If some people do not understand the situation profoundly and authentically, I just want them to learn more about it.

SOME CONCLUSIONS OF THE JEDWABNE DEBATE

The complexity of Polish–Jewish relations, and the emotional debate over Jedwabne, provide insight into universal challenges posed by the reconciliation process. We propose preliminary suggestions for the sequence of stages to be gone through when working towards intergroup reconciliation. The following processes may help improve relations.

Stages in Intergroup Relations

1.

Not violating the rights of either party. At a minimum level, the parties involved may function as the car drivers who do not care much about each other but want to avoid having trouble with policemen who monitor the relations. These supervising "policemen" are, for example, the *Anti-Defamation League* monitoring programs, or the Polish government, struggling with usage of the phrase "Polish concentration camps" instead of "Nazi camps." The major punishment is most often publicizing the misdeeds in reports, or exerting social or legal pressure to change the actions in question.

Positive and Negative Aspects

Positive aspects

- Educational. The actions undertaken by supervising institutions often teach the societies' values and vital needs that are violated or endangered by specific misbehavior.

- Direct defense. Through intervention, vital interests—especially those of the minority group—can be protected, regardless of the understanding and acceptance of other parties.

- Political. At best we have some sort of intergroup political dialogue.

Potential negative aspects

- The party with recourse to the policemen is often perceived as making problems even over small issues. For members of the other party, any contacts with the self-defending group may be perceived mostly as a troubling nuisance.

- Sometimes deadlock is caused by treating any criticism of the group as a manifestation of antisemitism or anti-Polandism. Fairly often in debates, these sorts of labels are treated as a tool in combating opponents. Such practices usually evoke resentment and hostility in return.

2.

Admitting truth regarding the past. (Here the issue of collective guilt is often involved.) The admission may assume different forms, including statements made by representatives of the persecuting group, publications in history books, or statements provided in court by those who committed the evil. Most important, the statements should be presented as "final" to prevent opponents from questioning them.

Positive aspects

- Spiritually and psychologically the admittance of truth about the past by members of the persecuting group provides the foundation for a lasting reconciliation. It also, and foremost, serves as a means of reestablishing the sense of moral justice for the victims themselves or their offsprings.

Potential negative aspects

- Group-based identities usually are broader aspects of our personal self-understanding and self-evaluation. Therefore, revelation of the unfavorable truth of the past of my group may evoke strong defense mechanisms, resulting in polarization of attitudes, counteraccusations, and decreasing openness to understanding the position of the other.

- The historical truth of the events is almost always complex. Therefore in the public discourse, we have to do with more or less overlapping interpretations of the past. Parties involved often have their own "true" histories of the events. Even acclaimed historians are sometimes at odds with their counterparts from the other group.

3.

Forced restitution or compensation. The most notable case in recent years is that of the valuables in Swiss banks, deposited mostly by Jews before World War II and reclaimed by their heirs. Other actions (e.g., of former colonies against colonizers, or Greeks attempting to reclaim their antiquities from Great Britain) have been in vain. Admission of truth first is common, but it is not a must (many Swiss people feel their country was treated unfairly in the case).

Positive aspects

- Giving back property that was illegally taken, or restoring rights to the group discriminated against, is an act and sign of justice. On the other hand, relations between the groups may forever be shadowed by the unresolved unjust practices of the past.

Potential negative aspects

- Return of property can be practically and morally difficult. Challenges arise over time due to missing documents, changing ownerships, and the material scale of compensations or restitution at stake.[40]

4.

Unforced restitution or compensation. This may imply moral and material actions, first and most notably represented by asking for apology[41] for the misdeeds. One of the most eminent examples of unprompted action for the sake of the persecuted "other" group are the unceasing initiatives of the Australian government and Anglican Church of Australia toward Aborigines.

Positive aspects

- The best quality of these practices in moral terms is their free-will character. Optimally, both individuals and their representations (governments, councils, legislatures, etc.) show that they are open to acting for the good of those victimized.

Potential negative aspects

- The act of paying debts, morally or financially, may be treated as a sort of end-station: "We did what we had to, and that's all." Therefore, expressing apology or giving back property to those deprived of it, or—as in most interstate relations—paying retributions, may close difficult chapters in mutual relations but not necessarily open new ones.

5.

Sustained compassion. This may pertain solely to some unique individuals in the given society or group. These people instantiate profound empathy, after Martin Hoffman's terminology (2000), for the distressed group.[42] They transcend pervasive cross-group borders as far as sometimes offering their lives for members of the persecuted group.[43]

Positive aspects

- Persons who attain this level are spontaneously active in helping and defending those directly victimized or their ingroup members. They are live signs of hope for the maltreated group. One of the worst things for Jews at the time of Shoah was the widespread indifference of many Poles who witnessed their calamity.[44]

Potential negative aspects

- Such spontaneous and unceasing defenders of the persecuted are often disliked or even hated by many of their own ingroup members. Sometimes they are called "group traitors," because they easily break with ingroup solidarity and do not hesitate to reveal evil past or current practices. [45]

Do We Really Need Reconciliation Between Groups?

The answer is yas, and for many reasons, moral and practical alike. Let us just mention here one of the practical ones. If the wounds of resentments about the past are not overcome, and the communities are living side by side largely unreconciled, if there is new persecution of one of the communities, the other one will, at best, be indifferent toward the sufferings of the first. Some people will even be happy about it. As we have already written, the overwhelming indifference experienced by many of those who underwent the Holocaust—for whatever reason this indifference occurred—was pervasively dispiriting, pushing the rescued Jews to leave territories their ancestors had settled generations before (Gutman 2001).

The public discussion over Jedwabne and other recent events in Polish–Jewish relations helped to lessen to some vital degree the attitudes of Poles toward Jews. Research by Ireneusz Krzeminski (2002) showed that aversion toward Jews rose, and understanding for the scope of World War II Jewish sufferings lessened as compared with data from research done in 1992.[46]

Daniel Bar-Tal (2002, 2004), an active spokesman of Arab–Jewish reconciliation and a scholar at Tel-Aviv University, maintains that if reconciliation is to be true, it [47] is in its very heart a matter of personal choice of people interwoven in a troubling mutual past.

Partnership and Mutual Just Treatment

Perceived lack of partnership and mutual treatment impedes advancement of reconciliation between groups. Polish (Christian)–Jewish relations are a good example of the challenges in this respect. Many Poles perceive the suffering of their countrymen as treated in the Polish–Jewish debate as being of minor moral importance and value. For many Jews, Polish resistance to moving a Catholic convent out of Auschwitz, and a few years later to removing a large Christian papal cross from the vicinity of the camp, were examples of fundamental lack of sensitivity. For many Poles, pressure from the Jewish community was perceived as degrading to the Poles and Christians who had suffered at the site. Neither party felt that its perspective of the historical suffering was adequately and honestly addressed by the other party. Similarly, Germans often feel that their suffering—due to the Allies' massive bombardment of Dresden and Hamburg and the banishment of their civilian countrymen from Poland and the Czech Republic after the war—is undermined by those who won the war. Discussing the suffering of one's nation, and in particular claiming some special rights based on such suffering, is a sensitive endeavor. The ideal situation is when the people representing one party understand the ordeals of the other and are capable of satisfying its relevant needs and expectations. This leads to a "win-win" solution in which both parties are relatively satisfied. However, when strong emotions are present and no clear-cut logical solutions are available, it is very difficult to arrive at a mutually satisfactory consensus.

Another factor in intergroup dialogue is the size and social power of the groups involved in the process. Like white Americans against indigenous Americans, and nonaboriginal Australians meeting with aborigines, Jews in many contexts worldwide—except in Israel and the United States, but including those in Poland—are faced with the fact that their numbers are so small compared to the other groups with whom they live. So while larger groups, like churches or nations, want reconciliation, often they do not understand that Jewish communities may feel uneasy at the approach of a larger partner, even if the partner's intentions are friendly. The encounter of an elephant with a mouse is a challenge, especially if the two have a troubled history; and it requires enormous sensitivity on the part of the elephant.

The last, and in fact the most important factor involved is the fundamental perception of members of the outgroup as inferior. A pervasive sense of superiority, or *Übermenscheit*, facilitates persecution of the inferior other. For generations Judaism was treated by Christians as a failed religion, and often Jews were believed to be morally and spiritually tainted by their alleged crimes against Jesus. The substantially more normal and partnerlike treatment of Jews after World War II bore the fruit of unprecendented openess for dialogue. The *Dabru Emet* (Speak the Truth) statement was signed by more than 150 rabbis and Jewish scholars from the United States, Canada, the United Kingdom, and Israel (Goodstein 2000). The statement documents how honestly treating the other as a legitimate partner in dialogue may effectively call for reciprocity. The rabbis wrote:

> We believe these changes merit a thoughtful Jewish response....We believe it is time for Jews to learn about the efforts of Christians to honor Judaism. We believe it is time for Jews to reflect on what Judaism may now say about Christianity.

Admission of Difficult Truth

Often in intergroup relations overshadowed by past misdeeds, acceptance of the truth of misbehavior by the ingroup members is a real challenge. We have seen that part of our personal identities and self-esteem come from characteristics of the groups with which we identify. This makes acceptance of an unpleasant truth difficult and sometimes painful. Moreover, revealing unfavorable information may result in strong defensive reactions, especially if the information challenges the dominating internal image of the group. For many Poles, including former President Aleksander Kwaśniewski, public revelations about Jedwabne and a series of similar events were a profound personal shock, because many Poles felt they had been victims of German and Russian oppression. Sometimes, for the sake of sustaining good relations, one of the groups involved may be hesitant in publicizing the truth. Shortly after the Second World War, Szymon Datner (1947) must have known much more about the pogroms than he actually reported. It seems he did not want to increase intergroup tensions by reporting the details of participation of Poles in these events. As a consequence of such actions, the truth of Jedwabne was kept from the public for almost 60 years, including 10 years after democracy was reestablished.

Is comprehensive truth about mutual past relations really necessary for establishing viable and friendly intergroup relations? National and international debate after Gross's *Neighbors* provides a complicated but generally positive answer. Admission of truth is important for offspring of both victims and perpetrators. The son of one of the murderers of the Radziłów pogrom confessed: "If we do not arrive at a true understanding of the events, the [morbid] situation will continue in oncoming generations of our children and grandchildren" (150). However, the majority of Jedwabne inhabitants denied active and free-will participation of Poles in the crimes. The official report of the National Remembrance Institute confirmed to a large extent that the thesis by Gross did not change many minds in this respect. Polish human rights activist Jacek Kuroń insightfully commented on the resistance to confront the dreadful past, when he said that a suppressed sense of guilt breeds hatred in a person's heart:

> Somewhere inside he actually knows that the nation perished here, and he profited from the situation as he is in possession of a formerly Jewish house or just a casual pillow. He does not want to confront the truth, and it results in rising hatred.

Telling the truth is also and foremost a form of moral debt toward those who perished; most often in the cases of the pogroms discussed, thereis not one of their family to remember them. Israel Gutman (2001), a scholar of the Yad Vashem Remembrance Institute, claims that crimes against Jews reflected profound moral crises of the perpetrators and that "telling the truth is an element of re-establishing the normal situation." Rabbi Jacob Baker, who had left Jedwabne before the war and attended the memorials of the sixtieth anniversary of the program, declared in the name of the murdered Jewish society: *"We want no revenge, but the memory."* The most notable example of the healing power of positive public confrontation of truth with evil was fruits of the actions undertaken by the Truth and Reconciliation Commission in South Africa.

We must remember that the revelation of truth is painful for all parties involved. Therefore it is ultimately crucial who reports and why and with what precision of detail. It is better if that reporting is done by representatives of the perpetrator party. Often, however, as in a long-lasting marriage, the misconduct is not attributable solely to one partner. Still, it is most appropriate to deliver critical information about one's own party's misdeeds. A member of the more victimized group may be oversensitive to its negative experience. It poses a moral challenge to describe atrocities committed against one's own group: I may imperceptibly become a judge—to some degree—of my own case, which is always problematic. Last, but absolutely not least, to consider in the process of truth telling is the perception of the motives that drive the truth revealer. In the Jedwabne case, negative attributions substantially blocked the openness of many Poles. Recurrent suspicion arose that Jewish lobbying groups planned to both humiliate the Polish nation internationally and to declare Polish guilt in order to get higher restitution: "The Jews are coming to recapture their possessions" (Gross 2006). Given that thousands of Polish citizens took profits from Jewish property, these suspicions easily evoked powerful defensive reactions; basic and existential needs were at stake.

Drawing conclusions from the foregoing, it would be better if the Jedwabne case were publicized by those who are perceived as Poles, or by independent bodies composed of representatives of both parties, to limit accusations of partiality. To some degree the official legal actions undertaken by the Polish Institute of National Remembrance (INR) could play this role of objective, impartial agent exploring the truth. Unfortunately, in some echelons of Polish society, the introductory debate on Jedwabne resulted in such strong fear and distrust that the INR report confirming much of Gross's findings was repeatedly contested.

The two principal authors who reported on the atrocities in Jedwabne, Jan Gross and Anna Bikont, define themselves as half Pole and half Jew.

Their backgrounds, coupled with the events they describe and the conclusions they draw, does not make the reconciliation process easier. Such people of mixed Polish-Jewish descent might appear to be a bridge of reconciliation, because they understand both parties and need some sort of internal reconciliation between their conflicted group-based identities. The problem is that whenever they articulate expectations that Poles feel guilty over anti-Jewish acts, they are easily perceived as Jews accusers who betray their Polishness. The life of Jan Gross, marked by his personal persecution during anti-Jewish events initiated by Polish Communists in 1968, followed by living in exile in the United States, does complicate matters—psychologically for him and in the social perception of the Polish side of the debate. However, the fundamental issue is that without the book by Gross, the truth of the Jedwabne crime and its victims would probably remain forever unrevealed to the broader public. President Kwaśniewski confessed that he was profoundly moved and shocked after reading the book. Several scholars in Poland, mostly historians, realized they had avoided confrontation with the traumatic events despite reestablished political freedom in the country. Similarly, Adam Michnik (2001), the editor-in-chief of *Gazeta Wyborcza,* a major Polish daily, wrote passionately in the *New York Times*:

> I do not feel guilty for those murdered, but I do feel responsible. Not that they were murdered—I could not have stopped that. I feel guilty that after they died they were murdered again, denied a decent burial, denied tears, denied truth about this hideous crime, and that for decades a lie was repeated.
>
> This is my fault. For lack of imagination or time, for convenience and spiritual laziness, I did not ask myself certain questions and did not look for answers. Why? Perhaps because I subconsciously feared the cruel truth [underlining by the authors] about the Jewish fate during that time.

Exploring further determinants of the truth-searching process, we also must focus on the issue that evoked the most furious objections, namely the credibility of data provided and generalizations made by Jan Gross. The situation is relevant to any other situation that explores a difficult intergroup past.

Poles resented the fact that Gross authoritatively announced in his book that 1,600 Jews were burned in the barn in Jedwabne on that sinister day of July 10, 1941. Gross relied on the statements provided by one of the very few rescuers, who reported as if he had been a personal witness of all the events described. It was proved afterwards that besides his own experiences, the "witness" had collected and summarized different stories heard after the pogrom. According to a large body of evidence gathered by the Polish Institute of National Remembrance in its official legal trial, 300 to 400 persons actually perished in the barn. This fact changes nothing of the ultimate horror of Jewish inhabitants assassinated in Jedwabne—including small children, the elderly, and women—but for many readers of Gross's book, this and other substantial inconsistencies and ungrounded statements undermine the credibility of Gross as an objective scholar and honest truth seeker.

It seems obvious that whoever takes responsibility for searching for the difficult truth in intergroup relations should be conservative in providing data. It would be better for the entire debate on Jedwabne if Gross had been much more cautious in describing his raw data and much more conservative in drawing relevant conclusions. In his book *Neighbors,* he proposes that the testimony of those who survived the Shoah be considered by scholars as an invaluable and reliable source of information about those days. But while survivors' reports most often are valuable, they cannot be automatically treated as reliable. Even without any intended bias in depicting reality, they may cover only selected fragments of truth as subjectively remembered, perceived, or heard by people under extreme stress. Such testimony treated as a literal source of data is likely to be contested by scholars and even more by general readers. This happened to some degree in Poland, where opponents of the "Jewish truth" on the Jedwabne case presented counter testimony that depicted the crime as solely a German affair and responsibility.

We will deal with the issue of making generalizations on the basis of collected data in the next section, devoted to attributing guilt to collectives.

Collective Guilt

Collective guilt can be dealt with from both subjective and objective perspectives. From the subjective perspective, collective guilt refers to the feelings and cognition a person may experience as a member of one or more groups—national, religious, or professional. The objective perspective implies it is legitimate, under some circumstances, to assign to a given person guilt for the misconduct of the group to which he or she belongs. These two perspectives are often confused. The way Jan Gross (2002) introduced the concept in his book, *Neighbors,* substantially affected its further reception. On the one hand, he clearly rejects the notion of collective guilt: "For each killing only a specific murderer or group of murderers is responsible" (89); however, he claims we cannot legitimately exclude from our identities extreme negative qualities of the past ingroup experience. Gross maintains that murders such as occurred in Jedwabne affects all people in a community over time. Here the moral taint seems unavoidable, independent of individual convictions. He finds any nation "a group with a distinctive collective identity," and by asking the reader if the nation can simultaneously be a victim and victimizer, Gross suggests the nation appears to be some kind of independent entity in which all its members participate in its "good" and "bad."[48]

This argument was resented by many, including those who did not deny the substantial free-will contribution of Poles in the crime. The famous Polish journalist Jacek Żakowski, known for his tolerance and promotion of democracy, wrote as a rejoinder to *Neighbors:*

> I got irritated by the language of large quantificators, which solely due to the fact that I am a Pole attempts to entangle me in the crime committed fifty years ago.

Membership in some organizations, if it is optional, may result in moral ostracism or even legal prosecution. Recently, the European public was moved by the case of Guenther Grass, the famous German writer and Nobel Prize winner, who admitted his service in a Waffen-SS unit. It caused storms of criticism, despite the fact he had never shot or killed anyone.

Morally, when we attribute positive qualities to the members of any nation, it does not do harm, regardless of whether the qualification accurately depicts the majority of a given group. But if you make negative generalizations, and especially if you attribute guilt to a nation, the consequences may be devastating.[49] Negative stereotypes, as we know, are a powerful vehicle for victimization of a group. Before World War II in Poland, the following saying was popular: "Jews and bicycle riders are accountable for all evil!" The response: "But why bicycle riders?"

Group Identification as a Personal Choice

It seems important to let all people of irreconcilable parties define themselves in relation to the difficult past. Foremost, it depends on which party you side with. Are you with us or against us? Are you friend or foe? These are questions people often ask in the context of past or current intergroup conflicts. World War II provides clear and dramatic examples: American citizens of Japanese descent detained in camps; Germans in the Soviet Union systematically and indiscriminately persecuted for their ethnic origin. Phenomenologically or psychologically, the identity issue is often much more complicated than the content of official forms. Adam Michnik (2001), the editor of *Gazeta Wyborcza,* wrote on this complexity:

> By coincidence I am a Pole with Jewish roots. Almost my whole family was devoured by the Holocaust. My relatives could have perished in Jedwabne. Some of them were Communists or relatives of Communists, some were craftsmen, some merchants, perhaps some rabbis. But all were Jews, according to the Nuremberg laws of the Third Reich. All of them could have been herded into that barn, which was set on fire by Polish criminals....
>
> Writing these words, I feel a specific schizophrenia: I am a Pole, and my shame about the [Jedwabne murders] is a Polish shame. At the same time, I know that if I had been there in Jedwabne, I would have been killed as a Jew. Who then am I, as I write these words? Thanks to nature, I am a man, and I am responsible to other people for what I do and what I do not do. Thanks to my choice, I am a Pole, and I am responsible to the world for the evil inflicted by my countrymen. I do so out of my free will, by my own choice, and by the deep urging of my conscience. But I am also a Jew who feels a deep brotherhood with those who were murdered as Jews (*New York Times*, 2001).

Michnik's problem rings true, especially in Poland, where thousands of people are of mixed Polish and Jewish descent. Reconciliation is not possible unless we consider and respect individual identities and relevant personal choices.

In conclusion, we have seen that collective guilt is a very complex topic, because the victimized group accuses victimizers who then question the motivation of the accusers. The fact of the murders at Jedwabne would have been less controversial had this tragic event been uncovered by both sides simultaneously, that is by Polish scholars and Jewish scholars. This difficulty exists in other countries where groups seek the truth. It also raises the question of whether a scholar has to belong to a group that has been victimized for the truth to come out. For instance, do you have to be a African-American scholar to disclose the horror of slavery in the United States? Do you have to be a Polish Catholic to uncover the truth of the Jedwabne Massacre? These controversies are permanently with us.

8
CONCLUSION

In our communities, anywhere we interact with others, there are opportunities to resolve painful hurts and help each other reconcile. There are positive benefits of forgiving and caring, not only for society, but for the caring person. Research has shown that people who are engaged in helping internalize the ethic of caring for others are more likely to forgive those who harmed them. While teaching a course on the sociology of altruism and compassion at Humboldt State University, I found that hundreds of students reported a positive influence on their lives simply by studying altruism and compassion and how it affects them in their daily lives. Pedagogical approaches in class that express the positive consequences of caring increase the likelihood that those students will discover their own compassionate natures. Acting in a caring and altruistic manner encourages even more caring and altruistic behavior in the future, which also includes empathy for others and willingness to forgive.

Professor Lawrence J. Walker, a prominent Canadian psychologist who has done empirical studies on moral development, has discovered some important attributes in those who help us emulate engaged spirituality. Emulation of moral exemplars and their ethical and moral behavior often produces compassionate and caring individuals. Fortunately, there are many to emulate: Gandhi and Martin Luther King, Jr., for example, and people we know who reflect those same kinds of values and behaviors on a smaller scale. Walker and Hennig (2004) propose three types of moral exemplars: the *just* moral exemplar, who reflects predominately conscientiousness; the *brave* moral exemplar, characterized by dominance, extroversion, and courage; and the *caring* moral exemplar, who has concern for others and puts the welfare of others alongside of his own.

Our current research on forgiveness indicates that the altruistic person is more humane, helpful, and hospitable, makes time for others, is willing to share, is unselfish and charitable, puts others first, is willing to volunteer on a sustained basis, and is usually more forgiving. Although these positive characteristics generally are not all found in one person, more of them are found among the types of individuals who have been spiritually and morally engaged. We wish to emphasize that these traits are *teachable* behaviors. A number of venues can be helpful in developing these attributes.

Individuals can help create a better world through the daily use of apology and forgiveness techniques. We can be role models to those around us, primarily as parents taking active steps to establish a structure that encourages our children to better understand the importance of helping those in need, apologizing when it is called for, and forgiving. Naomi Drew's (2006) website on building skills for peacemaking describes how parents can help their children develop compassionate listening skills that help resolve differences with others.

Try a game called "I Heard You Say." Take turns being the speaker and the listener. The listener asks a question; the speaker answers, then the listener paraphrases what was said, starting with the phrase, "I heard you say." Each time the listener paraphrases accurately, the speaker gives a thumbs up. Otherwise the listener must repeat what was said and try again. Avoid one-word responses, but keep what you say brief enough for the other person to remember. Or break your response into parts that can be paraphrased a little at a time. Questions you can use: Could you describe your favorite thing to do when you have free time? What is your earliest memory? If you could be anything you wanted, what would you be and why? What is your favorite holiday and why? What is your favorite book and why? What is something that really gets you mad, and why? If you could go anywhere in the world, where would it be and what would you do there? Who is someone you really admire and why? Playing this game will help your child master the complex skill of reflective listening, something especially valuable when conflicts arise.

Julia Keller (2005) reviews the importance of spiritual development in children and how recent research indicates that it is important to get children involved in helping others at an early age. This gives them a head start in the process of engaging with their community, and in that sense, some clues to answering the universal question about the meaning of life.

She quotes researcher Peter Benson, who says, "Spiritual development is likely a wellspring for the best of human life—generosity, sacrifice, altruism, social justice, stewardship of the Earth—as well as for its darker side—genocide, terrorism, exclusion" (Keller 2005: 37). Keller calls for further research into the importance and consequence of spiritual development in children, suggesting a more caring humanity for the future.

Parents have a responsibility to demonstrate genuine love to their children. Children deprived of parental love tend to be anxious and depressed; they suffer from low self-esteem and are less likely to be able to take the place of the other and act altruistically. Parents can teach love by modeling problem solving in the family; if parents are honestly willing to apologize for mistakes, as well as to forgive others, their children will emulate these behaviors. It is the "little things" that socialize us, so ethnic jokes, antigay rhetoric, anything that denies an individual's rights or helps to erect barriers between groups can "plant the seeds of injustice and hate" (Pon 2002: 13).

Schools can serve as a particularly effective source of positive influence in helping to teach our young. We all realize that reading, writing, arithmetic, physics, computers, and other topics are vital; in addition, we should be able to see the importance of teaching children about the consequences of indifference within human relations. Therefore, our schools need to become caring institutions, emphasizing the importance of love, civility, caring, and aiding a neighbor in need. Most importantly, they should convey how acting altruistically is helpful not only for the recipient but also for the giver.

It is the responsibility of all involved in education to participate in the dissemination of kindness and concern for others: teachers, students, janitors, bus drivers, presidents, and deans all have roles to play in attaining this goal. This is a choice that must be consciously thought of if it is to be implemented. School is a place for "practical idealism," where we can and must model and reinforce the processes of apology and forgiveness, where an atmosphere of reconciliation must prevail. To allow it to be otherwise leaves us in a state of dissatisfaction and alienation.

Our *leaders* also have the power and opportunity to model behavior that is honest and helpful to others. *Corporate leaders* can publicly take the high road in product safety, liability, and environmental and other community concerns that affect us all. *National politicians* and leaders have similar opportunities and responsibilities, because they have the advantage and aid of enormous resources, as well as a "bully pulpit." When our president apologizes to a group for some past injustice, it reinforces our common humanity and underlines the legitimacy of apology. *Religious leaders* and members of spiritual or moral communities have the opportunity to reinforce the values that make families strong and are perhaps our earliest recognized moral exemplars and role models.

Journalists can report, and editors can approve, feature stories about the many caring and compassionate events throughout the world. These stories can be helpful in countering the daily tidal wave of pessimistic and divisive reporting. We discern a new focus on morality beginning to show itself. What we can do now is to help encourage this new vision on the part of educators, movie makers, TV directors, and publishers of books, and we can help them devote more time to these topics. Many of us have the opportunity to pass along our own knowledge to new generations, whether through daily life experiences, teaching, or research. Currently, public sociology endeavors to establish in the field the understanding of how sociological research can help with problematic public issues (Buroway 2005).

The need to place blame resides closely to the moral center of individuals. Working for justice is a lifelong task of assessing guilt and defining responsibility, rather than pursuing processes based on punishment, shame, and blame. A significant movement toward forgiving begins when we quit blaming and move toward recognition of our joint participation by taking sole responsibility for our own actions and respecting the responsibility of others for their parts. Perceptions of love must be restored, and negotiations of trust must be resumed, which is equally demanding of the giver and receiver of forgiveness—both must trust and risk.[50]

Apology and forgiveness are becoming more evident throughout the world. People in public positions should use their exposure to model the kinds of behaviors that encourage caring among people and help resolve conflict. One good example is a group of doctors who are dedicated to saving lives in Haiti, one of the poorest nations in the world. Through their caring behavior, these doctors attempt to make amends for the neglect and oppression endured by the Haitian people. By providing children with the best available medical care, they share a view that the world can be a better place. The doctors come from family backgrounds that encourage them to help others, not simply to look out for themselves. They were willing to exchange personal and financial success in the United States in the hope of "triggering a chain reaction" (Kidder 2005: 6). Like most of the heroes we interviewed in 20 years of research on altruism, the doctors do not regard themselves as heroes. One of them said, "I am in a position to do something about that. It is not noble. It is simple. Because I have the choice, because I can I do it" (Kidder 2005: 6).

We believe that genuine apology and forgiveness are two sides of the same emotional coin. Charles Hauss (2003) informs us that they reflect constructive ways the oppressors and the oppressed in an intractable conflict can come to grips with the pain and suffering the conflict produced. Making apologies and granting forgiveness are integral parts of any long-term resolution of an intractable conflict. Without them, it is all but impossible to achieve genuine reconciliation and lasting peace.

Apology and forgiveness have produced different reactions in Germany and Japan. These two nations, guilty of similar crimes at the same time in history, have apologized to the people they murdered and abused. Though one may find faults with the German apologies, it remains true that every German government since the creation of the Federal Republic in 1949 has sought to establish good working relations with Israel and with their immediate neighbors. There has been a national examination of conscience about the crimes of the Nazi years and a society-wide grappling with that guilt.

Forgiveness is a gift and an act of reconciliation that has tangible consequences. Forgiving helps your body and mind to heal. It has spiritual consequences, because under the right conditions, it is able to reestablish a relationship between harmdoer and harmed. "I am sorry" is perhaps the most difficult phrase in any language. It is particularly crucial that a perpetrator acknowledges the truth and is willing to apologize when a relationship has been damaged. Many Germans feigned ignorance of Nazi crimes and were thereby stunted in their ability to apologize or be forgiven. Tutu notes that many white South Africans tried to find refuge in similar claims of ignorance. He said that such claims are often the result of not knowing because they do not want to know. "Like the three monkeys, they chose neither to hear, nor see, nor speak of evil… If the process of forgiveness and healing is to succeed, ultimately acknowledgement by the culprit is indispensable—not completely so but nearly so. Acknowledgement of the truth and of having wronged someone are important in getting to the root of the breach" (Tutu 1999: 270).

Forgiveness does not involve overlooking wrongdoing; forgiveness and reconciliation entail accepting the truth. True reconciliation exposes awful truths, abuse, pain, and degradation, and it can make things worse. It is a risky undertaking, but is worthwhile, because dealing with the situation helps healing. "If the wrongdoer has come to the point of realizing his wrong, then one hopes there will be remorse, or at least some contrition or sorrow. This should lead him to confess the wrong he has done and ask for forgiveness" (Tutu 1999: 271). Forgiving is not forgetting; on the contrary, it is important to remember the atrocities, so they do not happen again. Forgiving is not condoning what has been done; it means taking it seriously and not minimizing it. It involves trying to understand the perpetrators and having *empathy*—to stand in their shoes and appreciate the pressures and influences that might have conditioned them. "Forgiving means abandoning your right to pay back the perpetrator in his own coin, but it is a loss that liberates the victim" (Tutu 1999: 272). The victim may be ready to forgive, but it is up to the wrongdoer to appreciate the gift, acknowledge his wrongdoing, and let forgiveness enter his being. By forgiving, we are declaring faith in the future of a relationship and the capacity of the wrongdoer to make a new beginning.

Genuine attempts at apology and forgiveness constitute a second chance for new beginnings. Wrongdoers' actions and confessions are not the end of the process of forgiveness. Often the wrongdoer has affected the victim in a tangible, material way. "Confession, forgiveness, and reparation, wherever possible, form part of a continuum" (Tutu 1999: 273). If one cannot forgive on behalf of those who suffered and died in the past, those who did not suffer directly as a result of the reparations may be incapable of receiving forgiveness on behalf of the others. This means there is a massive block between the community of perpetrators and the community of victims. One way to deal with a sordid past is for descendants of victims to grant forgiveness, even symbolically, to compensate for the anguish. "True forgiveness deals with the past, all of the past, to make the future possible," Tutu said. "We cannot go on nursing grudges even vicariously for those who cannot speak for themselves any longer. We have to accept that what we do we do for generations past, present, and yet to come. That is what makes a community a community or a people a people—for better or for worse" (Tutu 1999: 279).

Most people, including a large percentage of our sample, have reported being seriously hurt. We are not speaking here of someone bumping into someone when walking on the street, but rather a serious and lasting hurt, which could be physical, psychological, or emotional in its effects. Some of the people who carry this pain have had negative personal or group consequences. Many individuals around the world would like relief from hurt and reconciliation with others. Harmdoers also carry burdens, mostly guilt, and the sensitive ones wish to reconcile and apologize. Most respondents in our study felt that interpersonal and intergroup apology is very important. If apology and/or forgiveness is genuine, then the possibility of reconciliation is likely.

Apology and forgiveness, both interpersonal and intergroup forgiveness, is an idea that is currently evolving throughout the world. Recently, the U.S. Senate apologized to the descendants of African-Americans who were victims of mob lynchings. We have seen that forgiveness can be motivated by altruistic inclination, along with social responsibility. Forgiveness is also motivated by unlimited love for the other. Internationally, forgiveness may be motivated by practical reasons: it improves cultural, political, and economic relations, and it heals historic wounds.

Although research into intergroup forgiveness is in its nascent stage, we have begun to see impressive evidence for positive outcomes in some countries where apologies have been made and forgiveness extended. One example that we have reported is the recent reconciliation between Ukraine and Poland, based on mutual apology and forgiveness for harms inflicted in the past. When apologies are genuine, when remediation is offered, changed behavior follows and harmony can prevail; this makes for a more peaceful world.

A number of other solutions have been suggested to bring about a more caring world. Buddhist monk Thich Nhat Hanh maintains that there is a need for revitalization of established religions, enabling them to be more relevant in our time. Religions seem to have stagnated in their practices and rituals, and this is responsible for the polarization among and between religions.

In this book we have stressed a relationship between altruism and forgiveness, altruism and apology, and altruism and reconciliation. If these correlations are accurate, how do we inculcate forgiving and bring about a more peaceful world? As proposed throughout this book, there are direct correlations among upbringing in a moral community, loving parents, and forgiveness. Therefore, parents are extremely important in teaching the importance of apologizing for harming others and forgiving those who have harmed us. Thich Nhat Hanh has stated that institutions need to practice moral virtue, including apology and forgiveness. These institutions should include the workplace, as well as educational institutions. Governments should practice caring for those for whom they are responsible, stressing the virtues of apology and forgiveness. It is healthy not only for individuals who have been hurt or who have hurt others to apologize and forgive, but it is also good for the institution, because there will be a more harmonious group of people as part of it. In an earlier work, the Oliners (1988) speak about "extensivity," including people outside of the family in one's sphere of care. An extensive orientation predisposes people toward altruism and includes the idea of reconciling with others by admitting fault and asking for forgiveness.

Apology and forgiveness as an intergroup process is effective. We saw that in the case of the Ukraine–Polish apology, in which surveys have shown that as a result of the two presidents' mutual apologies, the attitudes and perceptions among citizens of the two countries have improved substantially. Similarly, the apology by three Kentucky sister communities to African-Americans for slavery also had positive effects. And finally, the apology by Pope John Paul II to the Jewish community has also had a positive outcome. In fact, a group of rabbis and other members of the community we interviewed have pointed out that Catholic–Jewish relations have never been better in the last 2000 years.

We are optimistic enough to believe that a harmonious world is not an impossible dream. An altruistic world *is* possible; we see genuine acts of altruism every day that are the product of the environmental factors we talk about. Apology and forgiveness help reconciliation come about; we have seen several recent examples where a genuine apology was the first step in a healing process that might otherwise not have occurred. Empathy, altruism, apology, and forgiveness can rehumanize those we have excluded and reuniversalize those we have construed as members of outgroups, restoring balance in our interpersonal and intergroup relationships.

Appendix A
Methodology

Methods

Description of Sample

We have obtained data from a cross-cultural, comparative, nonrandom sample of 519 respondents; 435 Americans and 84 Poles. The sample consisted of the following groups:

A) The three Sister Communities in Kentucky: The Sisters of Charity of Nazareth, The Sisters of Laredo, and The Dominicans of Saint Katherine. We are particularly interested in these three because these convents inherited slaves in the beginning of the nineteenth century, who subsequently built their convents and churches in that part of Kentucky. The three Sister Communities decided to apologize to African-Americans at a church in Bartstown, KY, attended by 400 people. We wanted to find out why they apologized, what the responses were to the apology, and what the consequences of such an apology might have for future relations.

B) Humboldt County clergy who apologized to the offspring of the Wiyot People for the 1870 massacre of innocent victims sleeping on Indian Island near Eureka, California (Gordon 2004).

C) Clergy from different parts of the United States, including priests, nuns, rabbis, and moral exemplars (*moral exemplars*, who are nonclergy, are defined as individuals who perform altruistic acts for others on a consistent basis).

D) Students from the College of the Redwoods and Humboldt State University, both of which are located in Northern California.

E) Adults who are neither clergy nor students and who do not fit the criteria for moral exemplars.

The adult sample's age range was between 14 and 84, with a mean age of 32.

The interviews and mailed questionnaires were primarily aimed to elicit information about the following:

1) Peoples' attitudes about apology and forgiveness

2) Have they apologized to anyone they have hurt? Has anyone hurt them, and if so, have they received an apology?

3) What was the outcome? Did human relations improve? Did it lead to reconciliation?

4) Have their communities, of which they are members, apologized to other communities or their leaders for a contemporary historical harm committed?

5) Their attitude toward Pope John Paul II's recent apology to Jews, Muslims, and other people on behalf of Christian oppression

6) Additionally, the research gathered information about the demographics dealing with age, education, gender, and religiosity. Parts of the sample consisted of interviews, which were tape-recorded and transcribed. The students received questionnaires administered by various faculty at both Humboldt State University and College of the Redwoods.[51]

We used (SPSS) to analyze quantitative data. Our research team consisted of three individuals who analyzed the narratives (qualitative data) for emergent themes. We provided the three raters with motivational categories that tapped into the specific responses, such as caring, love, forgiveness, apology, reconciliation, religiosity, empathy, and a number of others. To determine our coders' liability, we reasoned that if any motivational categories had been checked either zero or three times, there was complete coder agreement. For example, if a particular subject received a zero, say for *empathy*, there was complete agreement that *empathy* was not a significant motivational factor in this person's explanatory acts. If *empathy* was checked three times, this indicated to us that the coded agreement was a salient factor in motivating this person to engage in exemplary acts in the community. To report on our coders' reliability, we combined the percentage of times that either "zero" or "three" was entered in each of the motivational categories. For example, if they all agreed that *empathy* was an important factor, then there was a 100 percent agreement between them; similarly with other categories listed, we found that there was approximately a 90 percent agreement between the raters in this study.

From both the quantitative and qualitative data, we were able to gain insight about the relationship among altruism, apology, forgiveness, empathy, religiosity/spirituality, social responsibility, self-esteem, and other variables.

Interviews were guided by some overarching themes. How do individuals and groups develop narratives that drive a conflict? How can these narratives sometimes exist in direct conflict with the historical facts? How is the construction and revision of narratives involved in the reconciliation process? Another consideration is the level of personal involvement with the conflict and the level of attachment to the group involved. In what ways can relationships change? How have the apology and forgiveness processes affected how groups view each other? The role of empathy and the ability to take the place of the other affects both the process of apology and of forgiveness. How can members of groups in conflict feel more empathy for members of the other group? Can a feeling of interconnectedness be generated? In terms of the roles of spirituality and religiosity affecting reconciliation, does it make a difference to be an active member of a moral community? Lastly, what is the outcome of apology and forgiveness? Has there been reconciliation? Or, at least, has the foundation been laid for reconciliation? Is rehumanization of the harmdoer possible?

Dr. Zylicz has supervised research in Poland. He was able to obtain a sample of 84 individuals (in Poland: the analysis of collective guilt reported in Chapter 7 reflected 100 respondents) using the same questionnaire and instruments utilized by our research team in the United States We were interested in comparing Polish individuals' responses to having been hurt and their attitudes and perceptions regarding the notion of collective guilt versus individual guilt, specifically the case of a Jewish massacre in the town of Jedwabne, Poland, which was committed by their Christian neighbors.

Table 1. Hurt and Forgiveness

	Total Sample* N=435	Moral Exemplars N=60	Clergy N=77	Students N=242	General Population** N=56	Polish Data*** N=84
Has been hurt	92.8%	86%	67.7%	97.9%	98%	84%
Has been asked for forgiveness	69.7%	80%	16.7%	76.5%	83.3%	73%
Has forgiven	82%	87%	75%	82.5%	87.3%	80%
Has hurt/ offended someone	91.7%	78%	67.2%	96.3%	94%	89%
Has asked for forgiveness	94.2%	91%	95.2%	93%	98.1%	69%
Has been forgiven	87%	94.6%	97.5%	83%	91%	82%
Believe apology is important	94.2%	90%	91%	96%	96.4%	90%
Believe apology leads to reconciliation	51%	64.9%	69.2%	41.4%	67.3%	68%
Believe forgiveness heals relations	70.7%	85%	92.7%	62.1%	80.4%	86%
Religious	89%	77%	96%	62%	80%	81%
Altruistic	87%	92.9%	89%	63%	86%	91%

*Total sample figures exclude Polish sample.
**General Population is a sample of adults who are neither students, moral exemplars, nor clergy.
***This column applies to Polish data only.

Analysis

Table 1 indicates that many people have been hurt at some point in their lives. Our study reveals that this is true; 92.8 percent of the total population sampled had experienced hurt of some sort at the hands of another, the highest percentages coming from within the student population and general population, both at 98 percent. Contrasted against the Polish sample, the numbers were slightly less: only 84 percent responded that they had been hurt.[52] For those who were hurt, 70 percent of the U.S. respondents were asked for forgiveness by the offender. The numbers were similar in Poland at 73 percent. Of those U.S. and Polish respondents, 82 percent (U.S.) and 80 percent (Polish) had forgiven the offender.

In contrast, of the total U.S. respondents, 92 percent indicated that they had harmed or offended another; the Polish data indicated that 89 percent of the respondents had harmed or offended another. The percentages increase when looking at whether they had asked the person they had offended for forgiveness. Ninety-four percent of the U.S. respondents indicated they had asked for forgiveness, whereas 69 percent of Polish offenders had. Of those people who attempted to mend their relationships with those they had hurt or offended, 87 percent of the U.S. respondents were forgiven, and 82 percent of the Polish respondents were forgiven.

The importance placed on apology is high among both the U.S. (94 percent) and Polish (90 percent), which we hope will lead to a true reconciliation. However, when asked whether forgiving someone leads to reconciliation, there were less who believed this to be true; 51 percent of the U.S. respondents and 68 percent of the Polish respondents felt reconciliation was not necessarily a result of forgiveness.

These lower percentages may shed some light on whether respondents felt the apology was valid or simply a gesture to get past the negative experience and social awkwardness of an interpersonal/intergroup feud. Looking further into reconciliation, a large percentage from both the United States and Poland feel that forgiveness heals relationships—71 percent of the U.S. sample and 86 percent of the Polish sample.

When broken down into the categories of moral exemplars, clergy, students, and the general population, we can see certain demographic characteristics that lend insight to the overall sample outcome. Ninety-seven percent of the student population claimed they had been hurt, whereas 86 percent of the moral exemplars and 68 of the clergy had responded that they had been hurt. However, the general population, with a response of 98 percent, reported being hurt the most.

The general population's percentages of having been hurt also coincided with whether the offender had asked them for forgiveness for their actions.

The general population, 83 percent, said they had been asked to forgive the offending party. Moral exemplars were next with 80 percent having been asked for forgiveness, and clergy represented the lowest number, at 17 percent.

Of those who forgave the offending party, the general population and moral exemplars reported an 87 percent forgiveness rating, students reported 83 percent, and the Polish population, 80 percent.

Looking at those who had offended someone in the recent past, our responses were similar to the percentages of those who had experienced *being* hurt; 96 percent of the student population responded that they had hurt or offended someone recently. This was followed closely by the general population (94 percent) and the Polish sample (89 percent). It is logical that the two categories of "been hurt" and "have hurt or offended someone in the recent past" show similar percentages; when we look at the total sample combined, 9 out of 10 people answered "yes" to these questions. Naturally, if someone is doing the hurting, then someone on the other end of the spectrum is receiving the harmful action.

Forgiveness is the first step towards reconciliation and mending a relationship. Earlier in our analysis, we observed respondents' answers to whether or not they had forgiven those who harmed them; 82 percent responded they had forgiven, but 87 percent believed they had been forgiven by those who they, the respondents, had offended or harmed. Clergy were among those less willing to forgive, yet 98 percent believed they had been forgiven by those they had offended. The lowest percentage of those who believed they had been forgiven came from the Polish sample at 82 percent, closely followed by 83 percent of the U.S. student population.

Overall, 91.7 percent of the U.S. sample surveyed believed apology to be important, contrasted to 90 percent of the Polish sample. 96 percent of the students and the general population sample believed apology to be important. However, when considering whether apology leads to reconciliation, only a little over half (51 percent) of the total population believed this to be true; 41 percent of the students represented the lower end of the spectrum, with 69 percent of clergy representing the higher end of the spectrum. The Polish respondents (68 percent) represented the second highest percentage, believing apology does lead to reconciliation.

When considering whether forgiveness leads to reconciliation, it was the clergy who truly believed, with 93 percent answering "yes". Eighty percent of the Polish sample felt this to be true, whereas only 62 percent of the U.S. student sample responded affirmatively to this possibility.

Collective and Individual Guilt

When the Polish sample was taken, we were interested in the collective and individual guilt displayed toward past harms done in their society, (i.e., the Jedwabne Massacre) and whether those alive during this time felt some sort of remorse or guilt for their action or inaction. 43 percent of those surveyed felt some sort of collective guilt as a result of harms perpetrated in the past by their government and peers, whereas 44 percent felt individual guilt. The difference between the two percentages is marginal but leads us to propose that perhaps those individuals felt they had the opportunity to *not* idly stand by and witness an act of injustice or harm toward another. However, for this study to accurately relate these differences to individual versus group responsibility for actions committed, further inquiry is required with a larger random sample.

An interesting finding was that there was no difference between males and females in the measure of forgiveness.

Lastly, we looked at how forgiving is related to education level. Respondents were asked to identify the highest level of education attained. Categories presented included some college, Bachelor of Arts or Bachelor of Science, postgraduate, and an advanced degree. Those with some college scored lower on the forgiveness scale, versus those with a Bachelor of Arts or Bachelor of Science degree, who scored higher. Those with a graduate degree scored highest on forgiveness. 79 percent of respondents strongly or mildly agreed that they could forgive a friend for almost anything, and 92 percent of respondents strongly or mildly agreed that people who apologize and truly want reconciliation should be forgiven by those they have hurt. Of the total sample, 97 percent of respondents believed that forgiveness helps to begin the reconciliation process, and 96.2 percent of respondents believed that when you forgive, you take an important step toward mending and rebuilding the relationship between the offended and the wrongdoer.

Other findings were that women in this sample were less impressed with the Pope's apology, because he did not say anything about women's access to the priesthood. Younger and more educated priests and nuns appeared to be more liberal and felt that apology and forgiveness were a very important step toward healing pain, and the sooner we begin to get consciously involved in this process, the better it will be for the harmed and the harmdoer.

There is a relationship between age and forgiveness; older respondents generally have a greater capacity to forgive. Additionally, on the measure of daily spiritual experience as gauged by the Daily Spiritual Experience Scale, data indicate that older respondents have a greater tendency toward spirituality. A sense of spirituality is also positively correlated with a sense of restorative justice, and forgiveness is correlated with a tendency toward restorative justice; that is, the more forgiving the person is, the higher they scored on the restorative justice scale. There is also a positive relationship between forgiveness and *agape* (selfless love). In general terms, the more forgiving individuals are, the greater their capacity for selfless love of others. Agape is positively correlated with a sense of restorative justice. Finally, there is a positive relationship between altruism and forgiveness.

Because this research is based on a nonrandom sample, our conclusions should be viewed in that light. A study with a larger, random sample should be taken to test our findings. Nevertheless, our research indicates valuable correlations among altruism, apology, forgiveness, and the likelihood of reconciliation.

APPENDIX B
LIST OF INTERGROUP APOLOGIES (NOT EXHAUSTIVE)

In the past two decades, there have been more than 100 intergroup apologies made. Here is partial list of those apologies. Although some of the them of dubious quality, and the long-term results of most are still in doubt, we are heartened by the fact that so many are finding the apology-and-forgiveness process of merit. Though some apologies have clearly been more effective than others, an apology can be a step in the right direction.

1. The Pope apologized for Catholic prejudice and dehumanization of Jews and Muslims; he also apologized for the Crusades and slavery.

2. Former U.S. President Bill Clinton apologized for the Tuskegee experiments.

3. The Mormon church apologized to black Mormons.

4. The Canadian government apologized to the indigenous peoples of Canada.

5. The Australian government apologized to Aborigines.

6. Rev. Jerry Falwell apologized for making comments disparaging Jews, including a focus on the biblical prediction that the Antichrist will be a Jewish man.

7. Hawaiian authorities apologized to native Hawaiian people.

8. Germany apologized to Jews and others for brutalities and genocide.

9. Dr. Laura Schlessinger apologized for degrading comments toward gays and lesbians.

10. The Japanese apologized for the rape and massacre at Nanking, China, as well as for the use of young Korean females as "comfort women" during the war.

11. The Truth and Reconciliation Commission, begun in 1995, sought justice through apology, forgiveness, and reparations.

12. Prime Minister Tony Blair (England) apologized to Ireland for the so-called Potato Famine.

13. America apologized to China for the bombing of the Chinese embassy in Belgrade.

14. In 1993 the U.S. government apologized for overthrowing the Kingdom of Hawaii in the nineteenth century.

15. The United Church of Canada apologized for its role in school tortures of indigenous peoples.

16. George H.W. Bush apologized to Japanese-Americans for the treatment they received during World War II (internment camps).

17. A Firestone CEO apologized to America for selling faulty tires.

18. NATO, in 1999, apologized for a bomb attack on Albanian Kosovar refugees.

19. Lech Walesa, President of Poland, apologized in Israel before the Knesset (parliament) for Polish antisemitism.

20. President Kwaśniewski of Poland apologized to Jews for the massacres committed against them by Poles during the German Occupation in 1942 in the town of Jedwabne.

21. In February 2003 British Columbia apologized for the treatment of its indigenous peoples and vowed to resolve land treaties ignored since the 1800's.

22. In September 1999, Cardinal John O'Connor made a public apology for the pain inflicted on the Jews by many Catholics over the last millennium.

23. In November 2003, villagers of the tiny settlement of Nubutautau wept as they apologized to the descendants of a British missionary who was killed and eaten by their ancestors 136 years ago.

24. In November 2003, President Morvic of Serbia and Montenegro apologized to Bosnia for the 1992–95 war in which some 200,000 people died, most of them Muslims.

25. The U.S. Southern Baptists declared, "We lament and repudiate historic acts of evil such as slavery."

26. The Evangelical Lutheran Church apologized for the antisemitism of its founder, Martin Luther, and the harm done to Jews in his name.

27. The United Methodists apologized for the 1864 massacre of 150 Cheyenne and Arapaho Indians, which was led by a Methodist preacher, Chin Chivington.

28. The Catholics in Brazil apologized for slavery and oppression of indigenous peoples.

29. German Christians in the Netherlands apologized to the Dutch for German atrocities during World War II.

30. The Dutch Reformed Church apologized to black South Africans for their role in providing religious justification for apartheid.

31. President Jacques Chirac apologized to the descendants of Alfred Dreyfus and Emile Zola for the Dreyfus Affair.

32. In Switzerland, the government apologized to Jews for its wartime role as a bank for the German regime.

33. In Benin (Africa), President Mathieu Kerekou sent a delegation to the United States to apologize to African-Americans for his country's participation in the slave trade.

34. Former U.S. President Bill Clinton expressed regret to various people in Africa for America's involvement in and condoning of the slave trade.

35. Johnson and Johnson apologized to consumers for the Tylenol tampering.

36. A letter from Cardinal John O'Connor, the Archbishop on New

York, regarded 2000 as the beginning of a new era for Christians in the spirit of Jubilee, with Ash Wednesday set aside for *teshuva,* or repentance, of Catholics' infliction of pain on Jewish people during the past millennium. This repentance was an attempt to build a new Catholic/Jewish relationship. The letter ended with an apology to Jewish people for sins committed against them by Catholics.

37. A Roman Catholic priest from the Cincinnati Archdiocese issued a statement in 2002 asking for forgiveness from people sexually abused by clergy members. This apology was given before a meeting in Indianapolis, where priests got together to try to understand the decline in the number of priests.

38. France's Catholic clergy apologized in 1997 for their silence during the Holocaust in a ceremony attended by 1000 Christian and Jewish people held the week before the war crime trials for Nazi Maurice Papon began. The French Catholic clergy confessed that silence was the failure of the Church and asked for God's forgiveness and for the Jewish people to hear their repentance. Jewish leaders welcomed the apology as a major turning point, but some people say it comes too late. The Pope encouraged the apology, but the Church continues to defend Pope John Pius XII (1939–58) against charges of remaining silent during the Holocaust.

39. Croatia's new President, Stefan Mesic, publicly apologized in 2002 for Croatia's World War II Nazi puppet regime. His predecessor, Franjo Tudjman, wrote a book denying Croatia's guilt in the death of 80 percent of their Jewish population during World War II.

40. The Catholic Church of Argentina asked for forgiveness in 2000 for its silence and participation during the country's 1976–83 military dictatorship and for not doing enough to fight antisemitism.

41. Christian churches in South Africa are active in condemning apartheid and in creating international awareness of governmental injustices in attempts to aid in the process of reconciliation.

42. In 1996, author Lynn Green was part of a Christian group that apologized for atrocities committed in the name of Christ dur-

ing the Crusades. This apology was given at a Turkish mosque as part of a five-month Reconciliation Walk from Cologne to Istanbul.

43. Nine Protestant churches met in Memphis, Tennessee in 2002 to launch a national campaign against racism designed to unify their 22 million congregation members. These church members sought forgiveness for the sin of division. Memphis was chosen as the location, because it is the city where Dr. Martin Luther King, Jr. was murdered.

44. The Slovakian town of Topolcany apologized to Jews for an organized pogrom against Jews who had just returned from Nazi concentration camps (Johnson 2006; *Together* April 2006: 10).

45. The northern branch of the Moravian Church publicly apologized for its past participation in slavery and vowed to eliminate racism in the church. (*Eureka Times-Standard* 2006: B–2)

APPENDIX C
SURVEYS AND SCALES

The scales used were 1) the Social Responsibility Scale (developed by L. Berkowitz and K. Luterman: 1968), which measured respondents' behaviors and attitudes toward being socially responsible; 2) the Self-Esteem Scale (developed by M. Rosenberg: 1965), which measures a respondent's self-esteem; 3) the Altruistic Personality Scale (developed by J. Phillippe Rushton, R.D. Christian, and G. Fekken: 1981), which assesses how often a respondent acted altruistically in certain situations; 4) the Daily Spiritual Experience Scale (DSE) (developed by Lynn G. Underwood: 1999), which draws upon respondents' spiritual connection to others and to creation in general; this scale was published in *Multidimensional Measurement of Religiousness/Spirituality for Use in Health Research: Report of the Fetzer Institute/National Institute on Aging Working Group*, October 1999; and 5) the The Traits of Forgiveness Scale (developed by Jack W. Barry and Everett Worthington, Jr.: 2001).

General Qualitative Interview Schedule

Transcriber's Name: Interviewer's Name:
Respondent's Name: Respondent Number: Date of Interview:

1. Respondent's ethnic background:

2. Age:

3. Place of birth:

4. Gender:

5.   Number of Siblings:

(a) Brothers:

(b) Sisters:

6.   Highest educational level attained:

7.   What did you major in?

8.   Your occupation:

9.   Mother's occupation:

10.   Father's occupation:

11.   Religion:

12.   Father's level of religiosity:

13.   Mother's level of religiosity:

14.   What does it mean to be a religious person?

14a. What does it mean to be a spiritual person?

15.   What are the most important lessons about life that you learned from your father?

15a. From your mother?

15b. From your siblings?

16.   Growing up, did you see yourself as emotionally close to your mother?

16a. Growing up, did you see yourself as emotionally close to your father?

17.   What are the most important lessons about life that you learned from your religious leaders?

18.   What are the most important lessons about life that you learned from other important people in your life?

19.   As a priest, I know you have been asked many times to give a speech to a group of high school or college students or other adults. What do you consider to be the most important message to leave with them?

20.   Who are the men/women that you most admire and why?

21.   Have you ever been hurt or offended by someone?

21a.   If yes, in what way?

21b.   Have they asked for forgiveness?

21c.   Have you forgiven them?

21d.   Why or why not?

21e.   What were the results?

22.   Have you ever hurt or offended someone?

22a.   If yes, in what way?

22b.   Have you asked for forgiveness?

22c.   Why or why not?

22d.   What were the results?

The following questions are about the recent apology made by:

The Government: ___(Go to 23)
The Pope: ___ (Go to 24—priests only)
Other: ___ (Go to 23) Who?_____

23.   To what group was the apology made?

23a.   What prompted the apology?

23b.   Under what conditions was the apology made?

23c.   Was the information disseminated among others in your group order (if nuns)?

23d.   Did your church take any steps to disseminate this information to your broader community?

23e.   If yes, what steps were taken?

23f.   Since the apology, what changes have you noticed in the behavior of those among your group, as well as those who were apologized to?

23g.   Since the apology, have your attitudes and/or behaviors toward the group apologized to changed?

23h.   If yes, in what ways?

23i.   Did you notice any changes in the behavior of the group apologized to?

23j.   If yes, what sort of changes?.

24.   Did you hear about the Pope's apology to the Jewish people?

24a.   If yes, how did you hear about it?

24b.   How was the apology made?

24c.   In your opinion, what prompted the apology?

25.   Did you hear about the Pope's apology to other groups (those harmed in the Crusades or during slavery)?

25a.   To what group was the apology made?

25b.   If yes, how did you hear about it?

25c.   How was the apology made?

25d.   In your opinion, what prompted the apology?

26.   How did you react to the apology?

27.   Since the apology, have your attitudes and/or behaviors toward the group apologized to changed?

27a.   If yes, in what ways?

28.   Did you disseminate the apology to your parishioners/convent?

28a.   If yes, how did your parishioners/convent respond to this apology?

29.   Did your church take any steps to disseminate this information to your broader community?

29a.   If yes, what steps were taken?

30.   Since the apology, have you noticed a difference in the behaviors and/or attitudes of your parishioners toward the group apologized to?

30a.   If yes, what sort of changes have you noticed?

31.   Did you notice any changes in the behavior of the group apologized to?

31a.   If yes, what sort of changes have you noticed?

32.   In your opinion, how important is apology in human relations?

33. In the future, are you planning on getting involved in the area of apology, forgiveness, and reconciliation? Why or why not?

34. Have you had an occasion to discuss with others some aspects of Jewish–Catholic relations?

35. Is there anything else that I should have asked you about this topic, your activities, values, and beliefs?

Scales for questions 1 through 42 comprise Self Esteem (SE), Social Responsibility (SR), Altruistic Personality (AP), and Daily Spiritual Experience (DSE).

Please place an "x" in the box that best represents your opinion

	Strongly Agree (1)	Mildly Agree (2)	Mildly Disagree (3)	Strongly Disagree (4)	Refused (5)	Don't Know (6)
1. Every person should give some time for the good of the town or country. (SR)						
2. I feel that I'm a person of worth, at least on an equal basis with others. (SE)						
3. It is the duty of each person to do the best s/he can. (SR)						
4. At times, I think I am no good at all. (SE)						
5. I have a positive attitude about myself. (SE)						

	Strongly Agree (1)	Agree (2)	Disagree (3)	Strongly disagree (4)	Refused (5)	Don't Know (6)
6. I feel that I have a number of good qualities. (SE)						
7. All in all, I am able to do things as well as most other people. (SE)						
8. Letting people down is not so bad, because you can't do good all the time for everybody. (SR)						
9. I wish I could have more respect for myself. (SE)						
10. All in all, I am inclined to feel that I am a failure. (SE)						
11. I feel very bad when I have failed to finish something I promised I would do. (SR)						
12. People would be a lot better off if they could live far away from other people and never have anything to do with them. (SR)						
13. I feel I do not have much to be proud of. (SE)						

14. It is no use worrying about current events or public affairs; I can't do anything about them anyway. (SR)						
15. I certainly feel useless at times. (SE)						
16. On the whole, I am satisfied with myself. (SE)						

	Never (1)	Once (2)	More than once (3)	Often (4)	Very Often (5)	Don't Know (6)
17. I have helped push a stranger's car out of the snow. (AP)						
18. I have given directions to a stranger. (AP)						
19. I have made change for a stranger. (AP)						
20. I have given money to a charity. (AP)						
21. I have given money to a stranger who needed it or asked me for it. (AP)						
22. I have donated goods or clothes to a charity. (AP)						
23. I have done volunteer work for a charity. (AP)						

	Never (1)	Once (2)	More than once (3)	Often (4)	Very Often (5)	Don't Know (6)
24. I have donated blood. (AP)						
25. I have helped carry a stranger's belongings (books, parcels, etc.). (AP)						
26. I have delayed an elevator and held the door open for a stranger. (AP)						
27. I have allowed someone to go ahead of me in a line (at a copy machine, in the supermarket, etc.). (AP)						
28. I have given a stranger a lift in my car. (AP)						
29. I have pointed out a clerk's error (in a bank, at the supermarket) in undercharging me for an item. (AP)						
30. I have let a neighbor whom I didn't know too well borrow an item of some value to me (e.g., a dish, tools, etc.). (AP)						
31. I have bought charity Christmas cards deliberately, because I knew it was for a good cause. (AP)						
32. I have helped a classmate who I did not know that well with a homework assignment when my knowledge was greater than his or hers. (AP)						

	Never (1)	Once (2)	More than once (3)	Often (4)	Very Often (5)	Don't Know (6)
33. I have voluntarily looked after a neighbor's pets or children without being paid for it. (AP)						
34. I have offered to help a handicapped or elderly stranger across a street. (AP)						
35. I have offered my seat on a bus or train to a stranger who was standing. (AP)						
36. I have helped an acquaintance move household. (AP)						
37. I experience a connection to all life. (DSE)						
38. I find comfort in my religion or spirituality. (DSE)						
39. I feel deep inner peace or harmony. (DSE)						
40. I feel God's love for me directly. (DSE)						
41. I am spiritually touched by the beauty of creation. (DSE)						
42. I feel a selfless caring for others. (DSE)						

30 Item Forgiveness Scale

Please assist us by completing the following survey:

		Strongly Agree (4)	Mildly Agree (3)	Mildly Disagree (2)	Strongly Disagree (1)	Don't Know (5)
1	It is easy for me to admit that I am wrong.					
2	I feel that apologizing for hurting someone will lead to healing the relationship between the offender and the offended, harmed, person, or group.					
3	I am able to make up pretty easily with friends who have hurt me in some way.					
4	I have forgiven myself for things that I have done wrong.					
5	I have forgiven those who hurt me.					
6	If I hear a sermon, I usually think about things that I have done wrong.					
7	I often feel that no matter what I do now, I will never make up for the mistakes I have made in the past.					
8	I try to forgive others, even when they don't feel guilty for what they did.					
9	I can never forgive and forget an insult.					
10	People who apologize and truly want reconciliation should be forgiven by those they have hurt, be it a person or a group.					

11	I like to apologize to the people I have hurt or offended.					
12	Forgiveness helps to begin the reconciliation process.					
13	I feel I have much in common with those I have hurt.					
14	When you forgive, you take an important step toward mending and rebuilding the relationship between you and the wrongdoer.					
15	When you forgive, you remove a burden that has been weighing you down.					
16	Forgiveness helps you to go on with your life instead of holding on to the past.					
17	Forgiveness makes you a better person and improves your overall mental and emotional health.					
18	I feel I have much in common with people who help others.					
19	I believe that when people say they forgive me for something I did, they really mean it.					
20	I have been hurt by people who never apologized to me.					
21	I find it hard to forgive myself for some things that I have done.					
22	I often feel like I have failed to live the right kind of life.					
23	I can forgive a friend for almost anything.					

24	If someone treats me badly, I treat him or her the same.					
25	People close to me probably think I hold a grudge too long.					
26	I feel bitter about many of my relationships.					
27	Even if I forgive someone, things often come back to me that I resent.					
28	There are some things for which I could never forgive even a loved one.					
29	I think forgiving someone who hurts you is a form of helping them.					
30	Those people who hurt others miss out because they lose relationships.					

ENDNOTES

1. These works come from a variety of academic and nonacademic fields. Given that our own backgrounds within sociology are quite diverse, we have been exploring literatures from the following fields: social psychology (for example, McCullough, Worthington, and Rachal 1997; Staub 2003); restorative justice (Sullivan and Tifft 2001; Galaway and Hudson 1996); alternative dispute resolution (Auerbach 2005, Hauss 2003, Bloomfield, Barnes, and Huyse 2003; Chaitan 2003; Hewstone, Cairns, Voci, Hamberger, and Niens 2006; public sociology (Burawoy 2004); sociology of race and ethnicity (Allport 1954), and the philosophy and sociology of love, altruism, and compassion (Kohlberg 1984; Post 2003; Shriver 1995; Sorokin 1954; Tavuchis 1991); and rescue (Fogelman 1995; Oliner 2000; Tec 1984; Paldiel 2000; Gushee 2003). We also looked at literature from faith-based perspectives (Perkins and Rice 2000; Washington and Kehrein 1993). Each of these has its strengths and weaknesses. Given the limited space available, we cannot critically evaluate each; instead, we note questions those authors and others have raised that are particularly compelling.

2. Moral exemplars individuals who have performed altruistic acts for others on a consistent basis.

3. Collective guilt can be understood from both subjective and objective perspectives. First, it refers to the feelings and cognition any person may experience as a member of different groups: national, religious, or professional. The latter implies it is legitimate, under some circumstances, to assign a given person guilt for the misconduct of the group to which he or she belongs. Individual guilt, often referred to as *moral guilt*, develops when an individual stands by and is able to avoid harm while harm is being committed toward another individual or group, therefore failing to do what they can to help. Subsequently, the individual experiences the emotion of guilt (Jaspers 1961).

4. See also Batson 1991.

5. Some "heroes" act "courageously" for other than moral reasons. For example, Hitler wanted to destroy whole nations and execute entire ethnic groups, because he claimed that Jews "stabbed Germans in the back" during World War I, and that other races and groups harmed the German people in other ways. Despite the illogic and brutality of Hitler's thinking, millions of Germans considered him a hero. However, our purpose is to discuss the motivations for positive actions.

6. Religion consists minimally of four attributes: 1) It is human involvement with what is considered to be the realm of the sacred, 2) It is expressed in thought, action, and social forms, 3) It consists of a total system of symbols in deep meaning, 4) It provides a path for ultimate transformation. One could add a fifth attribute: a deity is a necessary part of a religion (Ludwig 1996: 4). Spirituality is "the experience or relationship with the empowering source of ultimate value, purpose, and meaning of human life, producing healing and hope, and is articulated in diverse beliefs and practices of individuals and communities" (San Diego Hospice spiritual care).

7. See also Davidson and Dennis 1999. "Words of Faith: Dalai Lama Teaches Love, Kindness." *The Desert Sun*; Brandon, David. 1976. *Zen and the Art of Healing*. London: Routledge and Kegan Paul; Hevesi, Dennis. 1989. "Man in the News: Prophet of the Middle Way." The *New York Times*, Oct. 6: A6.

8. Numerous examples of God commanding Jews to aid the poor are to be found throughout the Jewish Bible. Jesus told his followers the parable of the Good Samaritan, instructing them to follow the example of the good neighbor who aided a poor, beaten man previously ignored by other passersby, including a priest.

9. Microsoft Encarta. 1995. "Mother Teresa of Calcutta (1910-1997)." Retrieved June 16, 1999 (http://www.netsrq.com/~dbois/m-teresa.html).

10. Ibid. See also Mother Teresa of Calcutta. Retrieved May 15, 1999. (http://www.netsrq.com/~dbois/m-teresa.html).

11. For further discussion of Islam and altruism, see Ross and Hills 1956; Templeton 1999; Beaver et al. 1982; Fisher 1994; and Ludwig 1996.

12. For further discussion of Islam and altruism, see Ross and Hills 1956; Templeton 1999; Beaver et al. 1982; Fisher 1994; and Ludwig 1996.

13. See, for example, (http://www.powerofapology.com).

14. This is similar to Jewish tradition, in which jubilee years were marked by acts of grace, such as forgiving debts and releasing prisoners.

15. Anthropologists speak about commemoration. "These accounts have studied sociopolitical functions of history, including myths and traditions. For example, there is a clear degree of similarity between the sociological use of the term commemoration (as in Connerton 1989), the anthropological use of the term "ritual" (for example, Eliade 1963), and historians' use of the term "invented tradition." The concept of invented tradition has been defined as "A set of practices, normally governed by overtly or tacitly accepted rules and of a ritual or symbolic nature, which seek to inculcate certain values and norms of behavior by repetition, which automatically implies continuity with a suitable historic past" (Hobsbawm and Ranger, cited in Devine-Wright 2002: 22).

16. Some Germans, including government officials, are beginning to question where collective guilt for the Holocaust ends. As one young German remarked, "We cannot be guilty of our grandparents' crimes" (Marzynski 2005). See Chapter 6 for further discussion of collective guilt.

17. Siemens, Krupp, and other large German corporations that employed slaves, and the American Ford Motor Company, still exist today. German and multinational corporations have offered compensation to slave workers employed during the Hitler years. Other corporate entities have been reluctant to offer compensation or apology to former slaves, became they are reluctant to admit guilt that may open them up to expensive litigation.

18. Story from *BBC News* published Mar. 26, 2007. Reported by BBC correspondent Chris Hoggs (http://news.bbc.co.uk/go/pr/fr/-/2/hi/asia-pacific/6495115.stm).

19. Story from the *New York Times* published Apr. 25, 2007. Article written by Norimitsu Onishi (http://www.nytimes.com/2007/04/25/world/asia/25japan.html).

20. Only 35 percent to 40 percent live in segregated communities; 95 percent of school-aged children attend denominated schools.

21. The study reanalyzed archival data sets, which methodologically possesses advantages and disadvantages. A primary disadvantage is that the current research objective differs from the original research, which makes "some of the key constructs...suboptimal."

22. After the war, the Polish Communist government accused the Lemko ethnic group of siding with the Ukranian Nationalists and being disloyal to Poland. The Lemkos (among whom Oliner resided until World War II began) inhabited the southeastern section of Poland, known as the Podkarptckie Region. The Lemkos speak a Slavic language related to Ukranian, they use the Cyrillic alphabet, and they belong to the Eastern branch of Christianity, using a version of the Byzantine Rites in their

church service. The Polish army fought the Ukranian insurgents' army (UPA), and the Lemko region was the battleground. Suspecting that the Lemko population supported the UPA, the Polish government resettled the Lemko in territories they had acquired from Germany, which became known as the Northern/Western Territories. In 1956 some Lemkos were allowed to return to their ancient homeland.

23. See Chapter 7 for further elaboration about the debates of the Jedwabne event and the discussion of collective versus individual guilt.

24. Article from the *Los Angeles Times*, published Mar. 19, 2007, written by Jenny Jarvie.

25. Elliot N. Dorff (1998) and Rye, Pargament, Amir, Beck, Hallisey, Narayanan, and Williams (2000) have addressed how forgiveness is manifested within Judaism. James G. Williams (1986) and Rye and colleagues (2000) address the same questions for Christianity, Islam, and Buddhism, and Guy L. Beck and Rye and colleagues (2000) for Hinduism.

26. Spirituality can be defined as "an inner sense of something greater than oneself; recognition of a meaning to existence that transcends one's immediate circumstances" (www.nature.com/nri/journal/v4/n11/glossary/nri1486_glossary.html), Spirituality has further been defined as "activities which renew, lift up, comfort, heal, and inspire both ourselves and those with whom we interact" (www.religioustolerance.org/gl_s1.htm).

27. Russian sociologist Piritrim Sorokin (1954); Stephen Post (2003); Michael E. McCullough, Kenneth I. Pargament. and Carl E. Thoresen (2000); and Dean Ornish (1998) all express in different ways that love is a life-giving force. For more on love, see: Brummer (1993), Olasky (1996), Nygren (1953), Soble (1989), Brehony (1999), Werber and Helmreich (1996), Werner (2002), and, Templeton (1999). For further discussion on altruism, see Oliner (2003; 1988).

28. For an elaboration of Dr. Carlson's research interests, visit http://whyfiles.org/087mother/4.html.

29. Printed in the *Naperville Sun* Apr. 25, 2007. Article by Britt Carson (http://www.suburbanchicagonews.com/napervillesun/news/356419,6_1_NA25_HOLOCAUST_S1.article).

30. Printed in the *New York Times* Apr. 25, 2007: A17.

31. *Dabru Emet* is a "proclamation dealing with Jewish–Christian relations signed by more than 150 rabbis and Jewish scholars from the United States, Canada, the United Kingdom, and Israel. It was published in the *New York*

Times and *Baltimore Sun* in late September 2000 in response to apologies put forth by various Church leaders. The statement notes at one point that many Protestant and Catholic religious leaders have "made public statements of their remorse about Christian mistreatment of Jews and Judaism. These statements have declared, furthermore, that Christian teaching and preaching can and must be reformed so that they acknowledge God's enduring covenant with the Jewish people'" (Haas 2004: 14–15).

32. Of course, there are many potential obstacles in such an undertaking: no sources of conflict may be present, no unequal power relationships may exist, and individuals must be perceived as typical examples of their group.

33. According to Chapman, "The precise number of countries and bodies depends on how strict a definition of *truth commissions* is applied. [As of 2001] Truth Commissions, or other mechanisms approximating a truth commission, have been set up in Uganda, Bolivia, Argentina, Zimbabwe, Germany, the Philippines, Uruguay, Chile, El Salvador, Rwanda, Ethiopia, Haiti, and Guatemala, as well as South Africa (Chapman 2001: 257).

34. Although the report was issued in 1998, the amnesty portion of the work continued for another two years.

35. This aid has contributed to "training lawyers, judges, investigators, and policemen; supporting reform of administrative and court procedures; funding the construction of courts, libraries, and prisons; paying for vehicles and fuel; supplementing the salaries of judges; and supplying technical assistance to the Ministry of Justice and the Supreme Court" (Bloomfield, Barnes, and Huyse 2003: 116).

36. Ecomog, comprising mostly Nigerian troops, was defending the government of President Ahmad Tejan Kabbah against rebels who seized large parts of the country. Ecomog's intervention allowed the president to return to power in March 1998 (BBC Online 1999).

37. Auerbach (2004) inspected and showed the links between personal religiousnes, the type of religion believed in, and openness to forgiveness for intergroup faults. All major religions, particularly Christianity, treat forgiveness as a core spiritual issue.

38. As nationwide research shows, 72 percent of Poles do not find reasons to feel intergroup guilt toward Jews (Krzeminski 2004).

39. Marek Edelman, while commenting about doubts of Simon Wiesenthal (1976), about whether he should have forgiven the dying Nazi criminal who was co-responsible for massive killing of Jewish civilians, was very much against it.

40. For instance, in the midst of the Jedwabne debate in May of 2001, two state legislators, Jeffrey Klein and Dov Hikind, urged the Port Authority of New York and New Jersey to revoke the contract with the Polish airline LOT to land in New York state. The action was the result of Poland's failure to pass a property restitution law that could compensate all former owners or their heirs who were deprived of property by Communists, including Holocaust survivors. As of 2006, the law had not been enacted. If the Polish legislature considered only Jews in the reprivatization process, it would significantly fuel intergroup resentments. The Polish authorities do not have enough resources either to compensate or reasonably restitute all the sufferers. As a result, the state of affairs is clearly unjust towards those deprived.

41. Apologizing in the name of the persecuting group, as was done by Pope John Paul II, is most often welcomed, as our reasearch showed. However, there may be a few problematic issues involved. Marek Edelman told us explicitly that only the victims themselves can actually forgive. In turn, others express concern that asking for forgiveness may be shallow and may prevent profound and adequate analysis of the roots of the evil committed, and thus hamper real reconciliation (Gutman 2001).

42. In his *Empathy and Moral Developent*, Hoffman (2000) wrote: "The combination of empathetic distress and the mental representation of the plight of an unfortunate group would seem to be the most advanced form of empathetic distress" (85).

43. For instance, Jan Karski, a Pole and pious Catholic, was such a person. As a messenger of the Polish government in exile, he visited the Warsaw ghetto and Bełżec death camp in disguise. Afterward, he became the most crucial witness and reporter to the Polish, British, and U.S. governments on the situation in Poland, especially the destruction of the Warsaw ghetto and the Holocaust at large. This unquestionable hero cried in profound compassion while telling the stories of the ghetto 40 years later, while during an interview with Claude Lanzman.

44. Feliks Tych (2001) of the Jewish Historical Institute in Warsaw calculated that about 10 percent of Polish society actively helped Jews, in spite of the death penalty faced by those who provided help and their families. This number shows the heroism of so many Poles, while 20 to 30 percent of Poles believed Hitler helped to solve the "Jewish problem," even as the rest were mostly indifferent to the Jewish fate.

45. The Polish priest, who in the course of the Jedwabne debate publicly claimed that the only righteous place for the Catholic priest of this locality during the massacre of Jews was in the barn to die with the victims. Afterward he encountered enormous criticism and social ostracism.

46. On both sides there are people who do not bother about reconciliation and sometimes are proud of it. For example, Claude Lanzman, a Paris-based filmmaker famous for making the outstanding documentary film *Shoah*, an oral history of the Holocaust, in one interview explicitly admitted he absolutely had not cared what Poles thought about the movie (Bikont 1997). In Poland the dominant, almost unanimous opinion is that Lanzman was dramatically selective in his use of Polish subjects to create the impression that Poles willingly cooperated with the Nazis; at the same time showed not one of the thousands who risked their lives to save Jews. In turn, he did not show anything of the French collaboration with Nazis. Such an approach to history is a very effective tool for anyone who does not want to lift the walls of mutual aversion in intergroup relations.

47. We see fundamental mistrust in many active participants of the debate over the Jewish–Polish past and present. One person, involved for several years as a key proponent of dialogue nowadays claims that Jews in the dialogue favor only these aspects of truth that are useful for their particular temporary needs.

48. This resembles religious understanding of spiritual community, which unceasingly continues in time and may be morally burdened or spiritually diminished due to the sins of its followers, even those remote in time. This is why the bishop could naturally ask Jews for forgiveness for the Jedwabne Massacre in the name of the Catholic Church.

49. Former Prime Minister of Israel, Yitzhak Shamir, in a moment of anger, once generalized: "Every Pole sucks antisemitism with his mother's milk." This cast an additional trouble-making shadow on Polish–Jewish relations.

50 See also Augsburger 1981.

51. For interview schedules, questionnaires and scales described, see Appendix D.

52. We define *hurt* or *harm* as "having serious effects on the victim." It is not just bumping into someone accidentally.

References

Adler, Jerry, Anne Underwood, Ben Whitford, Juliet Chung, Vanessa Juarez, Dan Berrett, and Lorraine Ali. 2005. "In Search of The Spiritual." *Newsweek*, Aug. 29–Sept. 5, 146 (9/10): 46–64.

Afrol News. 2002. "Belgium Admits Guilt in Lumumba Killing." Congo Kinshasa. Feb. 6, 2002. Retrieved October 6, 2005 (http://www.afrol.com/News2002/drc003_lumumba_bel.htm).

Agape Love Ministries. 2004. "Welcome and Be Blessed." Retrieved August 4, 2004 (http://www.ourchurch.com/member/r/ronlor777/).

Al-Mabuk, Radhi H., and Robert D. Enright. 1995. "Forgiveness Education with Parentally Love-Deprived Late Adolescents." *Journal of Moral Education* 24 (4): 427–445.

Aleksiun, Natalyia. 2007. "Polish Historians Respond to Jedwabne Debate" in *Rethinking Poles and Jews: Troubled Past, Brighter Future*, edited by Robert Cherry and Annamaria Orla-Bukowska. Lanham, MD: Roman and Littlefield.

Allen, N. and J. Phillippe Rushton. 1983. "Personality Characteristics of Community Mental Health Volunteers: A Review." *Journal of Voluntary Action Research* 12 (1): 36–49.

Allport, Gordon W. 1954. *The Nature of Prejudice*. Reading, MA: Addison-Wesley Publishing, Inc.

Alter, Susan. 1999. *Apologizing for Serious Wrongdoing: Social, Psychological, and Legal Considerations*. Ontario, Canada: Law Commission of Canada. Retrieved February 12, 2005 (http://www.lcc.gc.ca/research_project/ica/pubs/apology/toc-en.asp).

Amy Biehl Foundation. 2006. Retrieved June 7, 2006 (http://www.amybiehl.org/).

Anderson, Colt. 2002. "Bonaventure and the Sin of the Church." *Theological Studies* 63 (4): 667–89.

Astin, Alexander. 2003. "The Spiritual Life of College Students: A National Study of College Students for Meaning and Purpose." *Spirituality in Higher Education*. Los Angeles: Higher Education Research Institute, University of California.

Auerbach, Yehudith. 2004. "The Role of Forgiveness in Reconciliation" in *From Conflict Resolution to Reconciliation*, edited by Yaacov Bar-Siman-Tov: pp. 149–75. New York: Oxford University Press.

———. 2005. "Conflict Resolution, Forgiveness and Reconciliation in Material and Identity Conflicts." *Humboldt Journal of Social Relations* 29 (2): 40-81.

Augsburger, David. 1981. *Caring Enough to Forgive: True Forgiveness*. Ventura, CA: Regal Books.

Augustine, Saint. 1984. *City of God*. London: Penguin Press.

———. 1999. "World: Africa Massacre in Sierra Leone." BBC News. April 21, 1999. Retrieved December 29, 2006 (http://news.bbc.co.uk/2/hi/africa/325227.stm).

———. 2004. "Germany Regrets Namibia Genocide." BBC News World Edition. January 12, 2004. Retrieved June 11, 2004 (http://news.bbc.co.uk/2/hi/africa/3388901.stm).

Baier, Kurt. 1991. "Guilt and Responsibility" in *Collective Responsibility: Five Decades of Debate in Theoretical and Applied Ethics*, edited by Larry May and Stacey Hoffman: 197–218. Lanham, MD: Rowman & Littlefield Publishers, Inc.

Bakalar, Nicholas. 2007. "Most Doctors See Religion as Beneficial, Study Says." *New York Times*, April 17, 2007. Retrieved June 21, 2007 (http://www.nytimes.com/2007/04/17/health/17faith.html?_r=1&oref=slogin).

Barkan, Elazar. 2000. *The Guilt of Nations: Restitution and Negotiating Historical Injustices*. New York: Norton Company.

Barnett, Victoria J. 1999. *Bystanders: Conscience and Complicity During the Holocaust*. New York: Greenwood Press.

Baron, Lawrence. 1986. "The Holocaust and Human Decency: A Review of Research on the Rescue of Jews in Nazi Occupied Europe." *Humboldt Journal of Social Relations* 13 (1, 2): 237–59.

Bar-Tal, Daniel. 2001. "Why Does Fear Override Hope in Societies Engulfed by Intractable Conflict, As It Does in the Israeli Society?" *Political Psychology* 22: 601–27.

Bar-Tal, Daniel and G.H. Bennink. 2004. "The Nature of Reconciliation as an Outcome and As a Process" in *From Conflict Resolution to Reconciliation*, edited by Y. Bar-Siman-Tov: 11–38. Oxford: Oxford University Press.

Baskerville, Stephen. 1996. "Modern Collective Guilt Theory As Rooted in the English Revolution." *International Journal of Comparative Sociology* 37: 215–31.

Batson, C. Daniel. 1991. *The Altruism Question: Toward a Social-Psychological Answer.* Hillsdale, NJ: Lawrence Erlbaum Associates.

Bazemore, Gordon. 1998. "Restorative Justice and Earned Redemption: Communities, Victims, and Offender Reintegration." *American Behavioral Scientist* 41 (6): 768-813.

Beaver, R. Pierce, Jan Bergman, Myrtle S. Langley, Wulf Metz, Arild Romarheim, Andrew Walls, Robert Withycombe, and R. W. F. Wootton. 1982. *Eerdmans' Handbook to the World's Religions*. Grand Rapids, MI: Wm. B. Eerdmans Publishing Co.

Berg, Mathew Paul. 1997. "Challenging Political Culture in Postwar Austria: Veterans' Associations, Identity, and the Problem of Contemporary History." *Central European History* 30 (4): 513-544.

Berry, Jack. "Forgiveness Among the Virtues." *A Campaign for Forgiveness Research.* Retrieved March 28, 2004 (http://www.forgiving.org/campaign/press/altruism_jackberry.asp).

Berry, Jack W. and Everett Worthington. 2001. "Dispositional Forgivingness: Development and Construct Validity of the Transgression Narrative Test of Forgiveness (TNTF)." *Personality and Social Psychology Bulletin* 27: 1277–90.

Berry, Jack W., Everett L. Worthington, Jr., Nathaniel G. Wade, Charlotte van Oyen Witvliet, and Rebecca P. Kiefer. 2005. "Forgiveness, Moral Identity, and Perceived Justice in Crime Victims and Their Supporters." *Humboldt Journal of Social Relations* 29 (2): 136–62.

Better World Heroes. 2006. Rachel Carson: *American Environmentalist.* Retrieved June 19, 2006 (http://www.betterworldheroes.com/carson.htm).

Bikont, Anna. 1997. "And He Has Cried: You All Are Kapo!" *Gazeta Wyborcza*, 232, Oct. 2004–2005: 10.

―――. 2004. *My z Jedwabnego (We of Jedwabne)*. Warszawa: Proszyski I Ska.

Bindenagel, J. D. 2002. "U.S.–German Negotiations on an Executive Agreement Concerning the Foundation: Remembrance, Responsibility, and the Future." Presented at *the Asia Foundation Forum*, Tokyo, Japan, Feb. 5, 2002.

Bloomfield, David, Teresa Barnes and Luc Huyse, eds. 2003. *Reconciliation After Violent Conflict: A Handbook*. Stockholm, Sweden: International Institute for Democracy and Electoral Assistance.

Borer, Tristan A. 2003. "A Taxonomy of Victims and Perpetrators: Human Rights and Reconciliation in South Africa." *Human Rights Quarterly* 25: 1088–1116.

Botcharova, Olga. 2001. "Implementation of Track Two Diplomacy: Developing a Model of Forgiveness." in *Forgiveness and Reconciliation: Religion, Public Policy, and Conflict Transformation*, edited by Raymond G. Helmick and Rodney L. Petersen: 279–304. Philadelphia, PA: The Templeton Foundation Press.

Bowden, Maggie. 2006. "Native American Philanthropy." *Learning to Give*. Retrieved January 3, 2007 (http://www.learningtogive.org/papers/index. asp?bpid=34).

Braithwaite, John. 2006. "Doing Justice Intelligently in Civil Society." *Journal of Social Issues* 62 (2): 393-409.

Branscombe, Nyla and Bertjan Doosje, eds. 2004. *Collective Guilt: International Perspectives*. Cambridge, MA: Cambridge University Press.

Brehony, Kathleen A. 1999. *Ordinary Grace: An Examination of the Roots of Compassion, Altruism, and Empathy, and the Ordinary Individuals Who Help Others in Extraordinary Ways*. New York: Riverhead Books.

Bretherton, Di and David Mellor. 2006. "Reconciliation between Aboriginal and Other Australians: The 'Stolen Generations.'" *Journal of Social Issues* 62(1): 81–98.

Brinkley, Alan. 1999. "The Peacemaker: India Won its Freedom Without Firing a Shot." *The New York Times Magazine*, April 18: 116.

British Broadcasting Corporation. 1998. "Despatches: Vancouver." BBC News. January 7, 1998. Retrieved May 22, 2006 (http://news.bbc.co.uk/1/hi/despatches/45547.stm).

Brokenleg, Martin. 1999. "Native American Perspectives on Generosity." *Reclaiming Children and Youth* 8 (2): 66-68.

Brümmer, Vincent. 1993. *The Model of Love: A Study of Philosophical Theology.* Cambridge, MA: Cambridge University Press.

Burawoy, Michael. 2005. "For Public Sociology." *American Sociological Review* 70: 4-28.

Burton, J., M. Farrell, F. Lord, and R. Lord. 2000. "Confinement and Ethnicity: An Overview of World War II Japanese American Relocation Sites." No. 74 *Publications in Anthropology.* National Park Service. Retrieved March 9, 2006 (http://www.cr.nps.gov/history/online_books/anthropology74/ce3.htm).

CBOS (Centrum badania Opinii Społecznej/ Public Opinion Reseacrch Centre). 2001. "Polacy wobec zbrodni w Jedwabnem - przemiany społecznej świadomości." (Poles about Jedwabne crime). Report.

———. 2005. Por Kummunikat CBOS "Sytuacja Polski na arenie miedzynarodowej." *lipiec.* Retrieved June 15, 2006 (http://www.cbos.pl/SPISKOM.POL/2001/KOM088/KOM088.HTM).

Cairns, Ed and Micheal D. Roe, eds. 2003. *The Role of Memory in Ethnic Conflict.* New York: Palgrave Macmillan.

Carson, Britt. 2007. "I Refused to Die." *The Naperville Sun,* April 25.

Casarjian, Robin. 1992. *Forgiveness: A Bold Choice for a Peaceful Heart.* New York: Bantam Books. (*cited p. 130, from* Enright, Freedman, and Rique 1998: 51)

Caspi, Avshalom, Daryl J. Bem, and Glen H. Elder Jr. 1989. "Continuities and Consequences of Interactional Styles Across the Life Course." *Journal of Personality* 57 (2): 375-406.

Chaitan, Julia. 2003. "Narratives and Storytelling." *Beyond Intractability,* edited by Guy Burgess and Heidi Burgess. Boulder, CO: Conflict Research Consortium, University of Colorado. Retrieved June 28, 2006 (http://www.beyondintractability.org/essay/narratives/).

Chang, Iris. 1998. *The Rape of Nanking: The Forgotten Holocaust of World War II.* New York: Penguin.

Chapman, Audrey R. 2001. "Truth Commissions as Instruments of Forgiveness and Reconciliation" in *Forgiveness and Reconciliation: Religion, Public Policy, and Conflict Transformation*, edited by Raymond G. Helmick and Rodney L. Petersen: pp. 257–78. Philadelphia, PA: The Templeton Foundation Press.

Chapman, Gary and Jennifer Thomas. 2006. "The Five Languages of Apology: How to Experience Healing in All Your Relationships." Chicago, IL: Northfield Publishing.

Chilton, Robert Ruffner. 1992. "A Buddhist Practice of Altruism: Equalizing and Exchanging Oneself and Others." Master's Thesis, Department of Religious Studies, University of Virginia.

Chiu, Chi-yue and Ying-yi Hong. 1992. "The Effect of Intentionality and Validation on Collective Responsibility Attribution Among Hong Kong Chinese." *Journal of Psychology* 126: 291-300.

Chrystos. 1991. "Shame On." *Dream On*. Vancouver, BC: Press Gang Publishers.

Cleary, Thomas. 2001. *Wisdom of the Prophet: The Sayings of Muhammad.* Boston: Shambhala Publications, Inc.

Cobban, Helena. 2004. "Reflections on South Lebanon." *Just World News*. October 11, 2004. Retrieved June 23, 2006 (http://justworldnews.org/archives/000923.html).

Cohen, Jonathan R. 2001. "Legislating Apology: The Pros and Cons." Draft. Retrieved June 27, 2006 (http://papers.ssrn.com/sol3/papers.cfm?abstract_id=283213).

Compassionate Listening Project. 2006. "Compassionate Listening: Healing Our World from the Inside Out." Retrieved February 12, 2005 (http://www.compassionatelistening.org/articles.html).

Conflict Research Consortium. 2005. *Beyond Intractability Project*. Retrieved September 29, 2005 (http://www.beyondintractability.org/essays.jsp?nid=2167).

Confucius. c. 500 BCE. *The Analects*. Retrieved January 31, 2006 (http://classics.mit.edu//Confucius/analects.html).

Cowlishaw, Gillian. 2003. "Disappointing Indigenous People: Violence and the Refusal of Help." *Public Culture* 15 (1): 103–25.

Cox News Service. 2004. "Hill Weighs Apology to Indians." Washington-times.com. Retrieved May 22, 2006 (http://www.washtimes.com/national/20040525-113031-7766r.htm).

Cunnare, Richard D. 2005. "Forgiveness." Retrieved October 17, 2000 (http://www.deltadustoff.com/article.asp?ID=3).

Czíkszentmihályi, Mark. 2005. "Altruism in Chinese Religions" in *Altruism in World Religions*, edited by Jacob Neusner and Bruce Chilton: pp. 179–90. Washington, DC: Georgetown University Press.

Da Silva, Anthony, S. J. 2001. "Through Non-Violence to Truth: Gandhi's Vision of Reconciliation" in *Forgiveness and Reconciliation: Religion, Public Policy, and Conflict Transformation*, edited by Raymond G. Helmick and Rodney L. Petersen: pp. 295–318. Philadelphia, PA: The Templeton Foundation Press.

Dabru, Emet. 2000. *The New York Times*, Sunday, Sept. 10.

Dalai Lama. 1989. The 14th Dalai Lama Acceptance Speech—Nobel Peace Prize Citation, Oct. 5. Oslo, Norway. *The Foundation for Universal Responsibility of His Holiness the Dalai Lama*. Retrieved June 19, 2006 (http://www.furhhdl.org/speech.htm).

Dalai Lama. 2002. "Understanding Our Fundamental Nature" in *Visions of Compassion: Western Scientists and Tibetan Buddhists Examine Human Nature*, edited by Richard J. Davidson and Anne Harrington: pp. 66–80. New York: Oxford University Press.

Dalai Lama and Howard C. Cutler. 1998. *The Art of Happiness: A Handbook for Living*. New York: Riverhead Books.

Datner, Szymon. 1966. "Eksterminacja Żydów Okręgu Białostockiego," *Biuletyn Żydowskiego Instytutu Historycznego* 60: 1-29.

Davidson, Dennis. 1999. "Words of Faith: Dalai Lama Teaches Love, Kindness." *The Desert Sun*, March 20: D6.

Davidson, Keay. 2004. "Empathy Found to Have Basis in Brain Chemistry: Neurological Link Seen." *San Francisco Chronicle*, Feb. 20: A-2. Retrieved May 24, 2006 (http://www.sfgate.com/cgi-bin/article.cgi?file=/c/a/2004/02/20/MNGC65407H1.DTL&type=printable).

Davidson, Richard J. and Anne Harrington, eds. 2002. *Visions of Compassion: Western Scientists and Tibetan Buddhists Examine Human Nature*. New York: Oxford University Press.

Dawkins, Richard. 2006. *The God Delusion*. London: Bantam Books.

Degroot, Jacquelyn. N.d. "Jewish Philanthropy—The Concept of *Tzedakah*." Retrieved Oct. 6, 2005 (http://www.learningtogive.org/papers/index.asp?bpid=66).

Devine-Wright, Patrick. 2002. "A Theoretical Overview of Memory and Conflict" in *The Role of Memory in Ethnic Conflict*, edited by Ed Cairns and Micheal D. Roe: pp. 9–33. New York: Palgrave Macmillan.

Dickey, Walter J. 1998. "Forgiveness and Crime: The Possibilities of Restorative Justice" in *Exploring Forgiveness*, edited by Robert Enright and Joanna North: pp. 106–20. Madison, WI: University of Wisconsin Press.

Dilman, Ilham. 1998. *Love: Its Forms, Dimensions, and Paradoxes*. New York: St. Martin's Press, Inc.

Doosje, Bertjan, Branscombe Nyla, Russel Spears, and Antony Manstead. 1998. "Guilty by Association: When One's Group Has a Negative History." *Journal of Personality and Social Psychology* 75 (4): 872–86.

Dorff, Elliot N. 1998. "The Elements of Forgiveness: A Jewish Approach" *in Dimensions of Forgiveness: Psychological Research and Theological Perspectives*, edited by Everett L. Worthington, Jr.: pp. 29–55. Philadelphia, PA and London: Templeton Foundation Press.

Dozier, Rush W. 2002. *Why We Hate: Understanding, Curbing, and Eliminating Hate in Ourselves and Our World*. Chicago, IL: Contemporary Books.

Drew, Naomi. 2006. "Fostering Good Listening." *The Peaceful Parents Newsletter* 33. Retrieved June 20, 2006 (http://www.learningpeace.com/pages/newsletter.html).

Dwyer, Susan. 1999. "Reconciliation for Realists." Institute for Philosophy and Public Apology. Retrieved June 5, 2006 (http://www.publicpolicy.umd.edu/IPPP/spring_summer99/reconciliation.htm).

Eckstein, Menachem. 2001. *Visions of a Compassionate World: Guided Imagery for Spiritual Growth and Social Transformation*. New York and Jerusalem: Urim Publications.

Elder, Joseph W. 1998. "Expanding Our Options: The Challenge of Forgiveness" in *Exploring Forgiveness*, edited by Robert D. Enright and Joanna North pp. 150–61. Madison, WI: University of Wisconsin Press.

Eliade, Mircea. 1963. *Myth and Reality: World Perspectives*. New York: Harper and Row.

Engel, Beverly. 2001. *The Power of Apology: Healing Steps to Transform All Your Relationships.* New York: John Wiley & Sons, Inc.

Enright, Robert D. 1995. "The Psychology of Interpersonal Forgiveness." Paper presented at the National Conference on Forgiveness, Madison, WI, March 1995.

Enright, Robert D. 1998. *The Enright Forgiveness Inventory User Manual.* Madison, WI: The International Forgiveness Institute.

Enright, Robert D., Elizabeth A. Gassin and Ching-ru Wu. 1992. "Forgiveness: A Developmental View." *Journal of Moral Education* 21 (2): 99-114.

Enright, Robert D. and Joanna North, eds. 1998. *Exploring Forgiveness.* Madison, WI: University of Wisconsin Press.

Enright, Robert D., M. J. Santos and Radhi H. Al-Mabuk. 1989. "The Adolescent as Forgiver." *Journal of Adolescence* 12 (1) 95-110.

Enright, Robert D. and Richard Fitzgibbons. 2000. *Helping Clients Forgive: An Empirical Guide for Resolving Anger and Restoring Hope.* Washington, DC: American Psychological Association.

Enright, Robert D., Suzanne Freedman and Julio Rique. 1998. "The Psychology of Interpersonal Forgiveness" in *Exploring Forgiveness,* edited by Robert D. Enright and Joanna North: pp. 46–62. Madison, WI: University of Wisconsin Press.

Exline, Julie J., Everett L. Worthington, Jr., Peter Hill, and Michael E. McCullough. 2003. "Forgiveness and Justice: A Research Agenda for Social and Personality Psychology." *Personality and Social Psychology Review* 7 (4): 337–48.

Ferrucci, Pierro. 2005. *El Poder de la Bondad (Survival of the Kindest).* Barcelona, Espana: Ediciones Urano.

Fetzer Institute. 1999. "Multidimensional Measurement of Religiousness/ Spirituality for Use in Health Research: A Report of the Fetzer Institute and National Institute on Aging Working Group." Kalamazoo, MI: Fetzer Institute. Retrieved Oct. 11, 2005 (http://www.fetzer.org/PDF/Total_Fetzer_Book.pdf).

Fields, Bill. 2005. "Eight Steps to Biblical Forgiveness." Retrieved October 6, 2005 (http://www.peacemakers.net/peace/eight.htm).

Fisher, Mary Pat. 1994. *Living Religions* (2nd edition). Englewood Cliffs, NJ: Prentice Hall, Inc.

Fitzgibbons, Richard. 1998. "Anger and the Healing Power of Forgiveness: A Psychiatrist's View" in *Exploring Forgiveness*, edited by Robert D. Enright and Joanna North: pp. 63–74. Madison, WI: University of Wisconsin Press.

Flynn, Ray. 2001. *John Paul II: A Personal Portrait of the Pope and the Man*. New York: St. Martin's Press.

Fogelman, Eva. 1995. *Conscience and Courage*. New York: Random House.

Foley, Michael W. 1999. "Memory, Forgiveness, and Reconciliation: Confronting the Violence of History." Report on a Conference at the Institute on Conflict Resolution and Ethnic Conflict (INCORE) Derry/Londonderry, Northern Ireland, April 23-26, 1999.

Ford, Gerald R. 1976. "Proclamation 4417: An American Promise by the President of the United States of America." *Federal Register* 41: 35 (Feb. 20, 1976). Retrieved July 25, 2006 (http://academic.udayton.edu/race/02rights/intern03.htm).

Forgivenessweb.com. 2001. "Apology Room." Retrieved Mar. 21, 2006 (http://www.forgivenessweb.com/apologies.htm).

French, Peter A. 1991. "The Corporation as a Moral Person" in *Collective Responsibility: Five Decades of Debate in Theoretical and Applied Ethics*, edited by Larry May and Stacey Hoffman: 133–50. Lanham, MD: Rowman and Littlefield Publishers, Inc.

Galambush, Julie. 2007. "Interfaith Approach to Forgiving Trespass." *The New York Times*, Jan. 1: B7.

Galaway, Burt and Joe Hudson. 1996. *Restorative Justice: An International Perspective*. Monsey, NY: Criminal Justice Press.

Gerard, David. 1985. "What Makes a Volunteer?" *New Society*. 236–38.

Giddens, Anthony. 1991. *Modernity, Self, and Society in the Late Modern Age*. Palo Alto, CA: Stanford University Press.

Giraffe Project, The. 2006. "Giraffe Heroes." Retrieved June 7, 2006 (http://www.giraffe.org/hero_featured.html).

Giss, Gary. 2006. "Everest 2006: "To Help or Not to Help, That Is the Question." (http://www.everestnews.com/2006expeditions/tosummit05312006.htm).

Gold, Gregg J. and James R. Davis. 2005. "Psychological Determinants of

Forgiveness: An Evolutionary Perspective." *Humboldt Journal of Social Relations* 29 (2): 111–35.

Goldberg, Carey. 2003. "For Peace of Mind, It Is Better to Give, Science Suggests." *The Boston Globe* Nov. 28, Section One: 1.

Goldhagen, Daniel Jonah. 1996. *Hitler's Willing Executioners: Ordinary Germans and the Holocaust.* New York: Alfred A. Knopf.

Goodstein, Laurie. 2000. "Leading Jewish Scholars Extend a Hand to Christians." *New York Times* Sept. 2000. Retrieved July 18, 2007.

Gordon, John. 2004. "Massacre Site Given to Wiyot Tribe." *Indian Life* July 2004. Retrieved July 25, 2006 (http://www.findarticles. com/p/articles/mi_m0JJC/is_1_25/ai_n6361563).

Graybill, Lyn and Kimberly Lanegran. 2004. "Truth, Justice, and Reconciliation in Africa: Issues and Cases." *African Studies Quarterly* 8 (1): 1-18.

Green, William Scott. 2005. "Epilogue" *Altruism in World Religions,* edited by Jacob Neusner and Bruce Chilton: 191–94. Washington, DC: Georgetown University Press.

Griffin, Kathleen. 2004. *The Forgiveness Formula.* New York: Marlowe & Company.

Gross, Jan T. 2001. *Neighbors: The Destruction of the Jewish Community in Jedwabne, Poland.* New York: Penguin Books.

———. 2006. *Fear: Anti-Semitism in Poland after Auschwitz.* New York: Random House.

Gruber, Ruth E. 2001. "Against the Backdrop of a Poland in Denial, Jedwabne Apologizes." Jewish Telegraphic Agency. Retrieved Oct. 27, 2005 (http:// www.jewishsf.com/content/2-0-/module/displaystory/story_id/16430/ edition_id/322/format/html/displaystory.html).

Gulen, M. Fethullah. 2003. "Love, Compassion, Tolerance, and Forgiving: The Pillars of Dialogue." *Bloomington Muslim Dialog Group.* Retrieved Mar. 28, 2004 (http://en.fgulen.com/content/view/1339/13/).

Gushee, David P. 2003. *Righteous Gentiles of the Holocaust: Genocide and Moral Obligation.* New York: Paragon House.

Gutman, Izrael. 2001. Interview: "Odwaga Zbrodni" (Courage of crime). *Gazeta Wyborcza* 35, Feb. 10-11: 22.

Haley, John O. 1998. "Apology and Pardon: Learning From Japan." *American Behavioral Scientist* 41 (6): 842–67.

Hall, Tony P. 2000. "Resolution Apologizing for Slavery—Honorable Tony P. Hall (Extensions of Remarks, July 13, 2000). Address to the Congress, July 12, 2000. Retrieved May 22, 2006 (http://core.ecu.edu/hist/wilburnk/Africa/Reparations/TonyHall.htm).

Hanh, Thich Nhat. 1993. *For a Future to Be Possible: Commentaries on the Five Wonderful Precepts*. Berkeley, CA: Parallax Press.

Harris, Sam. 2004. *The End of Faith: Religion, Terror, and the Future of Reason."* New York: W. W. Norton & Company.

Hartwell, Marcia Byrom. 1999. "The Role of Forgiveness in Reconstructing Society After Conflict." *The Journal of Humanitarian Assistance*. Posted May 3, 1999. Retrieved Oct. 11, 2005 (http://www.jha.ac/articles/a048.htm).

Harvey, Richard and Debra Oswald. 2000. "Collective Guilt and Shame as Motivation for White Support of Black Programs." *Journal of Applied Social Psychology* 30 (9): 1790-1811.

Hass, Peter J. 2004. "Forgiveness, Reconciliation, and Jewish Memory After Auschwitz" in *After-Words: Post-Holocaust Struggles with Forgiveness, Reconciliation, Justice*, edited by David Patterson and John K. Roth: 5–16. Seattle, WA: University of Washington Press.

Hassel, David J. 1985. *Searching the Limits of Love: An Approach to the Secular Transcendent God*. Chicago, IL: Loyola University Press.

Hauser, Christine. 2007. "Virginia Tech sets out to Preserve Objects of Grief, Love, and Forgiveness." *The New York Times* April 25: A17.

Hauss, Charles. 2003. "Apology and Forgiveness." *Beyond Intractability*, edited by Guy Burgess and Heidi Burgess. Sept. 2003. Boulder, CO: Conflict Research Consortium. Retrieved Oct. 11, 2005 (http://www2.beyondintractability.org/m/apology_forgiveness.jsp).

Heider, Fritz.1958. *The Psychology of Interpersonal Relations*. New York: John Wiley and Sons.

Held, Virginia. 1991. "Can a Random Collection of Individuals Be Morally Responsible?" in *Collective Responsibility: Five Decades of Debate in Theoretical and Applied Ethics*, edited by Larry May and Stacey Hoffman: pp. 89–100. Lanham, MD: Rowman and Littlefield Publishers, Inc.

Helmick, Raymond G. and Rodney L. Petersen, eds. 2001. *Forgiveness and Reconciliation: Religion, Public Policy, and Conflict Transformation*. Philadelphia, PA: The Templeton Foundation Press.

Hevesi, Dennis. 1989. "Man in the News: Prophet of the Middle Way." *The New York Times* Oct. 6: A6.

Hewstone, Miles, Ed Cairns, Alberto Voci, Juergen Hamberger and Ulrike Niens. 2006. "Intergroup Contact, Forgiveness, and Experience of 'The Troubles' in Northern Ireland." *Journal of Social Issues* 62 (1): 99-120.

Hill, Julia. 2000. *The Legacy of Luna: The Story of a Tree, a Woman, and the Struggle to Save the Redwoods*. San Francisco, CA: Harper Collins.

Hitchens, Christopher. 1995. *The Missionary Position: Mother Teresa in Theory and Practice*. New York: Verso.

———. 2007. *God is Not Great: How Religion Poisons Everything*. New York: Hachette Books.

Hodgins, Holley S. and Elizabeth Liebeskind. 1999. "Apology Versus Defense: Antecedents and Consequences." *Journal of Experimental Social Psychology* 39 (4): 297-316.

Hoeger, Werner H. K., Lori Turner and Brent Q. Hafen. 2003. "Spiritual Wellness." *Wellness: Guidelines for a Healthy Lifestyle*. Georgetown University. Retrieved Mar. 28, 2004 (http://data.georgetown.edu/be/article.cfm?ObjectID=586).

Holy See, The. 2006. "Johannes Paul II: Predigt." Retrieved July 20, 2006 (http://www.vatican.va/holy_father/john_paul_ii/travels/documents/hf_jp-ii_hom_19990616_wadowice_ge.html).

Hosoi, Yoko and Haruo Nishimura. 1999. "The Role of Apology in the Japanese Criminal Justice System." Paper presented at the Restoration for Victims of Crime Conference, Australian Institute of Criminology, Melbourne, Australia, Sept. 1999. Retrieved June 23, 2006 (http://www.aic.gov.au/conferences/rvc/hosoi.pdf).

Hume, Robert E. 1959. *The World's Living Religions*. New York: Charles Scribner's Sons.

Humphrey, Michael. 2003. "International Intervention, Justice, and National Reconciliation: The Role of the ICTY and ICTR in Bosnia and Rwanda." *Journal of Human Rights* 2 (4): 495-505.

Huneke, Douglas K. 1986. "The Lessons of Herman Graebe's Life: The Origins of a Moral Person." *Humboldt Journal of Social Relations* 13 (1, 2): 320–32.

Huntington, Samuel P. 1996. *Clash of Civilizations and the Remaking of World Order*. New York: Touchstone.

———. 2004. *Who Are We: The Challenges to America's National Identity*. New York: Simon and Schuster.

Huyse, Luc. 2003. "Reconciliation After Violent Conflict." International Institute for Democracy and Electoral Assistance. Paper presented at the IDEA-OHCHR Seminar: From Divided Past to Shared Future: Reconciliation on Post-Conflict Societies. Retrieved June 2, 2006 (http://www.idea.int/conflict/sr/upload/Geneva_2.pdf).

Indian and Northern Affairs Canada. 1998. "Statement of Reconciliation: Learning from the Past." Retrieved May 22, 2006 (http://www.ainc-inac.gc.ca/gs/rec_e.html).

Institute for Research on Unlimited Love, Altruism, Compassion, Service. "Approaches to Defining Mechanisms by which Altruistic Love Affects Health." Research Topic White Paper #3, by Esther M. Sternberg, M.D. Retrieved July 28, 2006 (http://www.unlimitedloveinstitute.org/publications/pdf/whitepapers/Mechanisms_Altruistic.pdf).

Institute of National Remembrance. 2002. "Press Release: On Final Findings of Investigation S 1/00/Zn into the Killing of Polish Citizens of Jewish Origin in the Town of Jedwabne, on 10 July 1941, i.e. Pursuant to Article 1 point 1 of the Decree of 31 August 1944." Released July 9. Retrieved July 5, 2006 (http://www.ipn.gov.pl/index_eng.html).

Iritani, Frank and Joanne. 1995. *Ten Visits: Asian American Curriculum Project*, San Mateo, CA.

Jacobs, Jane. 1961. *The Death and Life of Great American Cities*. New York: Random House, Inc.

Jarvie, Jenny. 2007. "Slavery Apologies Debated Across U.S." *Los Angeles Times*, Mar. 19.

Jaspers, Karl. 1961. *The Question of German Guilt*. New York: Capricorn Books.

Jeffrey, Paul. 1999. "Guatemala Struggles to Find Peace." *New World Opinion: the Magazine of the United Methodist Church* July–Aug. Retrieved July 25, 2006 (http://gbgm-umc.org/NWO/99ja/guatemala.html).

Johnson, Eric. 2006. "Slovakian Town Apologizes to Jews." Deutsche Presse-Agentur. *Together* April: 10.

Johnson, Rolf, M. 2001. *Three Faces of Love*. DeKalb, IL: Northern Illinois University Press.

Jones, E. E., and K. E. Davis. 1965. "From Acts to Dispositions: The Attribution Process in Person Perception" in *Advances in Experimental Social Psychology*, L. Berkowitz, ed. v. 2: 219–66. New York: Academic Press.

Jones, James, M. 2006. "From Racial Inequality to Social Justice: The Legacy of Brown vs. Board and Lessons from South Africa." *Journal of Social Issues* 62 (4): 885-909.

Kaczynski, Lech. Address at a ceremony in the village of Pawlokoma, Poland, May 13, 2006. Retrieved July 5, 2006 (http://blog.kievukraine.info/2006/05/ukraine-polish-leaders-remember-1945.html).

Kalb, Claudia. 2003. "Faith and Healing." *Newsweek* Nov. 10: 44–56.

Kaminer, Debra, Dan Stein, Irene Mbanga, and Nompumelelo Zungu-Dirwayi. 2001. "The Truth and Reconciliation Commission in South Africa: Relation to Psychiatric Status and Forgiveness Among Survivors of Human Rights Abuses." *British Journal of Psychiatry* 178: 373-77.

Kanyangara, Patrick, Bernard Rime, Pierre Philippot, and Vincent Yzerbyt. 2007. "Collective Rituals, Emotional Climate, and Intergroup Perception: Participation in 'Gacaca' Tribunals and Assimilation of the Rwandan Genocide." *Journal of Social Issues* 63 (2): 387–403.

Kappen, Diane Marie. 2001. "Acknowledgment of Racial Privilege, Endorsement of Equality, and Feelings of Collective Guilt via Ingroup versus Outgroup Influence." *Dissertation Abstracts International: Section B: The Sciences and Engineering* 61 (9-B): 5056.

Keller, Julia C. 2005. "ABCs and 123s of Spiritual Development." *Science and Theology News* 6 (1): 36-37.

Keyes, Corey L. M. and Jonathan Haidt, eds. 2002. *Flourishing: Positive Psychology and the Life Well-Lived*. Washington, DC: American Psychological Association.

Khan, Taimur. 2003. "Lecture Discusses Virtues of Altruism and Islam." *Daily Pennsylvanian.com*, University of Pennsylvania. Retrieved Aug. 18, 2005 (http://www.dailypennsylvanian.com/vnews/display.v/ART/2003/10/06/3f8112704d8bf).

Kidder, Tracy. 2005. "Because We Can, We Do." Retrieved Oct. 10, 2006 *Parade.com*: (http://www.paradecom/articles/editions/2005/edition_04-03-2005/featured_0).

Kirkland, Russell. 1986. "The Roots of Altruism in the Taoist Tradition." Retrieved Oct. 25, 2005 (http://www.arches.uga.edu/~kirkland/rk/pdf/pubs/ROOTS.pdf).

Klein, Charles. 1995. *How to Forgive When You Can't Forget: Healing Our Personal Relationships*. New York: Berkley Books.

Knauer, Kelly. 1996. *Time: Great People of the 20th Century*. New York: Time Books.

Koenig, Harold G. 2001. *Handbook of Religion and Health*. New York: Oxford University Press.

Koenig, Harold G. 2002. *Spirituality in Patient Care: Why, How, When, and What*. Philadelphia, PA: Templeton Foundation Press.

———. 2007. "Altruistic Love and Physical Health" in *Altruism and Health: Perspectives from Empirical Research*, edited by Stephen Post: 623–51. New York and Oxford: Oxford University Press.

Kohlberg, Lawrence. 1984. *The Psychology of Moral Development*. New York: Harper and Row.

Kohut, Heinz. 1985. "On Courage" in *Self-Psychology and the Humanities*, edited by Charles B. Strozier: 5–50. New York: W.W. Norton and Company.

Kowal, Z., M. Tomashek and M. Zurowski. (n.d.) "Ukraine and Poland Reconciled." Retrieved May 18, 2006 (http://www.kirche-in-not.org/ut%20unum%20sint1.htm).

Krebs, Dennis L., and Frank Van Hesteren. 1992. "The Development of Altruistic Personality" in *Embracing the Other: Philosophical, Psychological, and Historical Perspectives on Altruism*, edited by Pearl Oliner, Samuel Oliner, Lawrence Baron, Lawrence A. Blum, Dennis L. Krebs, and M. Zuzanna Smolenska: 142–69. New York and London: New York University Press.

Kristeller, Jean L. and Thomas Johnson. "Cultivating Loving Kindness: A Two-Stage Model of the Effects of Meditation on Empathy, Compassion, and Altruism." *Zygon: Journal of Religion and Science*. In press.

Kristof, Nicholas D. 1998. "Burying the Past: War Guilt Haunts Japan." *New York Times* Nov. 30. Retrieved April 5, 2004 (http://www.mtholyoke.edu/acad/intrel/warguilt.htm).

Krzeminski, Ireneusz. 2004. "Polacy i Ukraincy o swoich narodach, o cierpieniu w czasie wojny i o Zagładzie Zydów" (Poles and Ukrainians on their Nations' Suffering During the War and Holocaust of Jews") in *Antysemistyzm w Polsce i na Ukarainie (Antisemitism in Poland and in Ukraine), edited by Ireneusz Krzeminski*: 108–68. Warszawa: Scholar.

Kuteeue, Petros. 2004. "No Apology, No Payout for Herero." The Namibian: *Local News* Jan. 12, 2004. Retrieved May 22, 2006 (http://www.namibian.com.na/2004/january/national/041A1EA3C5.html).

Kwaśniewski, Aleksander. 2001a. Interview for *Yediot Ahronot* March 2.

———.2001b. Interview for *Der Spiegel*, July 2.

———.2001c. "The Official Address Delivered by the President of the Republic of Poland on July 10 in Jedwabne, Poland." Retrieved March 9, 2006 (http://www.radzilow.com/jedwabne-ceremony.htm).

———.2007. Interviewed by Dr. Piotr Olaf Zylicz.

LaHaye, Tim and Jerry B. Jenkins. 1995. *Left Behind.* Wheaton, IL: Tyndale House Publishers, Inc.

Lama Surya Das. 1997. "Love and Forgiveness." A talk delivered in Cambridge, MA on January 27. *Dharma Talks*. Retrieved March 21, 2006 (http://www.dzogchen.org/teachings/talks/love.html).

Lazare, Aaron. 2004. *On Apology*. Oxford and New York: Oxford University Press.

Leitenberg, Milton. 1997. "Rwanda and Burundi Genocide: A Case Study of Neglect and Indifference" in Race, Ethnicity and Gender: A Global Perspective, edited by Samuel P. Oliner and Phillip T. Gay: 253–74. Dubuque, IA: Kendall/Hunt Publishing Company.

Levine, Amy-Jill. 2006. *The Misunderstood Jew: The Church and the Scandal of the Jewish Jesus.* San Francisco: Harper.

Lewis, H. D. 1991. "Collective Responsibility" in *Collective Responsibility: Five Decades of Debate in Theoretical and Applied Ethics,* edited by Larry May and Stacey Hoffman: 17–34. Lanham, MD: Rowman and Littlefield Publishers, Inc.

Lewis, Thomas, M. D., Fari Amin, M. D., and Richard Lannon, M.D. 2000. *A General Theory of Love*. New York: Random House.

Liberman, Kenneth. 1985. "The Tibetan Cultural Praxis: Bodhicitta Thought Training." *Humboldt Journal of Social Relations* 13 (1, 2): 113–26.

Lickel, Brian, Toni Schmader, and David Hamilton. 2003. "A Case of Collective Responsibility: Who Else Was to Blame for the Columbine High School Shootings?" *Personality and Social Psychology Bulletin* 29 (2): 194–204.

Lickel, Brian, Toni Schmader and Marchelle Barquissau. 2004. "The Evocation of Moral Emotions in Intergroup Contexts: The Distinction Between Collective Guilt and Collective Shame in *Collective Guilt: International Perspectives*, edited by Nyla Branscombe and Bertjan Doosje: 36–55. Cambridge, MA: Cambridge University Press.

Lifton, Robert J. 1986. *The Nazi Doctors: Medical Killing and the Psychology of Genocide*. New York: Basic Books.

Liptak, Adam. 2004. "Filing a Heartfelt Appeal Against the Legal System." *New York Times* May 15: A19.

Ludwig, Theodore M. 1996. *The Sacred Paths: Understanding the Religions of the World*. Upper Saddle, NJ: Prentice Hall.

Lumsden, Malver. 1997. "Focus On: Breaking the Cycle of Violence." *Journal of Peace Research* 34 (4): 377–83.

Luskin, Frederic. 2002. *Forgive For Good* (1st Edition). San Francisco, CA: Harper San Francisco.

———. 2003. "An Experience of Peace." *Ions Noetic Sciences Review* 65: 11–13.

———. 2004. "The Choice to Forgive." *Greater Good* 1 (2): 13-15.

Luskin, Frederic, Karni Ginzburg, and Carl E. Thoresen. 2005. Efficacy of Forgiveness Intervention in College Age Adults: Randomized Controlled Study." *Humboldt Journal of Social Relations* 29 (2): 164-184.

Mack, John E. 2003. "Deeper Causes: Exploring the Role of Consciousness in Terrorism." *Shift—Institute of Noetic Sciences Review* 64: 13-20.

Madre. 2005. "Demanding Justice: Rape and Reconciliation in Rwanda." *Madre*. Retrieved Sept. 5, 2005 (http://www.madre.org/articles/afr/raperecon-ciliation.html).

Marshall, Joseph M. III. 2001. *The Lakota Way: Stories and Lessons for Living.* New York: Penguin Compass.

Martin, Mike W. 1996. *Love's Virtues.* Lawrence, KS: University of Kansas Press.

Marty, Martin E. 1997. "Ethos of Christian Forgiveness" in *Dimensions of Forgiveness*, edited by Everett L. Worthington, Jr.: 9–28. Philadelphia, PA: Templeton Foundation Press.

Mathis, Nancy. 1997. "On Behalf of a Nation, an Apology." *Houston Chronicle* May 16, Retrieved Dec. 12, 2000 (http://www.chron.com/content/chronicle/page1/97/05/17/clinton.2-0.html).

May, Larry. 1991. "Metaphysical Guilt and Moral Taint" in *Collective Responsibility: Five Decades of Debate in Theoretical and Applied Ethics*, edited by Larry May and Stacey Hoffman: 239–54. Lanham, MD: Rowman and Littlefield Publishers, Inc.

May, Larry and Stacey Hoffman, eds. 1991. *Collective Responsibility: Five Decades of Debate in Theoretical and Applied Ethics.* Lanham, MD: Rowman and Littlefield Publishers, Inc.

McCullough, Michael E., Everett L. Worthington, Jr., and Kenneth C. Rachal. 1997. "Interpersonal Forgiving in Close Relationships [Interpersonal Relations and Group Processes]." *Journal of Personality and Social Psychology* 73 (2): 321–36.

McCullough, Michael E., Kenneth C. Rachal, Steven J. Sandage, Everett L. Worthington, Jr., Susan Wade Brown, and Terry L. Hight. 1998. "Interpersonal Forgiving in Close Relationships." *Journal of Personality and Social Psychology* 75 (6): 1586-1603.

McCullough, Michael E., Kenneth I. Pargament, and Carl E. Thoresen, eds. 2000. *Forgiveness: Theory, Research, and Practice.* New York: The Guilford Press.

McGarty, Craig and Ana-Maria Bliuc. 2004. "Refining the Meaning of the 'Collective' in Collective Guilt: Harm, Guilt, and Apology in Australia" in *Collective Guilt: International Perspectives*, edited by N. R. Branscombe and Bertjan Doosje: 112–29. New York: Cambridge University Press.

McLernon, Frances, Ed Cairns, and Miles Hewstone. 2002. "Views on Forgiveness in Northern Ireland." *Peace Review* 14 (3): 285–90.

McLernon, Frances, Ed Cairns, Miles Hewstone, and Ron Smith. 2004. "The Development of Intergroup Forgiveness in Northern Ireland." *Journal of Social Issues* 60 (3): 587-601.

McNamara, Marilyn R. and Mandeep K. Dhami. 2003. "The Role of Apology in Restorative Justice." Paper presented *at The 6th International Conference on Restorative Justice*, Simon Fraser University, BC, Canada, June 1-4.

McPherson, Dennis. 1998. "A Definition of Culture: Canada and First Nations" in *Native American Religious Identity: Unforgotten Gods*, edited by Jace Weaver: 77–98. Maryknoll, NY: Orbis Books.

Mellor, David and Di Bretherton. 2003. "Reconciliation between Black and White Australia: The Role of Social Memory" in *The Role of Memory in Ethnic Conflict*, edited by Ed Cairns and Micheal D. Roe: 37–54. New York: Palgrave Macmillan.

Michnik, Adam. 2001. "Poles and the Jews: How Deep the Guilt?" *New York Times* Mar. 17.

Midlarsky, Elizabeth, Eva Kahana, and Robin Corley. 1986. "Personal Situational Influences on Late Life Helping." *Humboldt Journal of Social Relations* 13 (1, 2): 217–33.

Miller, David. 2004. "Holding Nations Responsible." *Ethics* 114 (2): 240–69.

Mills, Nicolaus. 2001. "The New Culture of Apology." *Dissent* 48 (4): 113–15.

Montiel, Cristina Jayme. 2002. "Sociopolitical Forgiveness." *Peace Review* 14 (3): 271–77.

Montville, Joseph V. 2001. "Religion and Peacemaking" in *Forgiveness and Reconciliation: Religion, Public Policy, and Conflict Transformation*, edited by Raymond G. Helmick and Rodney L. Petersen: 97–116. Philadelphia, PA: The Templeton Foundation Press.

Morrow, Lance. 1984. "Why Forgive? 'I Spoke...As a Brother.'" *Time Magazine* Jan. 9: 27–33.

Murayama, Tomichi. 1995. "On the Occasion of the 50th Anniversary of the War's End." Statement by Prime Minister Tomichi Murayama, Aug. 15, 1995. The Ministry of Foreign Affairs, Japan. Retrieved Sept. 6, 2005 (http://www.mofa.go.jp/announce/press/pm/murayama/9508.html).

Nadler, Arie and Tamar Saguy. 2004. "Reconciliation Between Nations: Overcoming Emotional Deterrents to Ending Conflicts Between Groups."

The Psychology of Diplomacy, edited by Harvey Langholz and Chris E. Stout. New York, NY: Praeger.

National Park Service. 2000. "Confinement and Ethnicity: An Overview of World War II Japanese American Relocation Sites." *History*. Retrieved May 22, 2006 (http://www.cr.nps.gov/history/online_books/anthropology74/index.htm).

Neusner, Jacob and Alan J. Avery-Peck. 2005. "Altruism in Classical Judaism" in *Altruism in World Religions*, edited by Jacob Neusner and Bruce Chilton: 31–52. Washington, DC: Georgetown University Press.

Neusner, Jacob and Bruce Chilton, eds. 2005. *Altruism in World Religions*. Washington, DC: Georgetown University Press.

Niens, Ulrike and Ed Cairns. 2002. "Identity Management Strategies in Northern Ireland." *Journal of Social Psychology* 142 (3): 371–80.

North, Joanna. 1987. "Wrongdoing and Forgiveness." *Philosophy* 62: 499–508.

———. 1998. " 'Ideal' of Forgiveness: A Philosopher's Exploration" in *Exploring Forgiveness*, edited by Robert D. Enright and Joanna North: 15–34. Madison, WI: University of Wisconsin Press.

Nygren, Anders. 1953. *Agape and Eros*. Philadelphia, PA: Westminster Press.

O'Brien, Darcy. 1998. *The Hidden Pope: The Untold Story of a Lifelong Friendship That is Changing the Relationship Between Catholics and Jews: The Personal Journey of John Paul II and Jerzy Kluger*. New York: Daybreak Books.

O'Connor, Lynn E. 2002. Review of *A General Theory of Love*, by Thomas Lewis, Fari Amini, and Richard Lannon. *Human Nature Review* 2: 89–91. Retrieved Aug. 10, 2004 (http://human-nature.com/nibbs/02/leo.html).

Olasky, Marvin. 1996. *Renewing American Compassion: How Compassion for the Needy Can Turn Ordinary Americans into Heroes*. New York: The Free Press.

Oliner, Samuel P. 1993. "The Altruistic Personality: Rescuers of Jews in Nazi Europe." Paper presented at Prosocial Behavior Conference, University of Arkansas, Little Rock, AR, May 25, 1993.

Oliner, Samuel P. 2000 a. Interview with Julia Hill, March 3, 2000.

———. 2000 b. *Narrow Escapes*. New York: Paragon House.

————. 2003. *Do Unto Others: Extraordinary Acts of Ordinary People. How Altruism Inspires True Acts of Courage*. Cambridge, MA: Westview Press.

————. 2004. *Unlimited Love, Compassion, and Forgiveness: Acts of Moral Exemplars*. Unpublished manuscript.

————. 2005. "Altruism, Forgiveness, Empathy, and Intergroup Apology." *Humboldt Journal of Social Relations* 29 (2): 8-39.

Oliner, Samuel, P. and Kathleen M. Lee. 1996. *Who Shall Live: The Wilhelm Bachner Story*. Chicago, IL: Academy Chicago Publishers.

Oliner, Samuel P. and Phillip T. Gay. 1997. "Race, Ethnicity, and Gender: A Global Perspective." Dubuque, IA: KIendall/Hunt Publishing.

Oliner, Samuel P. and Pearl M. Oliner. 1988. *The Altruistic Personality: Rescuers of Jews in Nazi Europe*. New York: The Free Press.

Oliner, Samuel P. and Jeffrey R. Gunn. 2006. "Manifestations of Radical Evil: Structure and Social Psychology." *Humboldt Journal of Social Relations* 30 (1): 108–44.

Oman, Doug. 2007. "Does Volunteering Foster Physical Health and Longevity?" Pp. 7-36 in *Altruism and Health: Perspectives from Empirical Research*, edited by Stephen Post. New York and Oxford: Oxford University Press.

Onishi, Norimitsu. 2007. "Japan's Atonement to Former Sex Slaves Stirs Anger." *New York Times* April 24.

Ontario Consultants for Religious Tolerance. 2001. "Roman Catholic Apology for the Past Sins of Its Members." Retrieved March 18, 2004 (http://www.religioustolerance.org/pope_apo.htm).

Ornish, Dean. 1998. *Love and Survival: The Scientific Basis for the Healing Power of Intimacy*. New York: HarperColllins.

Paldiel, Mordecai. 2000. *Saving the Jews: Amazing Stories of Men and Women Who Defied the "Final Solution."* Rockville, MD: Schreiber Publishing.

Paolini, Stefania, Miles Hewstone, Ed Cairns, and Alberto Voci. 2004. "Effects of Direct and Indirect Cross-Group Friendship on Judgments of Catholics and Protestants in Northern Ireland: The Mediating Role of an Anxiety-Reduction Mechanism." *Personality and Social Psychology Bulletin* (30) 6: 770–86.

Parachin, Victor M. 2006. "How to Forgive: Ten Guidelines." *Unifier: European*

Unitarian Universalists. March Newsletter: 3.

Patterson, David and John K. Roth, eds. 2004. *After-Words: Post-Holocaust Struggles with Forgiveness, Reconciliation, Justice*. Seattle, WA: University of Washington Press.

Patton, J. 1985. *Is Human Forgiveness Possible? A Pastoral Care Perspective*. Nashville, TN: Ebington Press.

Pederson, Anne. 2003. "Social Justice and Collective Guilt: Diversity of Opinion and Practical Implications." *Australian Journal of Psychology* 55: 202–6.

Percival, John. 1985. *For Valor: The Victoria Cross: Courage in Action*. London: Thames, Nethuen.

Perkins, Spencer and Chris Rice. 2000. *More than Equals: Racial Healing for the Sake of the Gospel*. New York: Inter-varsity Press.

Pon, Cynthia. 2002. "Teaching Tolerance in a World of Violence." *Paths of Learning* Summer: 12–13.

Post, Stephen G. 2002. *Unlimited Love: What It Is and Why It Matters*. Institute for Research and Unlimited Love. Retrieved Oct. 5, 2006 (http://www.unlimitedloveinstitute.org/publications/pdf/UL_What_and_Why.pdf).

———. 2003. *Unlimited Love: Altruism, Compassion, and Service*. Philadelphia, PA: The Templeton Foundation Press.

Post, Stephen G., Byron Johnson, Michael McCullough, and Jeffrey Schloss. 2003. *Research on Altruism and Love*. Philadelphia, PA: The Templeton Foundation Press.

Post, Stephen G. and Jill Neimark. 2007. *Why Good Things Happen to Good People*. New York: Broadway Books.

Post, Stephen, ed. 2007. *Altruism and Health: Perspectives from Empirical Research*. New York and Oxford: Oxford University Press.

Prince, Russ Alan and Karen Maru File. 1994. *The Seven Faces of Philanthropy: A New Approach to Cultivating Major Donors*. San Francisco: Jossey-Bass.

Prince-Gibson, Eetta. 2004. "Despite Our Differences…" *Na'amat Woman Magazine* Summer. Retrieved Nov. 3, 2005 (http://www.naamat.org/Mag_articles.html#).

Ramose, M. B. 1999. "Truth the Liberator." *Newsletter on International Cooperation. APA Newsletter* 98 (2).

Rape of Nanking Redress Coalition. 2001. "50 years of Denial: Japan and Its Wartime Responsibilities." International conference held in San Francisco, CA, Sept. 6-9, hosted by Asian American Studies/Ethnic Studies, University of California, Berkeley. Retrieved June 23, 2006 (http://www.global-alliance.net/SFPT/SFPTEventCalendarAttach1.htm).

Reagan, Ronald W. 1988. "Ronald Reagan on Redress Act: Remarks on Signing the Bill Providing Restitution for the Wartime Internment of Japanese-American Civilians." University of Wisconsin. Retrieved May 22, 2006 (http://history.wisc.edu/archdeacon/404tja/redress.html).

Reconciliation Australia. 2000. "Australian Declaration: towards Reconciliation." Retrieved March 9, 2006 (http://www.austlii.edu.au/au/other/IndigLRes/car/2000/12/pg3.htm).

Reding, Andrew. 1999. "More Than an Apology Needed for America's Rwanda." Pacificnews.org. Retrieved April 20, 2006 (http://www.pacificnews.org/jinn/stories/5.05/990311-guatemala.html).

Reeves, Shawn. 2006. "The Twain Shall Meet." *Habitat World* March: 6-11.

Reykin, Andrew. 1990. *The Burning Season: The Murder of Chico Mendes and the Fight for the Amazon Rain Forest*. Boston, MA: Houghton Mifflin Company.

Roiphe, Anne. 2004. *"Poland Offers a Sorry Apology 60 Years Late." New York Observer*, March 17. Retrieved June 11, 2004 at (http://nl.newsbank.com/nl-search/we/Archives?p_product=NYOB&p_theme=nyob&p_action=search&p_maxdocs=200&p_text_search-0=Poland%20AND%20Offers%20AND%20a%20AND%20Sorry%20AND%20Apology&s_dispstring="Poland%20Offers%20a%20Sorry%20Apology%20&p_perpage=10&p_sort=YMD_date:D&xcal_useweights=no).

Rosenbaum, Thane. 2004. *The Myth of Moral Justice: Why Our Legal System Fails to Do What is Right*. New York: HarperCollins.

Rosenberg, Mica. 2006. "Guatemala Wants Probe into Civil War Disappeared." Reuters. Retrieved May 22, 2006 (http://news.yahoo.com/s/nm/20060519/wl_nm/rights_guatemala_dc_1).

Ross, Floyd H. and Tynette Hills. 1956. *The Great Religions by which Men Live*. Greenwich, CT: Fawcett Publications.

Roth, John K. 2005. *Ethics During and After the Holocaust*. New York: Palgrave Macmillan.

————. 2006. "The Ethics of Forgiveness." *Science and Theology News.* July/August.

Rye, Mark S., Kenneth I. Pargament, M. Amir Ali, Guy L. Beck, Elliot N. Dorff, Charles Hallisey, Vasudha Narayanan, and James G. Williams. 2000. "Religious Perspectives on Forgiveness" in *Forgiveness: Theory, Research and Practice*, edited by Michael E. McCullough, Kenneth I. Pargament and Carl E. Thoresen: 17–39. New York and London: Guilford Press.

Sachedina, Abdulaziz. 2001. *The Islamic Roots of Democratic Pluralism.* New Delhi: Oxford University Press.

Sacks, Rabbi Jonathan. 2005. *To Heal a Fractured World.* New York: Schocken Books.

San Francisco Chronicle. 1998. "The Amazon Still Needs Chico Mendes." Editorial, Dec. 31: A21.

Scheff, Thomas J. 1994. *Bloody Revenge: Emotion, Nationalism, and War.* Boulder, CO: Westview Press.

Schimmel, Solomon. 2002. *Wounds Not Healed by Time.* New York: Oxford University Press.

Schneider, Carl D. 2004. "What It Means to Be Sorry: The Power of Apology in Mediation." *Mediation Quarterly* 17 (3): 265–80. Retrieved Oct. 11, 2005 (http://www.divorcenet.com/md/mdart-14.html).

Schulweis, Harold M. 2000. "Forgiveness." Sermon delivered at Valley Beth Shalom. Retrieved Oct. 6, 2005 (http://www.vbs.org/rabbi/hshulw/forgive_bot.htm).

Seeds of Peace. 2006. "Advanced Coexistence Program: Acting out!" Retrieved June 7, 2006 (http://www.seedsofpeace.org/site/PageServer?pagename=centeradvcoex).

Shah, Parvin K. 1994. "Essence of World Religions: Truth is One, Paths are Many." Retrieved Oct. 11, 2005 (http://www.ibiblio.org/jainism/database/WORLDR/worldr.doc).

Sharma, Greesh C. 2000. "Relationships: the Fine Art of Apology." *Hinduism Today.* Retrieved April 5, 2004 (http://www.hinduismtoday.com/archives/2000/2/2000-2-12.shtml).

Sheffield, Jeffrey C. 2003. "An Investigation of the Relationships Between Forgiveness, Religiosity, Religious Coping, and Psychological Well-Being."

Ph.D. Dissertation, Department of Counseling and Special Education, Brigham Young University.

Shepard, Mark. 1987. *Gandhi Today*. Arcata, CA: Simple Productions.

Short, Damien. 2003a. "Reconciliation, Assimilation, and the Indigenous Peoples of Australia." *International Political Science Review* 24 (4): 491-513.

————. 2003b. "Australian 'Aboriginal' Reconciliation: The Latest Phase in the Colonial Project." *Citizenship Studies* 7 (3): 291-312.

Shriver, Donald W., Jr. 1995. *An Ethic for Enemies: Forgiveness in Politics*. New York: Oxford University Press.

Silverman, Jon. 2004. "Rwanda's Song of Reconciliation." BBC News UK Edition. Retrieved Sept. 5, 2005 (http://news.bbc.co.uk/1/hi/programmes/from_our_own_correspondent/3439525.stm).

Simon, Jean-Marie. 1988. *Guatemala: Eternal Spring, Eternal Tyranny*. New York: W. W. Norton and Company.

Simon, Sidney B. and Suzanne Simon. 1990. *Forgiveness: How to Make Peace with Your Past and Get on With Your Life*. New York: Warner Books.

Smedes, Lewis B. 1984. *Forgive: Healing the Hurts We Don't Deserve*. New York: Harper and Row Publishers, Inc.

————. 1996. *The Art of Forgiving: When You Need to Forgive and Don't Know How*. New York: Ballantine Books.

Smith, Peter. 2000. "African Americans Forgive Three Kentucky Orders." *The (Bardstown) Courier Journal* Dec. 4. Retrieved March 10, 2005 (http://www.courier-journal.com/localnews/2000/0012/04/001204nuns.html).

Smith, Tom W. 2003. "Altruism in Contemporary America: A Report from the National Altruism Study." The National Opinion Research Center/University of Chicago, report prepared for the Fetzer Institute. Retrieved March 14, 2006 (http://www-news.uchicago.edu/releases/03/altruism.pdf.

Smyth, Geraldine, O. P. 2001. "Brokenness, Forgiveness, Healing, and Peace in Ireland" in *Forgiveness and Reconciliation: Religion, Public Policy, and Conflict Transformation*, edited by Raymond G. Helmick and Rodney L. Petersen: 319–50. Philadelphia, PA: The Templeton Foundation Press.

Soble, Alan. 1989. *Eros, Agape, and Philia: Readings in the Philosophy of Love*. St Paul, MN: Paragon.

Sorokin, Pitirim A. 1954. *The Ways and Power of Love: Types, Factors, and Techniques of Moral Transformation.* Boston, MA: Beacon Press.

Sorry Works! Coalition, The. 2006. "Doctors, Insurers, Lawyers, Hospital Administrators, Patients, and Researchers Joining Together to Provide a 'Middle Ground' Solution to the Medical Malpractice Crisis." Retrieved June 27, 2006 (http://www.sorryworks.net/WhatIs.phtml).

Stanczak, Gregory C. and Donald E. Miller. 2004. "Engaged Spirituality: Spirituality and Social Transformation in Mainstream American Religious Traditions." Los Angeles: Center for Religion and Civic Culture, University of Southern California.

Standing, Jonathan. 2005. "Japan PM marks WW2 Defeat with Apology to Asia." Reuters News, Aug. 15. Retrieved June 19, 2006 (http://www.ezilon.com/information/printer_7977.shtml).

Stanley, Charles. 1996. *Experiencing Forgiveness: Enjoy the Peace that Comes from Giving and Receiving It.* Nashville, TN: Thomas Nelson Publishers.

Staub, Ervin. 2003. *The Psychology of Good and Evil: Why Children, Adults, and Groups Help and Harm Others.* Cambridge: Cambridge University Press.

Staub, Ervin and Laurie Anne Pearlman. 2001. "Healing, Reconciliation, and Forgiving after Genocide and Other Collective Violence" in *Forgiveness and Reconciliation: Religion, Public Policy, and Conflict Transformation,* edited by Raymond G. Helmick and Rodney L. Peterson: 205–27. Philadelphia, PA: Templeton Foundation Press.

Steele, Mark A. 1998. "Conflict Resolution among Religious People in Bosnia and Croatia" in *Religion and the War in Bosnia,* edited by Paul Mojzes: 246–56. Atlanta: Scholars Press.

Sternberg, Esther M. 2000. *The Balance Within: The Science Connecting Health and Emotions.* New York: W. H. Freeman & Co.

Stolberg, Sheryl Gay. 2005. "Senate Issues Apology Over Failure on Lynching Law." *New York Times,* June 14. Retrieved Oct. 11, 2005 (http://www.iht.com/articles/2005/06/14/news/senate.php).

Story, Donald C. 1992. "Volunteerism: The 'Self-Regarding' and 'Other-Regarding' Aspects of the Human Spirit." Nonprofit and Voluntary Sector Quarterly 21: 3-18.

Strehorn, Molly Ryan. 2004. "Restorative Probation in Franklin County, Massachusetts." Retrieved Oct. 11, 2005 (http://www.sfu.ca/cfrj/fulltext/strehorn.pdf).

Suchocki, Marjorie. 1995. *The Fall to Violence*. New York: Continuum.

Sugimoto, Naomi. 1997. "A Japanese-U.S. Comparison of Apology Styles." *Communication Research* 24 (4): 349–69.

Sullivan, Dennis and Larry Tifft. 2001. *Restorative Justice: Healing the Foundations of Our Everyday Lives*. Monsey, NY: Willow Tree Press.

Summerfield, D. 1995. "Raising the Dead: War, Reparations, and the Politics of Memory." *British Medical Journal* 311: 495–97.

Svidercoschi, Gian Franco. 1994. *Letter to a Jewish Friend*. New York: Crossroads/Herder and Herder.

Svoboda, Elizabeth. 2005. "School Spirit." *Science and Spirit* Sept.–Oct.: 15–17.

Swanbrow, Diane. 2002. "People Who Give Live Longer, ISR Study Shows." Retrieved Jan. 2, 2007 (http://www.umich.edu/~urecord/0102/Nov18_02/15.shtml).

Tajfels, Henri. 1982. "Social Psychology of Intergroup Relations." *Annual Review of Psychology* 33: 1–39.

Tajfels, Henri and John Turner. 1986. "The Social Identity Theory of Inter-Group Behavior" in *Psychology of Intergroup Relations,* edited by S. Worchel and L. W. Austin: 7–24. Chigago, IL: Nelson-Hall.

Takaku, Seiji. 2001. "The Effects of Apology in Perspective Taking on Interpersonal Forgiveness: A Dissonance-Attribution Model of Interpersonal Forgiveness." *Journal of Social Psychology* 141 (4): 494–509.

Tavuchis, Nicholas. 1991. *Mea Culpa: A Sociology of Apology and Reconciliation*. Stanford, CA: Stanford University Press.

Tec, Nechama. 1984. *Dry Tears: The Story of a Lost Childhood*. New York: Oxford University Press.

———. 1986. *When Light Pierced the Darkness: Christian Rescue of Jews in Nazi-Occupied Poland.* New York and Oxford: Oxford University Press.

Templeton, John Mark. 1999. *Agape Love: A Tradition Found in Eight World Religions*. Philadelphia, PA: The Templeton Foundation Press.

Thomas, W. I. 1923. *The Unadjusted Girl: With Cases and Standpoint for Behavior Analysis*. Boston: Little, Brown, and Company.

Tipping, Collin C. 2002. *Radical Forgiveness: Making Room for the Miracle*. Marietta, GA: Global 13 Publications, Inc.

Touber, Tijn. 2005. "Survival of the Kindest." *Ode* 3 (3): 42–47.

Tutu, Desmond. 1999. *No Future Without Forgiveness.* New York: First Image Books.

———. 2004. "Truth + Reconciliation." *Greater Good* 1 (2): 10–12.

Tych, Feliks. 2001. Inte Historia Musi Polegać na Prawdzie Rzeczpospolita 04.06.2001n.

Umbreit, Mark. 2005. "Peacemaking and Spirituality: Touching the Soul Within the Energy of Conflict and Trauma." *Center for Restorative Justice and Peacemaking.* Retrieved June 26, 2006 (http://www.rjp.umn.edu/img/assets/13522/Peacemaking_%20&_%20Spirituality_%20Touching_%20the_%20Soul.pdf).

Umbreit, Mark S. and William Bradshaw. 2001. "Assessing Victim Satisfaction with Victim Offender Mediation and Dialogue Services: The Development and Use of the Victim Satisfaction with Offender Dialogue Scale (VSODS)." St. Paul, MN: Center for Restorative Justice and Peacemaking, School of Social Work. Retrieved Aug. 6, 2004 (http://2ssw.che.umn.edu/rip/Resources/Documents/V-Scale.MON.pdf).

Underwood, Lynn G. 1999. "The Human Experience of Compassionate Love: Conceptual Mapping and Data from Selected Studies" in *Altruism and Altruistic Love: Science, Philosophy, and Religion in Dialogue,* edited by Steven G. Post, Lynn G. Underwood, Jeffrey P. Schloss and William B. Hurlbut: 72–88. New York: Oxford University Press.

USA Today. 2004. "What is Spirituality?" Sunday, March 28. Retrieved June 30, 2007. (http://proquest.umi.com/pqdlink?PMID=7631&TS=1150734727&SrchMode=3&SrtM=0&PCID=15012901&VType=PQD&VInst=PROD&aid=1&clientId=17853&RQT=572&VName=PQD&firstIndex=60).

Van der Merwe, Hugo. 2003. "National Narrative Versus Local Truths: The Truth and Reconciliation Commission's Engagement with Duduza" in Commissioning the Past: Understanding South Africa's Truth and Reconciliation Commission, edited by Deborah Posel and Graeme Simpson: 269–81. Johannesburg, South Africa: Witwatersrand University Press. Retrieved June 23, 2006, Center for the Study of Violence and Reconciliation (http://www.wits.ac.za/csvr/papers/papvdm4.htm).

Van Evera, Stephen. 1994. "Hypotheses on Nationalism and War." *International Security* 18 (4): 5-39.

Van Gelder, Sarah Ruth. 2006. "Holy Impatience—An Interview with Matthew Fox." *Yes! A Journal of Positive Futures,* winter: 4-5.

Vinsonneau, Genevieve and Etienne Mullet. 2001. "Willingness to Forgive Among Young Adolescents: A Comparison Between Two Groups of Different Cultural Origins Living in France." *International Journal of Group Tensions* 30 (3): 267–82.

Vrba, Rudolf. 1964. *I Cannot Forgive*. Vancouver, BC: Regent College Publishing.

Walker, Lawrence J. and K. H. Hennig. 2004. "Differing Conceptions of Moral Examplarity: Just, Brave, and Caring." *Journal of Personality and Social Psychology* 29: 859–82.

Washington, Raleigh and Glen Kehrein. 1993. *Breaking Down Walls: A Model for Reconciliation in an Age of Racial Strife*. Chicago: Moody Publishers.

Weaver, Jace, ed. 1998. *Native American Religious Identity: Unforgotten Gods*. Maryknoll, NY: Orbis Books.

Weigel, George. 1999. *Witness to Hope: The Biography of Pope John Paul II*. New York: HarperCollins.

Werber, Jack and W. B. Helmreich. 1996. *Saving Children: Diary of a Buchenwald Survivor and Rescuer*. New Brunswick, NJ: Transaction Publishers.

Werner, Emmy E. 2002. *A Conspiracy of Decency: The Rescue of the Danish Jews During World War II*. Boulder, CO: Westview Press.

Wiesel, Elie. 1999. "The Perils of Indifference." Address to the United States Congress delivered April 12 in Washington, DC. Retrieved July 5, 2006 (http://www.americanrhetoric.com/speeches/ewieselperilsofindifference.html).

Wiesenthal, Simon. 1998. *The Sunflower*. New York: Randomhouse.

Williams, James G. 1986. "The Sermon on the Mount as a Christian Basis of Altruism." *Humboldt Journal of Social Relations* 13 (1, 2): 89–112.

Wilson, Nicholas. 2000. "We Did It!" *Auto-Free Times* Issue 17 spring: 35.

Wink, Walter. 1998. *When the Powers Fall: Reconciliation in the Healing of Nations*. Minneapolis: Fortress Press.

Witvliet, Charlotte V. 2001. "Forgiveness and Health: Review and Reflections on a Matter of Faith Feelings and Physiology." *Journal of Personality* 59: 281–312.

Wolf, Naomi. 1998. "Apologize for Slavery? Without an Apology, Blacks and

Whites Will Never Get Along." Retrieved Oct. 11, 2005 (http://www.rpi.edu/dept/union/bsa/public_html/wwwboard/messages/20.html).

Wolniewicz, Joanna. 2002. "Korelaty współodpowiedzialności w świetle dwóch koncepcji psychologii moralności" ("Correlates of Collective Responsibility in Perspective of Two Moral Psychology Concepts"). Unpublished manuscript.

Works of Love. 2003. Scientific and Religious Perspectives on Altruism Conference, Villanova University, May 31-June 5. Retrieved Sept. 15, 2004 (www.metanexus.net/conference2003/).

Worthington, Everett L., Jr. 1997. "Interpersonal Forgiving in Close Relationships." *Journal of Personality and Social Psychology* 73 (2): 321–36.

———. 2004. "The New Science of Forgiveness." *Greater Good* 1 (2): 6-9.

Yablo, Paul. 1991. "A Cross-Cultural Examination of Altruism and Helping Behavior: Thailand and the United States." Microfilm.

Zahn, Paula. 2003. "Faith in America," CNN Broadcast. Dec. 25, 2003.

Ziniewicz, Gordon L. 1996. "Confucius: Humanity, Character, and Altruism." Retrieved Feb. 9, 2006 (http://www.fred.net/tzaka/confuc.html).

Zorbas, Eugenia. 2004. "Towards Justice and Reconciliation in Rwanda: Taking Stock." Canadian Centres for Teaching Peace. Retrieved Sept. 5, 2005 (http://www.peace.ca/aftowards_justice_and_rec_rwa.htm).

INDEX